POLITICAL ECONOMY OF MODERN CAPITALISM

To the memory of
Andrew Shonfield

POLITICAL ECONOMY OF MODERN CAPITALISM

Mapping Convergence and Diversity

Edited by
COLIN CROUCH & WOLFGANG STREECK

SAGE Publications
London · Thousand Oaks · New Delhi

Chapters 4, 8 and 9 translated from the French by Simon Lee

First published 1997. Reprinted 1998, 2000

Originally published in French as *Les capitalismes en Europe* by
La Decouverte, Paris, 1996.

SAGE Publications Ltd
6 Bonhill Street
London EC2A 4PU

SAGE Publications Inc
2455 Teller Road
Thousand Oaks, California 91320

SAGE Publications India Pvt Ltd
32, M-Block Market
Greater Kailash – I
New Delhi 110 048

British Library Cataloguing in Publication data

A catalogue record for this book is
available from the British Library

ISBN 0 7619 5652 2
ISBN 0 7619 5653 0 pbk)

Library of Congress catalog card number 97-068597

Typeset by Type Study, Scarborough
Printed in Great Britain by The Cromwell Press Ltd,
Trowbridge, Wiltshire

CONTENTS

LIST OF CONTRIBUTORS

Robert Boyer is an economist, CNRS Director of Research, and Director of Studies at the Ecole des Hautes Etudes en Sciences Sociales in Paris. His present field of study is the performance and development of the labour market and the context of regulation. His publications include: *Labour Market Flexibility in Europe*, 1988; *The 'Regulation' School: A Critical Appraisal* 1990; (with Jean-Pierre Durand) *Post-Fordism*, 1997; and (co-edited with Yves Saillard) *Théorie de la régulation. L'état des savoirs*, 1995.

Philip G. Cerny is Professor of International Political Economy at the University of Leeds and has a special interest in the liberalization of global markets. He has published: *The Politics of Grandeur: Ideological Aspects of De Gaulle's Foreign Policy*, 1980; *Socialism, the State and Public Policy in France* (with Martin A. Schaia), 1985; *The Changing Architecture of Politics*, 1990; and *Finance and World Politics*, 1993.

Colin Crouch is Professor of Comparative Social Institutions at the European University Institute of Florence, Professor of Sociology at the University of Oxford and a Fellow of Trinity College, Oxford. His area of study covers trade union organizations, industrial relations, occupational training and the social structure of western European countries. He has published: *Class Conflict and the Industrial Relations Crisis*, 1977; *Trade Unions: the Logic of Collective Action*, 1981; and *Industrial Relations and European State Traditions*, 1993.

Philippe d'Iribarne, who is Director of Research at the CNRS (Gestion et Société), is concerned with the cultural milieu relating to systems of production characterizing different countries. He is the author of *La Logique de l'honneur. Gestion des enterprises et traditions nationales*, 1989; *Le Chômage paradoxal*, 1990 and *Vous serez tous les maîtres*, 1996.

Ronald Dore is Senior Research Fellow at the Centre for Economic Performance, London School of Economics and Political Science, at which he was some time Professor of Sociology. He is a member of the British Academy, the Japan Academy and the American Academy of Arts. His publications include: *British Factory: Japanese Factory*, 1973; *Flexible Rigidities*, 1986; *Taking Japan Seriously*, 1987; and *Will the Twenty-First Century be the Century of Individualism?*, 1990.

Jean-Paul Fitoussi is an economist and teaches at the Institut d'Etudes Politiques in Paris. His publications include: *Le Fondement micro-économique* *de la théorie Keynésienne*, 1974; and (with E.S. Phelps) *The Slump in Europe*, 1988.

Andrew Graham is Fellow and Tutor in Economics at Balliol College, Oxford. He was economic adviser to the British Prime Minister 1966–69 and 1974–76, and to the Leader of the Labour Party 1992–94. With A. Seldon, he is co-editor of *Governments and Economics in the Post-War World*, 1990 and with Garyn Davies he is the co-author of *Broadcasting, Society and Policy in the Multimedia Age*, 1997.

J. Rogers Hollingsworth is Professor of Sociology and History at the University of Wisconsin, Madison, and the author of a number of books and articles on comparative political economy. With J.L. Campbell and L.N. Lindberg, he has co-edited *The Governance of the American Economy*, 1991; with P. Schmitter and W. Streeck, *Governing Capitalist Economies*, 1994; and with Robert Boyer, *Contemporary Capitalism: The Embeddedness of Institutions*, 1997.

Jonas Pontusson is Associate Professor of Government at Cornell University and specializes in the problems of political economies of the Scandanavian social-democratic type. His publications include *The Limits of Social Democracy*, 1992 and (co-edited with Miriam Golden) *Bargaining for Change: Union Politics in Europe and North America*, 1992.

Marino Regini is Professor of Industrial Relations at the Università degli Studi, Milan, and has published numerous books and articles on industrial relations in Italy and other western European countries. These include: *I dilemmi del sindacato*, 1981; (with P. Lange) *State Market and Social Regulation*, 1989; and *Uncertain Boundaries: The Social and Political Constitution of European Economies*, 1995.

Susan Strange, Professor of International Political Economy at the University of Warwick. Formerly at the London School of Economics and European University Institute of Florence, she is one of the founders of the study of the international political economy. She has published several books, among them: *Sterling and British Policy*, 1977; *Casino Capitalism*, 1986; (with J.M. Stopford) *Rival States, Rival Firms*, 1991; *States and Markets*, 1988 and 1994; and *The Retreat of the State*, 1996.

Wolfgang Streeck is Co-Director of the Max-Planck Institut für Gesellschaftsforschung in Cologne and specializes in the sociology of economics and of labour. His publications include: (with P. Schmitter) *Private Interest Government*, 1985; (with R. Hyman) *New Technology and Industrial Relations*, 1988; *Social Institutions and Economic Performance*, 1992; (with J.R. Hollingsworth and P. Schmitter) *Governing Capitalist Economies*, 1994; (with J. Rogers) *Works Councils: Consultation, Representation and Co-operation in Industrial Relations*, 1995.

PREFACE

A full quarter century separates the publication of Andrew Shonfield's *Modern Capitalism* in 1965 and Michel Albert's *Capitalisme contre Capitalisme* in 1991, but in many respects the books are remarkably similar. Both are by men busily engaged in the world's affairs but capable of deep reflection on the wider implications of the changing economic environment. Both books rapidly had an impact on public debate in a number of countries. Both analysed and revealed the institutional underpinnings of government policy and social organization that are fundamental to the operation of economics but which are often ignored by academic economic science.

There is however a major difference in the economic climate within which these works appeared. When Shonfield was writing his immediate British public was keen to hear of new ways that economies might be managed other than through the stereotypical alternatives of free markets and state ownership – though the variety and subtlety of his discussion of national forms of capitalism tended to be temporarily lost in the general desire to concentrate on one form in particular: *planification à la française*. Ironically, the Frenchman, Albert, is less interested in his own country's specific approach than in the confrontation between institutional and free-market capitalism, captured largely in a comparison between German and US models. But the main difference in the climate of the 1990s compared with the 1960s is that there is less sympathy, at least among elites, for discussions of institutional arrangements. The prevailing orthodoxy emphasizes neo-liberal policies, deregulation and flexible labour markets, and treats most other forms of economic institution as sources of rigidity and inefficiency. At the precise time of publication of Albert's book the mood was different, which was one reason why it attracted so much attention. Since 1992 however, in the wave of disillusion with the scope for constructive public policy-making that seemed to follow the Treaty of Maastricht, an uncritical neo-liberalism has come to dominate thinking in many national governments as well as in international organizations.

Why is this so? Is this convergence on a preference for free markets a well-founded or a panic response to intensified global competition? What are its likely implications for the institutional diversity of the advanced economies? Will they all converge on an imitation of the USA? How do the very different arguments that have led to attempts to imitate Japanese economic institutions relate to this?

It is to answer questions of this kind that this book has been prepared. Its origins lie in the different activities of two other thinking men active in public life, and again an Englishman and a Frenchman. Sir Arthur Knight, with some associates, founded the Andrew Shonfield Association in the mid-1980s to try to bring together business people, people active in public life, journalists and academics to continue the kind of work that Shonfield had started in his several books: the practical but intellectually informed analysis of the public policy issues facing business in western Europe and elsewhere at a time of rapid change in the global economy. It was within the framework of debates within the Association that the ideas in the present volume took shape. René Monory, past president of the Senate of France, chairman of the Conseil Régional de la Vienne, founded some years ago at Poitiers the Observatoire du Changement Social en Europe Occidentale, with similar objectives of bringing together academics and *hommes des affaires* to consider the future challenges confronting Western Europe. A joint initiative by the Association and the Observatoire enabled the editors to organize in October 1994 a seminar at the Observatoire in Poitiers and a larger conference in Paris, from which the chapters in this volume developed. We are indebted to all involved in both organizations, and to all who attended the two meetings, for having made our venture possible. The editors and individual contributors are of course solely responsible for the contents of the chapters, which do not necessarily reflect the views of others associated with either the Association or the Observatoire.

CC
WS

INTRODUCTION: THE FUTURE OF CAPITALIST DIVERSITY

Colin Crouch and Wolfgang Streeck

Institutional capitalism: diversity and performance

Interest in the diversity of modern capitalist economies became wide-spread as far back as the late 1960s, when a new generation of social scientists began to challenge the then ruling 'convergence theory' of 'pluralist industrialism'.[1] The scholars associated with this emerging tradition were sociologists and political scientists at least as much as economists, and the diversity in which they were interested was seen as resulting from differences in the institutional structures of societies, not only purely economic institutions but also political and wider social ones. This is why what has by now become a broad stream of theory and research is often referred to as 'new institutionalism' (for a selection of recent studies see Berggren, 1991; Dore, 1986; Jürgens et al., 1989; Maurice and Sorge, 1989; Best, 1990; Sako, 1992; Kogut, 1993; Hollingsworth et al., 1994).

For the new institutionalists, the differences they found in the social organization and the modus operandi of modern capitalist economies were of more than merely aesthetic interest. Describing and analysing them served to make a fundamental political point: that, contrary to the demoralizing message sent by Kerr et al. (1960), technologies and markets were far from fully determinative of social life under capitalism, and that societies had non-trivial alternatives with respect to how they wanted to run their respective capitalisms and, by implication, what kind of society they wanted to be. It was true that sometimes these choices had been made long ago and were now deeply entrenched in an established 'culture' that was, at least in the short term, beyond the reach of contemporary actors. Nevertheless, the very idea of alternatives and choice implied that, to some extent at least, purposeful collective action – in one word: politics – could make a difference even and precisely for the nature of advanced capitalism. Observed and relentlessly documented capitalist diversity stood for the promise that, provided one could create the 'right' political conditions,[2] people in twentieth-century societies did have a capacity to reorganize their capitalist economic systems in line with collective preferences, within a broad band of meaningful alternatives.

Very importantly, the politics that was supposed to generate capitalist diversity was national. This was not because of any inherent affinity of institutional analysis to the nation-state, nor because of normative preferences on the part of theorists for markets to be interfered with only by national and not by other agents of collective intervention. Instead it reflected the historical fact that it happened to be mainly through and within nation-states that twentieth-century capitalism was organized and regulated by twentieth-century society,[3] and that in particular it was only at national level that societies were able through democratic politics to 'talk back' to their economies. For popular-democratic intervention in the economy, the nation-state simply was the only game in town, like it or not – and indeed many of the post-1968 generation did not like it at all and remained profoundly uncomfortable with it.

Mapping capitalist diversity

In the 1980s a welter of studies showed advanced capitalist societies to vary profoundly in the way they dealt with the two core institutions of capitalism: competitive markets and property rights based organizational hierarchies. Markets and hierarchies were found to differ between countries, not just in their scope or reach, but also in their mode of operation. Just as in some societies markets tended to be more flexible and 'liquid' than in others, managerial hierarchies, rather than always being operated unilaterally, had to differing degrees to be negotiated between their participants.

Moreover, research into Japanese firms in particular suggested an important refinement to the concept of hierarchy. Any large firm is likely to have a structured set of relationships through which orders are transmitted, making companies into social institutions and not just clusters of individual exchanges. Some firms, however, go considerably further than this and generate entire cultures and communities within themselves. A company culture embodies certain values about specific ways in which work is considered to be conducted in that firm, and becomes the basis for appeals to loyalty. Companies of this kind usually develop internal labour markets and encourage long service among their employees, to the extent of developing a company level of social policy. While these firms can exist within highly competitive product markets, they do suspend the operation of market rules in their labour relations. They can be identified as institutional companies to distinguish them from mainstream hierarchical firms.

Institutionalist analysis also urged recognition of at least three other, equally important, mechanisms of economic governance. Not only did these differ even more strongly between countries, but they also formed a wide variety of configurations with markets and firms, embedding the latter to different degrees and in different ways in broader social contexts and thereby further defining their jurisdiction and operation. First, far from being limited to the maintenance of public order and the enforcement of contracts, states were found to be deeply and variously involved in the management of capitalist economies, so much so that different 'state traditions' made for quite different rules and outcomes of economic action. Second, formal associations, such as *Kammern* and trade unions, organized cooperation between competitors and negotiated collective rules of exchange between groups with opposing interests, thereby both modifying the functioning of markets and firms and adding to the variety among states. Third, informal communities and networks apparently controlled a significant share of certain economies' transactions, and in varying degrees helped to sustain as well as transform the other mechanisms of governance.

Capitalist diversity was found to affect wide areas of economic activity. More importantly, some national economies were found to be more 'institutional' than others, in that they tended to subject a wider range of economic activities to governance mechanisms other than and in addition to market exchange and managerial prerogative, while typically also modifying the two through various forms of social intervention. It was the presence of these 'institutional economies' that most strongly supported the claim that capitalism was more than one system, and that modern capitalist economies were open to, and indeed required, defining influences of a social as well as an economic kind.

Performance and competitiveness

From the beginning, the new institutionalists took a strong interest in how different institutionalizations of capitalism related to different economic performance patterns. Increasingly during the 1970s and 1980s, and with rising confidence derived from a growing stock of evidence, claims were made that the typical performance pattern of institutional economies gave them a competitive advantage over economies operated by free markets and unfettered hierarchies. Apparently this was because institutional economies could combine keen competitive behaviour with the pursuit of collective goods, from which they derived advantage over economies that were locked into short-term market maximization. For example, it has been argued that during the 1980s the greater capacity of the German economy for producing the collective good of a skilled workforce enabled that country's motor industry to produce high-quality vehicles of a type that eluded its British competition. In analyses like these, diversity residing in social–institutional differences was understood as constituting factor advantage or disadvantage, in the same way as natural resources. Conventional economics was more reluctant to recognize this, because institutions often operate on economic behaviour in a way that neo-classical theory has to regard as a distortion. However, more flexible forms of economic analysis have demonstrated a capacity to adapt and take account of institutions in theory (see Soskice, 1990; Crafts, 1992).

The 1980s were the decade in which the competitive advantage of institutional capitalism was celebrated in the academic literature. Obviously this was a period when various continental European economies as well as Japan were outperforming the two countries that seemed to correspond most fully to a 'pure' free market model: the UK during the 'de-institutionalizing' Thatcher period, and the USA. Work done at the time showed, for example, the importance for competitive economic performance of formal and informal links between competing firms in the German, Italian and Japanese economies, although such links operate in very different ways in each of these countries (Bagnasco, 1977; Dore, 1986; Sabel et al., 1989). 'Networks' of this kind enable profit-seeking companies to cooperate with one another in the pursuit of collective goods despite their competition, with cooperation requiring only limited recourse to the sort of state action that is often considered indispensable for collective goods production. Differences in the model of cooperation between institutional economies were, again, regarded as functionally equivalent means for securing identical ends: like, for example, the differences between the formal associational structures of German business on the one hand, and the informal community links that bind central Italian firms on the other; or between either of these and the coordinative role of the French state. The notion of functionally equivalent institutions opened up an even richer landscape of possibilities of how to make an internally and externally competitive market economy compatible with a desirable society, and by implication once more underlined the economic significance of 'culture' and, embedded in it, politics.

Over time, several 'models' of institutional economies had their theoretical and political conjunctures, depending in part on their economic fortunes, but also on changing perceptions of their operation and on shifting political values. For a while, Sweden was widely regarded as the foremost example for the national–political malleability of capitalism. Later it was increasingly joined by (West) Germany, whose prestige with the left rose inexorably in the 1980s, in spite of the Kohl government, while it declined somewhat among the right, which was compelled to recognize that the 'social market economy' was a good deal more social than many of its admirers had believed. Japan came to be embraced by conservatives for its 'work ethic' and the apparently unlimited willingness of its workers to accept managerial authority – social contributions that even the freest of the free marketeers would rather not want to miss. More seriously, Japanese economic success provided others, like Ronald Dore (see this volume), with evidence that, *pace* Adam Smith, it is not just the self-interest of the butcher but also his benevolence – his commitment to ethical values restraining that self-interest – on which the performance of a modern capitalist economy depends.

The message all this was to convey was that attempts to impose social control on capitalism were not at all doomed to failure by the 'economic realities' that were so confidently invoked against them by mainstream free market economists. Quite to the contrary, the superior performance of countries like Japan and Germany, but also very much northern and central Italy, seemed to indicate that economies which refused to be talked back to, and insisted on extricating themselves from political and social regulation, were *ipso facto* and on their own terms deficient – ultimately reflecting the fundamental fact that economic action is always and inevitably social action, and for this reason depends for its successful conduct on a supportive social context.

The study of capitalist diversity and its implications for competitiveness supported a common, generalizable conclusion, one that went far beyond the technicalities of macro-economic management and the apparently technocratic details reported in Shonfield's book. While Shonfield had made visible the diversity of national economic regimes, what he really meant to demonstrate was a general need for all countries, albeit each according to its traditions and politics, to build strong non-market institutions for governing their economies. In this respect, his work was not just about diversity, but also about 'convergence' – convergence of the variety of democratic ('modern') capitalist nations on and under the 'embedded liberalism' (Ruggie, 1983) of the post-war period, that is, on a common practice of internationally protected and socially protective institutional regulation of capitalist economies by and within sovereign but similar and cooperating nation-states.

The crisis of institutional capitalism: back to convergence?

The deep recession of the German and Japanese economies in the early 1990s caused a change in the perception, and perhaps indicated a change in the reality, of the economics of capitalist diversity. With the USA and the UK beginning to expand at a time when in Japan and many of the continental European economies unemployment was still rising, old claims about an inherent lack of competitiveness on the part of institutional economies were again heard, and were more confidently made than ever before. At the time of writing it is not possible to decide whether this was based on purely temporary, conjunctural phenomena associated with the timing of national economic cycles. Something rather similar had, after all, happened for a brief period in the mid-1980s with respect to the continental versus British economies, and it is quite compatible with the notion of short-termist economies that their initial recoveries may be more rapid than those of countries locked into longer term behaviour.

The new competition

Still, there is no doubt that institutional economies, and most of all German-style, high-wage, high-cost and high-quality regimes that allow for only limited wage differentiation (see the chapters by Pontusson and Streeck, this volume), have come under pressures for change that would have been hard to foresee only a few years ago. In part this seems to reflect a declining capacity of such economies to avoid price competition by specializing on less price sensitive quality markets. Technological developments and improved managerial and accounting systems seem to widen the price differentials between advanced industrial nations and low-cost producers in the Far East and, increasingly, Eastern Europe, to a point where many consumers' trade-off between price and quality has become affected. Moreover, in some areas of production it is not even clear that there is still a quality difference. While new production technologies may originate among the institution-rich economies of the West and Japan, they seem to be increasingly amenable to being applied by poorly skilled workers in poorly equipped infrastructures, to turn out products that are not only cheap but also of high quality.

In addition, accelerated technological change, renewed price competition and the globalization of financial markets have combined to produce a world economy in which a premium seems to be placed on speed of reaction: on rapid product change and an ability to cut costs fast. To the extent that this favours decision-makers who can act without having to seek agreement within their organizations, it challenges the viability of institutional economies which, depending as they do on 'voice' mechanisms for change and improvement, assume committed resources and make change dependent on broad consensus. On the other hand, the force of this argument is reduced by at least two important considerations: first, unilateral fast decisions by non-responsive leaderships may generate mistrust and thus necessitate cost-intensive legal–contractual regulation; second, they may also be less than constructive where organizations depend on widespread employee commitment (Sako, 1992).

Certainly the last word on the social conditions of competitiveness is far from spoken. Today the socio-economic model of a high-wage economy with relatively egalitarian wage dispersion and effective democratic participation, in the political system and the workplace, appears on the defensive. If advantages lie overwhelmingly with fast moving, low-cost, unregulated market behaviour, then economies of the institutional type that refuse to admit increased inequality, stepped-up pressure on individuals, families and communities, and greater discretion in decision-making by managers and investors may be doomed, and only deregulated, finance-driven capitalisms of an Anglo-American kind may stand a chance of meeting the Far Eastern and Eastern European competition. But this argument is itself not without problems. At some point it will need to clarify whether it is really expected that British and American wages and social and infrastructural costs can be forced down to a point where they can compete on straight cost terms with the Far East and Eastern Europe, or, alternatively, whether it is assumed that inheritance of certain institutional and infrastructural features will provide advantages that compensate for higher costs. Answering the former in the affirmative creates a real credibility problem, while the latter does not differ very much from arguments in defence of institutional economies: it simply asserts that effective competition will take place at a point of lower cost and quality trade-off.

The economic capacity of institutions

Generally, there is a need to proceed beyond crude distinctions between institutional and pure market economies, and between strategies likely to succeed and to fail. More differentiated typologies of governance mechanisms – like markets, firms, states, associations and communities – make one less likely to run to easy conclusions concerning the general or overwhelming superiority of any particular kind of economy. For example, formal associations are likely to be more associated with a strong collective goods potential than market systems, but less with adaptability. However, one must again be cautious of asserting too many a priori rules. Associations might be prone to rigidity because there must usually be widespread consultation before they can act. But the high trust that can be established through associational networks may also increase the speed of decision-making, by reducing the need for formal transactions, avoiding costly trial and error, and accelerating the diffusion of best practice. Alternatively, while pure markets are usually associated with short-term actions and exchange rather than long-term enhancement, there are niches within pure market systems for firms specializing in research-based technologies.

Undoubtedly institutions may sometimes have a negative effect on economic performance, or they may outlive an earlier usefulness; but discovery of this will have to be the result of detailed theoretical and empirical investigation, not a conclusion to be derived axiomatically. At the same time, failure to recognize the role of institutions in, for example, sustaining creative entrepreneurial behaviour may lead, and indeed is currently leading, to the false conclusion that markets alone can sustain economic dynamism. This is particularly observable in the former Soviet bloc countries. The communist system allowed no true markets, and eventually produced economic stagnation; therefore it may seem that all that is needed for economic dynamism is free markets.

The point is, however, that communism destroyed not only markets, it also destroyed – or in many parts of Eastern Europe, took advantage of the absence and prevented the formation of – the very associational and community networks that are central to the Western concept of civil society. It is often accepted in the West that civil society is important for things that the economy cannot provide: for example, welfare, a sense of collective identity, and control of deviant behaviour. But civil society also produced such institutions as the Japanese employment system, the small-firm communities of central Italy, or indeed the dense web of relations that bind the firms of the British financial sector – the 'City of London' – into something far more than just a multitude of competing companies. Indeed, in some respects the move from state socialism to pure capitalism that seems to be the current fate of much of Eastern Europe is among the easier transitions for that part of the world to make. While in the past people in these societies were told that economic success came from the state, all that has changed now is that the state has been replaced in the message with the market – again leaving out the crucial role played by social institutions.

Competitiveness re-examined

A useful starting point for re-examining the problem of performance and competitiveness is the insight that economic success often depends on finding niches of some kind that provide temporary relief from immediate competitive pressure. After all, what the individual entrepreneur requires is not maximal competition, but sufficient security and confidence to risk investment in major projects. Schumpeter recognized this in his argument on the paradox of monopoly, but a more flexible and more generally applicable argument has recently been developed by Kay (1993) in his analysis of successful competitive strategies. The aim of really successful firms, he argues, is to find niches where there is a temporary distinctiveness of some kind – not to find the anonymous, purely competitive position of 'average' firms around which economic theory is axiomatically built. Of course, if such a situation persists without challenge for a prolonged period, the lethargic symptoms of uncompetitiveness will set in; but where there is nothing but relentless competitive pressure, it is likely that only the most short-term forms of trading or petty production will become established. If Soviet Eastern Europe provided abundant cases of the former weakness, in the new Eastern Europe there are many instances of the latter.

As Kay himself argues, this reasoning can be extended to countries. German apprenticeships, Japanese consumers' resistance to imported products and the ability of the French state to regulate competition constitute distinctive features of national societies that help domestic producers to gain a competitive edge. But Kay's theory also allows us to deal with the case of the USA. While the USA is often seen as the purest example of a market economy among developed nations, it is also the world's dominant political and military power, with a unique investment of state resources in defence and aerospace technology; it has a distinctive commitment to expenditure, private and public, on higher education; and it has exceptionally high rates of immigration, and consequently a higher birth rate and a more multi-ethnic population, than almost all other industrial nations. None of these attributes can be derived from the pure concept of the free market, but all in their way constitute distinctive resources at the disposal of US companies.

For example, it is true that the US economy lacks traditional community ties and widely accepted customs of the kind that bind, say, Japanese businesses, with each other and with their employees. However, precisely because of the ethnic diversity that is a major cause of this, distinctive sub-cultures and ethnic communities have often been the base for econ-omic organization and the establishment of trust networks. One may go even further and argue that the very lack of collective identity that under-lies much of the individualism of American life, has made it possible for some of the large corporations to manufacture a sense of company iden-tity and loyalty among their employees that transcends the simple wage–effort bargain. This may be very different from the kind of loyalty on which Japanese employers are able to draw, but it sometimes seems to have similar results. Both defenders of the 'American way' as the way of pure markets and individualism, and critics of its anomie and lack of relationships other than contract and short-term obligation, miss this important characteristic of many of its most dynamic firms.

In addition and even more importantly, the present resurgence of the American economy indicates that certain assumptions underlying some of the work of the 'new institutionalists' were, from their perspective, excessively optimistic. Claims, however implicit and qualified, that an economy can be competitive only with a benevolent politics and a co-hesive society were clearly premature. While for a time it seemed evident that a socially cohesive society was capable of being economically com-petitive, Hollingsworth shows in his contribution to this volume how the American example today indicates that in turn competitiveness may well be compatible with social decay, at least in certain conditions and for a con-siderable length of time. Large US firms, rather than having to wait for a political restoration of American society, made their comeback in the 1990s in an environment of progressive infrastructural decline, growing social inequality, and accelerating destruction of the social fabric at the lower end. To the extent that their recovery required social relations other than pure markets and hierarchies, they were apparently able to generate these in-house, applying social engineering technologies like human resource management and corporate culture building.

Far from needing an institutional economy to surround them, insti-tutional firms of this sort seem to be able to achieve a remarkable degree of autarky from their social and political environment,[4] which among other things enables them to cross national borders with great and growing ease. The formation of such firms, which increasingly seem to occupy the place of more traditional communities and social identifi-cations, is one of the most consequential developments in the recent history of capitalism, one that must be seen in the context of another fundamental transformation, the globalization of markets and the resul-tant attrition of the governing capacity of nation-states.

The future of capitalist diversity

The full extent of the challenge of globalization to capitalist diversity, and in particular the impact of international financial markets, are pursued in later chapters by Susan Strange and Philip Cerny. Jean-Paul Fitoussi and Philippe d'Iribarne take further some of the implications of the pursuit of pure free-market strategies for the distinctiveness of economies and societies in both Western and Eastern Europe. Our task in the rest of this introductory chapter is to consider the consequences for political and economic performance of one specific aspect of globalization: the decline of the governing capacity of the nation-state and its impact on capitalist diversity.

Globalization and political performance

The rapidly advancing attrition of national state capacity in relation to the economy does not mean the end of national politics, or of the assertion of national interests in the international arena. (1) While economic globaliz-ation places strong pressures on national economic policies for deregu-lation and privatization, formally ratifying the loss of national control over the economy, surrender to such pressures may well be offered in the name of national interest and national sovereignty. (2) Indeed the process may be accompanied by strong nationalist rhetoric and ideology. In part such symbolism may help conceal the loss of economic 'fate control' suffered by national political communities. But it also unwillingly sustains a poten-tially destabilizing 'democracy illusion' among citizens, to the extent that these continue to expect national politics to offer them protection against market forces. Finally and ironically, (3) defence of national democratic sovereignty constitutes a roadblock against the construction of supra-national sovereignty, that is, the rebuilding of economic governance above the old nation-states, and in this way further advances the release of the globalized capitalist economy from public–political control. We shall con-sider these three points in turn.

1 National political systems embedded in competitive international product and capital markets and exposed to ungoverned external effects of competing systems are tempted to protect their formal sovereignty, or the appearance of substantive sovereignty, by devolving responsibility for the economy to 'the market' – using what little has remained of their public powers of economic intervention to limit once and for all the claims politics can make on the economy, and citizens on the polity. If citizens can be made to believe that economic outcomes are, and ought to be, the result of com-petitive markets, and that national governments are therefore no longer to be held responsible for them, national sovereignty and political legitimacy can be maintained even in conditions of tight economic interdependence.

In many countries today, the rapidly proceeding disengagement of poli-tics from the economy through deregulation and privatization is defended with reference to international economic constraints that would frustrate any other policy. Deploying public power to liberate and accommodate market forces instead of trying to domesticate them may indeed have become the last national political programme that can be imposed on internationalized national economies without inevitably being frustrated by global economic forces that would expose to the citizens the obsolescence of the national state. Note that domestic deregulation tends to be presented by national governments as the only economically rational political response to internationalization, especially to international competition, and the only promising way of defending the national interest in competitiveness.

2 As nationally based democracy is increasingly preempted or constrained by the nation-state's loss of economic control, the political space provided for popular participation becomes available for symbolic performances of all sorts. Politicians have strong incentives to make their voters believe that they are in control, or in any case could and should be. The British example in particular shows that radical economic internationalism may easily be combined with nationalist rhetoric, and suggests that the latter may be fiercest where economic sovereignty is most energetically abandoned to the forces of the market. For a time, symbolic politics may help governments to neutralize citizen demands for economic protection that the nation-state can, and will, no longer satisfy. But as the gap between formal and effective sovereignty widens and the economic purchasing power of citizenship deteriorates, demagogically cultivated popular beliefs in the lasting efficacy of national democracy, running up against the realities of a global economy, are likely to have quite different consequences. Having kept alive illusions of national political capacity, politicians may find themselves in need of foreign scapegoats on which to blame their impotence, while citizens torn between their increasingly undeniable dependence on an internationalized economy and their desire to control their collective fate may begin to suspect that it was their 'sovereign' governments that had abandoned them to anonymous forces outside their comprehension and control.[5]

Political regression has many faces; in coming years nationally confined political democracy under international economic interdependence may offer ample opportunity to explore them in detail. Somewhat as in the world of the gold standard, as described by Karl Polanyi (1944), national governments must today simultaneously satisfy two constituencies: their national citizenry and the international capital market. Arguably, the much increased sensitivity of the latter (the small group of international bankers that embodied Polanyi's 'haute finance' has today been replaced by a faceless multitude of computer-linked bonds and securities traders), as well as the democratic character of today's polities have made this task even more difficult than it was in the nineteenth century. Hesitant to reveal to their voters the dirty secret that it is no longer they who determine their country's economic policies, national governments must somehow manage to extract from the democratic process policies that conform to the 'general will' of global capitalism: the will of 'the markets'. While these, at least for the time being, prefer democracy over dictatorship, and indeed place a premium on 'democratic stability', the democracy they reward is a strictly liberal one – one that keeps a country open to the world economy, bars itself constitutionally from using the tool kit of the nation-state for 'irrational' measures like capital controls or confiscation of private property, and keeps itself electorally vulnerable to middle-class concerns about the negative effects of a 'loss of confidence' among international investors. The difficult task of governments, then, is to ensure that their countries remain 'stable democracies' without generating policies that interfere with the free play of internationalized market forces.

3 How insistence on national sovereignty can help cement the liberalization of an increasingly global economy is exemplified by the politics of European integration. While European nation-states have progressively lost the capacity to impose a political will on the 'free play' of market forces on their territories, they have remained uniquely viable as political organizations and as foci of collective identification. Having lost their internal sovereignty over their economies, they have remained in control of international relations, including those within the European Union, enabling them to use an increasingly important political resource in a rapidly internationalizing world to protect their external sovereignty. In this, they continue to draw legitimacy from their historical association with democracy and 'cultural diversity'. Although the global market has grown far beyond the scope of democratically organized national political and cultural identities, defenders of the nation-state seem to find it easy to convince citizens that supranational governance would detract from democracy and replace citizen participation with bureaucratic rule.

Within the European Union, nationalism today takes the form of resistance against supranationalism and defence of inter-governmentalism. Rhetoric aside, and all their many disagreements notwithstanding, European nation-states have throughout the history of European integration carefully protected their status as the masters of their union. Nationalism thus ensured that the integrated European economy remained largely free from integrated public–political interference. Governance capacities that were lost at national level failed to be replaced at supranational level, due to the vigilance with which nation-states defended and defend their national sovereignty. This is not to say that the emerging international economy, in Europe and beyond, is or will be without any governance institutions at all; but whatever these may be like, they will probably lack the specific 'market distorting' capacities of the traditional European nation-state. The historical alliance of nationalism and neo-liberalism, as embodied most visibly but by no means exclusively by Margaret Thatcher, has many facets, domestic as well as international, and has for some time in both arenas clearly been the most powerful force in the European political economy.

Globalization and economic performance

The demise of national state capacity under globalization is likely (1) to destroy a range of governance mechanisms in institutional economies whose performance depends indirectly on the support of a strong state and public power; (2) to favour those national capitalisms that have in the past done with comparatively little state intervention, over those institutional economies that required a high level of state-mediated political organization, thereby affecting the relative competitiveness of alternative performance patterns; and (3), to the extent that national politics was an important source of capitalist diversity to promote convergence of capitalist economies on an institutional monoculture of deregulated markets and hierarchies, thereby reducing the overall diversity of available governance arrangements and potentially causing a net loss in overall performance capacity.

1 At present there is wide consensus that competitiveness will be improved, and there will be general gain, if national and other regulatory barriers to free trade are broken down. However, gains from deregulation need to be offset against losses. As Streeck has argued (1993), some economically beneficial institutional arrangements within civil society depend directly or indirectly on the presence of public regulatory regimes. For example, associations may derive their strength within their constituency of firms from their role in administering government policies or regulations, and may only or mainly for this reason be able to ensure the production of the collective goods which make for their constituency's competitive niches.

While Streeck has extracted his argument from the German case, another example is offered by the tripartite structure of Swedish active labour market policy (King and Rothstein, 1993). In the past, tripartism has contributed to the mobility of Swedish labour, which has in turn been a source of competitive advantage. The involvement of unions in the running of active labour market policy led workers to trust the policy commitment to full employment, and they were willing to accept job changes. Currently tripartite control of policy instruments is challenged in the name of liberalization, and the role of representative associations of business and labour is being brought in line with what is perceived as an American model of lobbying (see Pontusson, this volume). The effect may well be a loss of useful distinctiveness for the Swedish economy.

The indirect effects of deregulation are likely to operate differentially in different economies, as some non-market economic institutions do not in this way depend on public regulation. Those that operate more informally may stand a chance of emerging more or less unscathed. The complexities of this can be gleaned from the response of US trade policy to what it perceives as 'Japanese protectionism'. Bewildered by the resistance of Japanese consumers to buying foreign goods, the American government seems to assume that the cause must be some state practice, threatening sanctions if the Japanese government fails to ensure that Japanese customers buy certain amounts of American goods. The problem is that American policy can only rarely if at all point the finger to any observable protectionist measures, as consumer resistance seems to be based on far more subtle aspects of behaviour.

The impact of indirect dependence of non-state social institutions on state intervention needs to be explored more fully. While the central Italian small-firm sector thrives on the highly 'inaccessible' institutions of local community, and indeed often on opposition to the central state, an important part of its support and even definition is provided by government action. For example, legislation defines what a 'small firm' is and determines its exemption from certain kinds of regulation and its eligibility for certain kinds of subsidy (Weiss, 1988). Further, regional and local government regulation is often an important component of the local institutional base (Bagnasco, 1977; Becattini, 1987).

Paradoxically, with global competition involving many new low-cost producers, European-level political intervention might be the most promising means to preserve niche-creating national or subnational institutional specificities. As pointed out, however, political nationalism creates a deregulatory bias which in fact limits the scope for national specificity, exposing more complex social institutions to the erosive force of markets and hierarchies by refusing to build supranational protection for them. Since in contrast with Japan and the USA, the economic institutions of most Western European countries, even those that are not directly state dependent, tend to be of the kind that will be negatively affected by public deregulation, the failure to establish a European state capacity would seem to be particularly devastating to the social base of the European economies.

2 The destruction or devaluation of national state capacity under globalization discriminates against institutional economies that are socially governed by politics at national level, as opposed to those that derive their institutional advantages from subnational–regional or firm-based social arrangements. At the same time, it improves the relative competitiveness of the more open economies of the Anglo-American kind that have long learned to operate without the succour of an interventionalist state and in the absence of strong social cohesion. If the global orientation of the City of London has in the past made the access of British manufacturing industry to capital difficult and precarious, in an internationalized capital market the manufacturing industries of all other nations will ultimately face the same condition, levelling the playing field for everybody, albeit downward. And as Italian banks start playing in the internationalist casino, the privileged access of the famed networks of small central Italian firms to credit may dry up, effectively preempting whatever may have been the economic advantages of an integrated civil society. With the absolute performance of institutional economies declining in a deregulated world economy, the relative performance – the competitiveness – of their de-regulated competitors is bound to increase.

Most endangered of all are performances exclusively associated with the state, like the French form of state regulation (see Boyer, this volume), which all too easily fall foul of deregulationist drives.[6] Also threatened are universalism of provision, of infrastructures as well as minimum income levels, across an entire population and an entire territory, and effective redistribution, of capacities and resources, between regions and firms. Market-driven systems cannot, and do not want to, ensure the former; firm-based systems fail to provide for inter-firm redistribution; and regionally based systems are incapable of redistribution between regional economies.

Also though somewhat less vulnerable is German-style economic governance through formal, often corporatist associations, discussed here in the chapter by Streeck. Although these mechanisms are not as statist as in the French case, they often derive part of their role and authority within their constituencies from state regulation. Further, at a time when many companies feel constrained by economic difficulty to jettison long-term and collective commitments, there is considerable temptation to cut loose from constraints of the kind that formal associations often impose. In the pure German case, but less so in Scandinavian systems, these problems may be offset by a degree of flexibility accorded to individual firms within associational discipline.

Japanese firms and networks and Italian networks (discussed in this volume by Dore and Regini respectively), different as they undoubtedly are from each other, may be less threatened, provided it turns out to be actually the case that they can perform their organizing functions independently from national political protection and regulation. They, too, may experience tendencies among firms to seek to reduce external obligations. On the other hand, to the extent that they can rely on diffuse community or cultural supports, they may be largely inaccessible to deregulatory measures targeted on formal rules, and relatively unaffected by the declining capacity of the nation-state.

3 A deregulated international economy subdivided into deregulated national economies would be an institutional monoculture that may lead to a net loss of performance capacity. To the extent that national or other institutional specificities serve as niches allowing firms and economies to develop competitive new products and processes, their disappearance must diminish the aggregate entrepreneurial creativity and vitality of capitalism as a system. It is furthermore highly unlikely that any one approach to running a capitalist economy will monopolize all the virtues – which would seem to offer good Popperian, or even Hayekian, reasons for seeking to preserve the innovative potential inherent in a healthy level of 'socio-diversity' within global capitalism.

Today such diversity, or 'requisite variety', is seriously threatened by a number of factors. The USA continues, by virtue of its sheer size and political dominance, to be able to impose its practices on other countries, and make sure that their policies suit its needs and capacities.[7] Also, it so happens that the dominant school of economic theory is intellectually and institutionally wedded to free market models, and promulgates them whenever asked for advice. Perhaps most importantly, free market solutions offer the easiest short-term escape route for firms under destabilizing competition and afraid of the costs of building and rebuilding social infrastructures, especially if they can hope to internalize and privatize such infrastructures by turning themselves into institutional firms.

Unless governability is recovered at national level, which seems most unlikely, capitalist diversity in the future will not primarily reside in national differences. This is not to say that there will be no diversity at all, or that a denationalized global capitalism will be entirely unregulated. More than by nations and the outcomes of national politics, economic governance regimes will vary between subnational regions, international sector and globally operating institutional firms. And instead of being imposed on markets and hierarchies by public power, with a capacity to redistribute resources and decision rights for the purpose of protecting social cohesion, regulation will increasingly be private and market accommodating. It is worth noting that markets inhabited by strategic alliances of transnational corporations are hardly the open, easily entered and perfectly competitive markets celebrated in neo-liberal ideology.

In all systems there is probably a future for firms that have, either within a wider supportive culture as in Japan, or as substitutes for such a culture like in the USA, an institutional base of their own that motivates and retains employees and sustains capital market support for R&D and technical development. However, while these will fare better than firms that face the market with no institutional support at all, this hardly favours the egalitarian high-wage model of capitalism. Individual firms may be able to build company communities that integrate their workforces regardless of a lack of institutions counterbalancing hierarchical managerial unilateralism. However, being only company-wide, these mechanisms do not enable us to draw conclusions about the general state of the societies in which they are located; if anything, isolated firms of this kind are likely to imply considerable social inequality.

If company communities seem the most viable future source of institutional diversity, we face the question whether their rise will unite with market pressures to crowd out such 'republican' institutions as associations, collective bargaining, democratic government regulation and social policy, with the consequence of economic and social decay at the bottom levels of society. It is in this context that the secular decline of the nation-state as an economic community of fate becomes most relevant. The very concept of inequality, not to mention the possibility of its social containment, seems to presuppose the existence of a territorially bounded community capable of effective collective action. If nation-states give way to consensually organized international firms as the most salient foci of economic solidarity, increasingly segmented national societies and politics will be reduced to accommodating the demands of such firms, having to reward them for creaming off the top ranks of national labour markets with all sorts of infrastructural and political inducements. National differences, even where they persist, will then cease to be associated with different social performances. While different countries may continue to be differently competitive, competitiveness may come to mean nothing more than the capacity to move away faster than others from the constraints of egalitarianism and high social protection.

The all-important question today, we believe, is how to recapture public governance of the private economy at some international level, after the national one has become obsolete. Domestic democratic sovereignty over the economy, the one sovereignty that really counts, can be restored only if it is internationally shared, that is, if the reach of what used to be 'domestic' political intervention is expanded to match an expanding market. National social institutions and national democratic politics can support internationally viable, egalitarian high-wage economies only in a conducive international context, and it is only within such a context that they can continue to generate and maintain capitalist diversity and its beneficial consequences for economic performance. Existing national institutions, economically successful as they may or may not have been in the past, can today be no more than the building blocks of a new, larger institutional structure that must supersede them in order to preserve their contribution to the task of civilizing a, by now, globally integrated capitalist market economy.

Notes

This introductory chapter is a considerably revised version of the authors' preparatory paper for the Poitiers conference. The authors are grateful to conference participants, in particular Susan Strange, for helping to clarify a number of critical points.

1   Andrew Shonfield's (1964) pioneering work within the field dates, of course, already from the early 1960s. To many of the new institutionalists he was one of their most significant sources of inspiration and encouragement.

2   Where 'right' was, of course, often left or social-democratic. It is important, however, that the interest in and search for diversity was not limited to the political left. In France, for example, there is a long common tradition across the political spectrum that insists on and takes pride in the uniqueness of the French economy and society. Also, while Shonfield was without doubt a social democrat, the country he seemed to prefer in *Modern Capitalism* was France, at a time when French socialism and social democracy were virtually dead. Although French 'statism' tends to be associated with highly inegalitarian outcomes and regressive distributional effects, the very fact of the distinctiveness of its political economy could add credibility to the claim that there were alternatives within capitalism, and that convergence upon 'pluralist industrialism' was not inevitable.

3   This is an unspoken premise of Shonfield's book – one that must have seemed so self-evident to him that he felt no need to justify it.

4   A major factor that seems to assist them in this is the very destruction that the forces of the market are inflicting on older, pre-economic social relations. As families and communities dissolve, the workplace becomes for a growing number of people the only place that offers them an opportunity to socialize. This provides employers not only with a steady supply of willing labour, but also with workers who, often in spite of declining wages and benefits and deteriorating working conditions, are eager to develop strong moral bonds even with a formal organization, that is, a social entity that has a strategy instead of a morality. Unlike Japanese

firms that legitimate their managerial authority by invoking an image of the family village that is still culturally viable, American institutional firms may thus become functional villages in a desert of anomie, and indeed ones without spatial limits.

5   See the widespread conspiracy theories in the USA that accuse the Bush and Clinton administrations of having surrendered American sovereignty to, of all things, the UN. The code word is Bush's 'New World Order'. NAFTA, GATT and the Mexican bail-out figure prominently in the fantasies of a neo-isolationist movement that has for some time grown influential among Republican constituencies. Gun control legislation is regarded by its adherents as a step in the disarmament of the American people, in preparation for a take-over by UN 'peace-keeping forces'. The neo-regionalist 'militia' movement, which has formed in recent years to defend American society against its constitutional government was involved in to the bombing of a government building in Oklahoma in spring 1995, resulting in many deaths.

6   It should however be noted that state regulation is by no means the only source of distinctiveness in the French economy, many firms having achieved the capacities of institutional companies.

7   Post-war 'embedded liberalism' was strongly dependent on American concerns that if other countries were not allowed a measure of economic and institutional autonomy, their populations might 'go communist'. No such inhibitions any longer exist.

1

THE DISTINCTIVENESS OF JAPAN

Ronald Dore

A good way to approach the question of different kinds of capitalism is to start with a rough classification of the variety of ways in which, currently, people of various persuasions, nationalities and social situations view the nature of the private-sector business firm in capitalist societies. Broadly, I think, one can distinguish four major positions. One may call them: the Property View; the Entity/Community View (two sub-versions); and the Arena View.

The Property View is the dominant one among business practitioners in the Anglo-Saxon world. It is represented, for instance, in the reigning assumptions underlying the Cadbury Report on company governance. The key assumption is that the legal situation, as set out in the British Companies Act, represents social reality. A company is an entity set up by its capital-providing members to further their own material interests. The managers are their agents with a duty to give priority to that shareholder interest, and the careful buying of the best labour as cheaply as they can is as much part of their duty as getting the best bargain out of their suppliers of raw materials. To be sure, the analogy cannot be quite exact because the people who provide the labour have passions and sentiments and respond in a variety of ways to a variety of approaches. These interactions differ from the relationship with external suppliers of, say, molybdenum. Hence, policies of 'worker involvement', paternalistic welfare policies and premium wages above market 'going rates' may all be permissible tactics, provided that they are 'manipulations' designed to yield better value for money in the purchase of labour.

The Entity/Community View sees the company, by contrast, as something like a nation. Company chairmen talk about 'the future of our great company' much as presidents and kings talk about 'our nation's future'. Two things are involved: the company is, as it were, reified. It is seen as an entity which transcends the participating work life of the individuals involved. Second, that entity is at any one time concretely embodied in a particular set of people who, as in a nation, constitute a community, tied together by bonds of mutual interest in the community's fate, obligations of cooperation and trust, the sharing of similar risks. The boundaries of that community can vary. They may be limited to the group of senior managers, or senior and middle managers, or may be extended to the whole body of people who work in the firm, blue collar and white collar, ('core' workers, that is, not usually 'peripheral', temporary and part-time workers). This suggests a distinction between what one might call the Managerial Community View and the Employee Community View. The latter, the view that the firm is a 'community of people', to use the Pope's phrase in his recent encyclical,[1] implies that the shareholders are just one of the groups of outsiders who have to be taken into account for the community to survive and prosper.

The Arena View is one favoured by academic analysts – professional economists, business school teachers, etc. The firm is seen as an arena in which individuals or groups of individuals (for example, 'managers', 'skilled workers', 'suppliers' – groups usually referred to as 'stake-holders') make, often implicit, contracts of various kinds. The organization of a firm can be 'dissolved' into a network of contracts; productive activities are pursued as the fulfilment of bargains motivated exclusively by individual self-interest. 'Principal-agent theory', now a substantial body of economic writing, can be fitted into either the Property View or the Stakeholder–Arena View; sometimes it may be not incompatible with the Managerial Community View, but never with the Employee Community View.

National contrasts

To summarize the contrasts: in the USA and the UK, the Property View dominates, with some deviation, especially in the USA, though increasingly in the UK with the growth both in management buy-outs and share options, towards the Managerial Community View. The dominant concept in Japan corresponds to the Employee Community View, that is, the employee version of the Entity/Community View.

Why does one make these judgements? What are the behavioural manifestations of the imputed differing underlying views? Listen, somebody told me once, to a company chairman addressing shareholders at an annual general meeting. In the USA and UK he's likely to talk about 'Your firm, ladies and gentlemen, over the last year'. His Japanese counterpart (although likely to have far less in the way of shares and stock options) is much more likely to talk about 'our firm'. But the evidence from behaviour is far more complex and comprehensive than that. Let me list some features in summary form.

The employment relation

Employees in large Japanese firms, both blue collar and white collar, are not people who have applied for and been given 'jobs' in the firm. They are people who – at a very early age, usually as soon as they leave school or university – have successfully applied to 'become members' of a firm. 'Membership' means that they can have the expectation (sufficiently often fulfilled for it to be a very confident expectation) that they will not just 'do jobs' but 'make a career' in the firm. This pattern of employment is rare in the USA and the UK, especially in the private sector. It is confined principally to the armed forces of both countries, the pre-Thatcher UK civil service, parts of the US civil service (for example, the State Department), and the managerial ranks of those private sector companies which deviate most towards the Managerial Community View, for example, Shell, Unilever, Phillips, IBM, Hewlett Packard.

Recruitment selection focused not so much on specific vocational capacities, but on personal qualities, general intelligence and learning ability, is consequently standard practice – and quite expensively rigorous – for blue-collar and routine manual workers as well as for managerial workers in Japanese firms. Such selection methods are confined to the very limited managerial segments listed above in the USA and UK.

The individual's identification with the firm that is bred by this 'lifetime commitment' is such as to make it unthinkable for say, a senior manager with a career in Hitachi to move into a comparable position in a directly competing firm such as Toshiba. This would be like a captured British officer joining the German army. He might join a steel firm, but, if he was a senior manager, only with Hitachi's blessing. It is said that the UK banking world was once rather similar; a Barclays Bank manager would never move to Midland. Perhaps one needs to draw a distinction, though, between the more institutionalized and quite stable collectivist communitarianism of the contemporary Japanese firm and the British bank case which might be interpreted as the survival of more paternalistic versions of the 'firm as family'. Even these succumbed, in the end, to the determined onslaught in the 1980s of the reinvigorated Property View, laced perhaps with the Arena View. In the capitalist arenas, all contracts are one-off. An individual's involvement in the contract making arena of one firm should not preclude his taking off and entering a different arena.

Indeed, such sentiments of 'loyalty' and 'paternalistic duty' were under direct attack as impediments to efficiency – thanks to the ideological hegemony exercised by the ineffable exponents of a rigid neo-classical economics. But more of this in the final section.

A UK or US chief executive can expect an income from salary, stock options and bonuses that is tens or even hundreds of times larger than the average salary in his firm if he has served his shareholder principals well by efficiently maintaining earnings and share prices, including effective restraint on wage costs. A Japanese chief executive in any of the large quoted companies can expect a multiple barely into two figures, only a little more than the other directors from whose ranks he has been promoted; in almost exactly the same way, and by the same criteria, as permanent secretaries are promoted from under-secretaries in the British civil service. The salary differences in the two cases are similar. The relationship of the levels of income inequality within the firm to the sense of the firm as community hardly needs pointing out.

Labour and trade unions in the USA and UK try to bring together all the people offering the same occupational skills in the market, hoping to maintain the market 'going rate' for those skills. In Japan the enterprise unions bring together all the people who have committed their future to membership in a particular firm. Their function is: (a) to monitor the possibility of unfair treatment of individuals at lower levels of the hierarchy (juniors on managerial career tracks as well as blue collars); (b) in wage bargaining, to represent the interest those furthest from the centres of power have in getting more jam today, as against the tendency of the 'responsible' people at the top to be more conscious of competing obligations to banks and shareholders, and to want to invest to gain more jam tomorrow.

The investments in training made by a Japanese firm are considered to enhance the firm community's pool of skills. In the USA and the UK skills are viewed as the property of the individual. Skills acquired in one firm are frequently taken to another; Silicon Valley would not exist without the skill/enterprise spin-off from Intel, TI, Hewlett Packard and IBM.

Enterprise behaviour

It is easy to see how all these different employment institutions are congruent with on the one hand the Property View and on the other the Employee Community View of the firm. There are equally characteristic differences in the way firms are managed. First, US and UK managers measure performance above all by return on investment over a relatively short time frame while Japanese managers focus on increase in market share. Second, Japanese firms have a much greater capacity to invest for the long term, if necessary thereby forgoing immediate profits. Third, US and UK managers seek to maintain dividend payments in order to hold share values in the depth of a recession, and may even draw down reserves in order to do so, while at the same time vigorously pruning payrolls – 'letting staff go'. Japanese managers will cut dividends for several periods before they resort to the traumatic experience of forced redundancies – and that only after they have been through the preceding stages of managerial pay cuts, voluntary early retirement or outposting of staff to related companies. Fourth, Japanese companies rely a good deal more on the cooperation of other firms in order to produce their final goods and services. The wholesale/retail sales ratio (about 4:1) is approximately double Britain's, partly for that reason. Extra layers in the distribution system account for the other part. Trading relations between firms in Japan are also characteristically different from those in Anglo-Saxon countries.

As stated earlier, everybody recognizes to some degree that the people who sell a firm labour are different from the people who sell the firm molybdenum in that their passions and sentiments, their capacity for resentment or loyalty, have to be taken into account when dealing with them. The Japanese assume that the sellers of molybdenum also have to be treated in the same way.

British or American businesspersons are apt to think that the efficiency of their business depends on always keeping an eagle eye open for trends in the market. They should always be comparing the deal they are getting from a particular supplier with what they could get elsewhere – and switch without compunction if they find a better combination of quality and price. The Japanese, by contrast, operate with a sense of obligation. Trading relations are seen as generating mutual obligations; as long as the supplier is fulfilling his part of the bargain, 'genuinely and sincerely doing his best' to maintain quality and delivery times, to sink capital in the relationship in order to speed up the joint development of new products, to cooperate in cost cutting when the market turns down, he has a right not to be abandoned because, perhaps for circumstances beyond his control, another supplier offers a better deal. A list of the sixty-odd members of Toyota's first-line suppliers' club in 1990 has only two or three names not present in 1970, and only two or three of the names which figured in the earlier list have now disappeared.

Finally, there is a sharp difference in the way in which industrial firms are financed. Japanese firms have traditionally relied less than Anglo-Saxon firms on the equities market and much more on long-term bank loans. Managers thereby put the firm in the power of similar managers (often from the same universities) who can be persuaded of their projects on the same terms as they justify them to themselves.

This is not to say that equity is unimportant, particularly in the late 1980s when what seemed like an irreversible tendency for share prices to rise continually made investors satisfied with tiny dividends because the capital gains kept them happy. But the pattern of equity holding is distinctive. Banks own shares in the companies to which they make substantial loans, and those companies own shares in their banks. Similar cross-holdings are found between firms and the fire and accident insurance companies that insure their operations, the life insurance company that offers special schemes for their employees or runs their pension funds, other firms that supply their raw materials or buy their products or those with which they have joint ventures or strategic tie-ups to develop new business.

Major Japanese firms have deliberately built these cross-holdings to the point at which they represent a sizeable proportion of their equity – on average about 70 per cent. The stock market handbooks list the percentage, the other 30 per cent on average, of a company's shares which are 'floating shares', that is to say, shares which are freely bought and sold in the market without consultation with the issuing firm.

It is partly because the floating shares on which a raider might lay hands are scarce that no one gets much of a chance to overcome any traditional inhibitions (based on the notion that firms are communities and not pieces of property) and to acquire a taste for the hostile takeover. The Japanese stock market is not a market in corporate control. In turn, this is why Japanese industrial managers do not turn first to the stock price pages in their newspapers and boards of directors do not spend a large part of their time discussing how to present their interim results in a way that makes them most acceptable to 'the markets'. They can, in fact, show indifference to what the shady manipulations of the security companies may be doing to their share prices from day to day. This freedom from the fear of takeover and the ability to contemplate a temporary decline in stock prices, provided the growth indicators are good, are reasons why they can spend so much time thinking about, and can so readily commit the necessary funds to, long-term investment.

A system?

To what degree can one consider the features of Japanese economic organization described above to constitute an integrated national system – labour markets and personnel matters, capital markets, research and development, production methods and work organization, and marketing – in the sense that changes in one area would have to be accompanied by changes in the others?

One notion which is suggested in the introductory chapter of this volume, if not fully expanded, is that national systems can be characterized by the the relative importance in, as it were, the total cake of 'institutions of governance' of the various ingredient institutions. The chapter develops a typology of such institutions derived from Hollingsworth and Streeck (1994) which includes, between the two 'extremes' of state regulation and competition in 'pure' (in economists' terms, efficient) markets: regulation by formal associations such as chambers of commerce; regulation through informal networks and communities, like those reported for clusters of manufacturing firms in central Italy; regulation through 'institutional companies' which develop some form of internal community.

Can one say that any one of these three is more central to the governance of the economy in Japan than elsewhere? It is certainly true that Japanese corporations are the archetype par excellence of the 'institutional company'. The institutions of particular firms (which are very similar across companies) play a much more important role relative to that of labour markets in regulating employment relations in Japan than in, say, the UK or the USA (unless one persists in misnaming the Japanese POCADS – Personnel Office Career Deployment System – as an 'internal labour market'). But this is a matter which specifically concerns employment relations, rather than the whole range of economic transactions. Whether it carries more weight in the sum total of 'governance' than, say, the informal networks of subcontracting between firms, or the quite tough competition in consumer goods product markets, is difficult to conceptualize.

There are also problems in assigning features of the Japanese economy to the other two categories – formal associations and informal networks and communities. First, let us consider the formal and the informal. The merely implicit, not contractually spelt out, lifetime employment guarantee in Japanese large firms could well be considered informal. But case law regarding 'unfair dismissal' and the priority of wages and redundancy compensation in bankruptcy proceedings are ways in which state organs have formally reinforced and sanctioned the practice. Likewise, subcontracting networks are informal, but the state has created Subcontracting Complaints Tribunals to give summary hearings to allegations of unfair trading by the weaker parties to the relationship. It has thereby given certain parameters of the relationship formal status. 'Formal' and 'informal' are therefore a matter of degree.

Second, the dichotomization of 'community' and 'association' has been giving sociologists trouble for over a century, because what are formed as associations of individuals combining to pursue their individual interests more effectively, often develop community-like characteristics in the sense of fostering fellow feeling among members and becoming objects of loyalty. One can in some senses justly describe a Japanese firm as a 'community', but membership is not ascribed by birth like membership in a village community; it is achieved through a quite rigorous selection process (though this achievement has such importance for life chances that it might almost be called a process of 're-ascription'). The Japanese Iron and Steel Association is as formal an association as its British or American counterpart, but the managers of its constituent firms, as Rodney Clark first pointed out many years ago (1978), have a far more lively (and constraining) sense of belonging to a 'community of the steel industry' than their counterparts in Britain or the USA.

There is another way of referring to these phenomena which, being at a higher level of abstraction, has a much more 'across the board' relevance. This is to say that economic transactions in Japan are much more commonly 'embedded' in face-to-face social relations. But note that this is not at all the Polanyi type of social embeddedness, the disentangling of which he sees as the precondition for the emergence of modern market capitalism.[2] The difference lies in the ascription point made above. Polanyi referred to ascribed social relations – between uncle and nephew in an extended family, or neighbours in the same village. In contrast, social relations in which Japanese economic transactions are embedded are achieved. Membership in the firm, for instance, is obtained through selection tests designed to make sure that each set of new employees starts on its appropriate career track as an ability-homogeneous group; or, to take a similar example, subcontractors have to work their way through Categories C and B before they can become Category A suppliers of Toyota. The greater tendency of Japanese associations to develop community-like characteristics is part of this more general syndrome: the embedding of economic transactions in (achieved) social relationships.

Institutional interlock

The most obvious way in which the institutions of any country's capitalist system may be described as being really a 'system' is through the jigsaw-puzzle 'fitting' of one institutional practice with another. Take, for example, the three salient features of the Japanese system:

1 lifelong rather than highly mobile employment relationship;
2 long-term, obligated, rather than auction-market mobile, supplier relations;
3 patient, long-term committed, rather than short-term, returns-sensitive, equity capital and the consequent absence of takeovers.

Some of the obvious interconnecting 'fits', already hinted at above, include:

1 Supplier relations can more easily rest in part on verbal understandings and trust because the assembler's purchasing manager, as a lifelong member of the firm who identifies with it, can commit not just himself but the firm. Although he is likely to move on to something else at his next posting, his successor will feel bound by the promises given by his predecessor, who will still be around in the firm to give his version of what those promises might have been. Lifetime employees have a strong and shared interest in the firm's reputation.
2 People who have committed their working lives to a particular firm are more prone to take a long-term view, to have a low time discount. The firm's future is their future – an important precondition for the long-termism which informs both the supplier relations and stable shareholding.
3 Managers who have to watch their share prices in volatile stock markets to avoid takeovers cannot afford to keep underemployed workers on their books through recessions. Only managers who can cut back on profits and dividends in recessions are able to do so. The cross-shareholdings and committed capital are, therefore, preconditions for lifetime employment.
4 Managers do not treat these cross-shareholdings primarily as a source of profit; they are willing to sacrifice gains they might make by selling them and investing in something with higher returns, in order to retain the long-term business relationship with the issuing firm. That long-term interest is more likely to be appreciated by lifetime managers. Lifetime employment was thus a precondition for the initial creation of cross-shareholdings and of the conventions which surround them.

There is, also, of course, institutional interlock between economic and not primarily economic institutions – the structure of the family and employment institutions, for example. The distinctness of male and female roles in the marriage relationship, and in society generally, determines the acceptability of the sharp difference between the terms and conditions under which young unmarried and older married women are usually hired. The 'male as breadwinner' assumption affects the acceptability of the lifetime distribution of male wages. It may also be the case that first-generation industrial workers from a farming background were attracted into initially low-wage career employment patterns because their families had given an assured future to the eldest sons with the inheritance of the farm and therefore accepted the need to 'set younger sons up for life'.

Motivational congruence

But there is another mechanism which can make for coherence in social systems, one hinted at by Crouch and Streeck as 'aspects of behaviour' – long termism, adaptability, cooperativeness, etc. This concerns the motivational or cathectic consistency of behaviour. In all the institutional practices described, is there a similarity in the values which seem to be maximized, in the moral constraints that seem to be obeyed, which would make it plausible to state that people brought up in Japanese families and schools are largely predisposed to behave in this way, and to take happily to this kind of institutional practice, whereas people brought up in British or American schools are predisposed to behave differently and to fit into different kinds of institution? (Japanese or Americans, on average, that is to say). It is not necessary to postulate that no one brought up in the USA could fit happily into a Japanese-type firm, or that no Japanese could fit into the individualistic short-term life of a British company. The range of behavioural predispositions is large in both societies. We are referring here only to central tendencies.

Note that I speak of 'behavioural dispositions', avoiding the word which the new institutionalists fear – 'culture'. There are other good reasons for not resorting to use of the word 'culture' beyond the desire not to offend any sectarian group. It is a protean concept and often includes behavioural dispositions, but is usually extended to cover all those cultural artefacts – family relationships and ideas about proper family relationships, patterns of toilet training or gift giving, the social organization and curricula of schools, poverty and affluence and its distribution, explicit systems of Christian or Confucian morality, dominant ideologies with assumptions about the nature of human motivation, dominant interpretations of national history, which currently reinforce and sustain those dispositions.

It is true that if one seeks to explain those dispositions, or to speculate as to how they might change, or be changed by design, one has to take account of all those currently operating factors involved in reinforcement and reproduction of the dispositions – and then start delving back into history. How do current notions of right and wrong derive from those of previous generations? What relation does the current interpretation of history bear to the actual facts of history? How did that history – the experience of being a pioneer or late developer, the experience of victory or defeat – shape the formative institutions of school or family? What role is played by the form of agriculture and the pattern of settlement, or (whisper it not to anyone susceptible to the charge of racism) the predominance in the population gene pool of those genes that tilt the aggression/passivity balance, or the deference/self-assertion balance one way or the other? It is true that the explanation of behavioural dispositions involves all this, but the observation and description of behavioural dispositions can be a separate and independent activity. And appeal to the tendency in human personalities to avoid cognitive and cathectic dissonance as a reason for expecting the various institutional spheres of society to be congruent – in the sense that they appeal to the same sort of behavioural dispositions – is valid to the extent that the experiments of social psychologists confirm that tendency to exist (which is to say moderately valid, with all sorts of qualifications).

This congruence is assumed to have emerged over time through the following process. Social change constantly provides new, relatively unstructured or weakly structured situations, or those for which established institutionalized responses are inadequate. Individuals are required to choose. The way they choose to behave in such unstructured or weakly structured situations is determined by the behavioural dispositions they have acquired in the context of well-established institutions, and the way they behave determines the form that emerging or changing institutions take. The almost totally unstructured pattern of Japanese post-war industrial relations, for example, gradually became structured under the influence of – and in their final institutionalized form reflected the nature of – the behavioural dispositions dominant among the workers and managers involved.

To revert from this methodological digression to the differences between Japanese and Anglo-Saxon society, how might one define the behavioural dispositions which give each society the character of integrated 'systems'? I can think of three dimensions of difference.

1 Anglo-Saxons behave in ways designed to keep their options open – to keep their freedom to change jobs and loyalties, to shift investments, as soon as the prospect of advantage offers. Japanese are much more willing to foreclose their options by making long-term commitments from which, they accept, they can only disengage themselves with great difficulty.
2 In making their choices, Anglo-Saxons give greater weight to their own immediate welfare or that of their family or personal friends. Japanese

are much more likely, by virtue of their long-term commitments, to have diffuse obligations to promote the welfare of others – the other members of the firms they have joined, their partners in long-term trading relationships. Put starkly, this is a difference in the selfishness/altruism dimension.

3 The third difference in behavioural dispositions is rather more often made into an explicit cultural ideal than the previous two – a difference in the evaluation, and hence in the willingness to undertake, different kinds of economic activity. In Japan, producing goods and services which directly enhance the lives of others is good. Spending one's life in the speculative purchase and sale of financial claims is bad.

This 'productivist ethic' is far from absent in Anglo-Saxon countries, but, in all the ways described by Wiener (1981) in *English Culture and the Decline of the Industrial Spirit*, it has become far more attenuated than in Japan. The direct transition of the gentry to gentlemanly banking rather than to entrepreneurship helped to produce this result in Britain. In the USA, the sanctification of time and the foundation of charitable trusts have made folk heroes out of the Rockefellers and Morgans, and allowed economists to argue that it is a far more effective form of altruism to make as much money as one can in whatever way one can and then give it away (*à la* Soros) than to reduce one's profits by harbouring tender feelings about losers such as one's employees or business partners.[3] In the Anglo-Saxon countries there is a much greater disposition to nod sagely when economists demonstrate that speculation in secondary markets is the way in which the invisible hand ensures that markets get the prices right so that the producers of goods and services get the best possible signals on which to base their production decisions. We need derivatives, it is believed, and society is well served when it devotes a significant number of its cleverest brains to that particular form of what looks like gambling and is gambling, but is also a crucial mechanism for balancing fluctuations in trade.

There are Japanese – certainly a majority of Japanese American-trained economists – who hold the same beliefs. There was a time during the late 1980s asset price bubble, amid rumours of fantastic salaries to be made in the financial sector, when newspaper leader writers, reflecting the dominant 'productivist' morality, noted with alarm that some physicists, engineers and mathematicians from the top universities were beginning to take jobs with securities companies and banks rather than in industry – something which their Oxbridge equivalents had been doing as a matter of course for decades. Such seductions have become rarer recently. In spite of what the economists say and the growing number of returned MBAs, it is still, probably, the dominant view in, say, the Ministry of Finance that (a) the proliferation of secondary markets in Anglo-Saxon economies goes well beyond what the production of adequate market signals for producers requires; (b) even if speculation is a partially beneficial evil in its consequences, it is still to be deplored that clever people should make gambling not an occasional recreation but a way of life. It might be better to sacrifice some degree of allocative efficiency through the market in order to maintain the 'productivist ethic' and to channel the flows of human talent in desirable directions. The advantage will be still greater if that sacrifice of market efficiency is more than adequately compensated for by enhancing those other kinds of efficiency which come from people having greater security and stability in their lives and being able to cooperate with and trust each other – so that in fact by that sacrifice of market efficiency one ends up with higher growth rates, as well as a more equal distribution of income.

Does it matter?

But does it matter, in practical terms, whether one can justly say that Anglo-Saxon capitalism and Japanese capitalism are different systems, with different integrating principles?

It does if one is trying to change things. Take the institutional interlock point. There are many exponents of 'human resource management' in Britain, for example, who urge that firms should become more like communities, that workers should be 'involved' and made to feel more like respected members of their firms as seems to be the case in Japan. But if there is no change in the owner dominance of British firms and the priority given to shareholder returns, the flexibility in hiring and firing required for maximizing those returns through technical change and business cycles makes it unlikely that managers will be able to deliver the job security which is an essential element of Japanese employees' involvement.

Or take the behavioural disposition point. If people in Anglo-Saxon societies are generally disposed to want to keep open their options in order to seize the short-term advantage of new opportunities, an employer who does seek 'involvement' of his workers by offering them complete job security may well not gain the advantages of Japanese firms from training investments, and from the ability to do long-term manpower planning, because the workers may choose to go elsewhere when better jobs are on offer.

But that is obviously not to say that the economic systems of societies are so tightly integrated that nothing can change. Piecemeal change does occur. Change in one set of institutional practices can induce complementary change in others. Even assumptions about the purpose of human life and the most effective and most moral means of achieving it can change. The post-Thatcher British economy is different in many respects from the economy in the days of Butskellism. Japanese capitalism in the 1930s was much more like contemporary Anglo-Saxon capitalism than it is today. The mutual security, cross-shareholding system is largely a creation of the last thirty years. Three-quarters of a century ago lifetime employment was confined, as in Britain, to the public service and the managerial ranks of banks and a small number of large industrial firms. In the depression of the mid-1950s, the willingness of large firms to cut out subcontractors and take work in-house was remarked on as a feature of the ruthlessness of Japan's 'dual economy' capitalism. Historians have recently documented the transition which clearly had roots in some of the larger firms' labour management policies in the 1920s, but seems to have been definitively promoted by wartime controls which produced a managerial revolution and led to the dethronement of the shareholder.[4] Postwar labour militancy and the resulting compromise – the stable enterprise union pattern – consolidated the change, as, subsequently, did the deliberate development of cross-shareholdings.

Now all the talk is of change in the other direction, celebrated in numerous articles in the *Wall Street Journal* and the *Economist* under such titles as 'The demise of the Japanese model'. So far substantial change in employment or share-holding patterns, as distinct from much talk by management gurus about the advent of such changes, is hard to discern in spite of the strains of five years of recession. But as a long-run perspective the reversion to the Anglo-Saxon model scenario has plausibility. Some human institutions require more coercive constraints – because they involve trained repression of basic urges – than others. In that sense the Japanese system is more constraining than the Anglo-Saxon. What, for the older generation, enforced those constraints and made them acceptable was in part poverty. Affluence, it can be argued, brings greater security and willingness to take risks, including the risks involved in 'defecting' from the established rules. When defecting snowballs, which is more likely to happen when backed by the legitimacy lent by what Albert calls US 'cultural power' – then institutions change. One can equally argue the reverse, of course, as I have previously done (Dore, 1987). Affluence takes the edge off ruthless competitiveness; people come to be able to afford greater consideration for others. They are more likely to value the social benefit of good personal relations even at the expense of turning an extra penny. Only time will tell which effect is the stronger.

Systems and ideologies

There is another reason why it matters whether or not these societies present alternative systems. The system that is the real economy of the USA mirrors the value system that is implicit in neo-classical economics. The general propensity to keep one's options open is what ensures the maximum mobility of resources. In societies where people always keep their options open – where markets are mobile because people can, from moment to moment, choose and rechoose where to spend their time and money – the resources of labour and capital get allocated to the uses which yield the highest return, and the equilibrium of maximum efficiency is most closely approached. Flexibility, flexible and rapid response to market signals, is the root of dynamism and growth; locking resources into long-term commitments is a recipe for stagnation.

It would not matter if neo-classical economics claimed only to be an apologia for the American way of life. Instead it claims universal truth, containing prescriptions valid for all times and places. There is some point, therefore, particularly for the Russians or the Chinese, say, who are having those prescriptions urged on them with such total self-assurance and self-righteousness by World Bank and IMF economists, to reflect on the fact that there can be an alternative system with its own, different, coherence, and one which so far seems to have performed pretty well.

Notes

This chapter makes some use of material included in the author's chapter 'What makes the Japanese different?', in C. Crouch and D. Marquand (eds) *Ethics and Markets*. Oxford: Blackwell, 1993.

1 *Centesimus Annus*, 1991.
2 Karl Polanyi (1944) *The Great Transformation*. New York: Rinehart.
3 See, for example, G.S. Becker (1980).
4 T. Okazaki (1994).

2

GERMAN CAPITALISM: DOES IT EXIST? CAN IT SURVIVE?

Wolfgang Streeck

Does it exist?

In the roughly four decades between the end of World War II and German unification, West German society gave rise to a distinctive kind of capitalist economy, governed by nationally specific social institutions that made for high international competitiveness at high wages and, at the same time, low inequality of incomes and living standards. Already by the late 1980s, when the differences in performance and social organization between the West German economy and its main competitors came to be widely noticed, the continued economic viability of the 'German model' began to appear doubtful to many. Shortly thereafter, the survival of the German version of advanced capitalism became tied to its successful extension to the former East Germany. With the 1992 completion of the European Internal Market, it became in addition dependent on the compatibility of German economic institutions with the emerging regime of the integrated European economy.

At the time of unification, West Germany was internationally the most successful of the major economies (Table 2.1). More exposed to the world market than both Japan and the USA, the country accounted for a significantly larger share in world visible exports than Japan, with roughly half its population, and for about the same share as the USA, which has a population twice the Japanese. West German trade and current account balances, expressed in percent of GDP, exceeded those of Japan, and presented a stark contrast to the chronically deficitarian Anglo-American economies. This was in spite of the fact that German wages had long been considerably higher than Japanese and American wages.

Characteristically, the international success of the West German high-wage economy was accompanied by comparatively little internal inequality. The difference between high and average wages, as measured by the ratio of the ninth over the fifth decile of the wage spread, was much lower in Germany than in its major competitor countries. Similarly, German low

Table 2.1   *The comparative performance of the German economy*[a]

	Trade in goods and services, in % of GDP[b]		Visible exports in % of world total exports[c]		Trade (current account) balance in % of GDP				Hourly wage of workers, US = 100[d]
	·1988	1994	1988	1993	1988		1994		1992
Germany	54.9	51.0	12.0	10.1	6.5	(4.0)	2.7	(–1.1)	160	(119)
UK	48.7	50.8	5.4	4.8	–4.5	(–3.1)	–2.1	(–1.8)[e]	91	(82)
Japan	18.0	16.7	9.8	9.6	3.3	(2.8)	3.4	(3.1)[e]	100	(66)
USA	19.6	21.8	12.0	12.3	–2.6	(–2.6)	–2.5	(–2.3)	100	

[a] 1988: West Germany. 1994: United Germany.
[b] Trade data calculated on a balance of payments basis. Sources: IMF, *International Financial Statistics Yearbook, International Financial Statistics*, June 1995.
[c] Exports calculated on an international transactions basis.
[d] In parentheses: in purchasing power equivalents. Source: Freeman (1994: 31), based on data from US Bureau of Labor Statistics, *Hourly Compensation Costs for Production Workers in Manufacturing*, 1992. German data refer to West Germany only.
[e] 1993.

wages, as represented by the first decile of the distribution, were significantly higher in relation to the median (Table 2.2). Moreover, during the 1980s, at a time when in all other industrialized countries the wage spread increased, the relation of the high German wage to the median remained essentially unchanged, whereas the low wage increased substantially, from 61 to 65 per cent of the median wage. Furthermore, intersectoral wage dispersion was dramatically low in West Germany compared to both Japan and the USA, and so were the earnings differentials between workers in small and large firms (Table 2.3). In the latter respect, it is important to note that the employment share of small and medium-sized firms in West Germany was far higher than in Britain and the USA, and close to Japan in spite of a comparatively low wage differential. Finally, the ratio of German chief executive salaries over skilled wages, while higher than in Japan, was lower than in Britain and, in particular, the USA.

The economic institutions of postwar German capitalism

The West German combination of external competitiveness and normalized high-wage employment reflects the operation of a distinctive set of socio-economic institutions. These, in turn, reflect a complex historical compromise between liberal capitalism, as introduced after World War II, and two different countervailing forces, Social Democracy and Christian Democracy – as well as between traditionalism and two alternative versions of modernism, liberalism and socialism, and of course between capital and labour. This compromise was struck, and became firmly institutionalized, at a time when both the communist wing of the labour

Table 2.2   *Wage spread*

	D9:D5[a]		D1:D5[b]	
	Early 1980s	Early 1990s	Early 1980s	Early 1990s
Germany	1.63	1.64	0.61	0.65
UK[c]	1.72	1.99	0.68	0.59
Japan[c]	1.63	1.73	0.63	0.61
USA	2.16	2.22	0.45	0.40

Germany: gross monthly earnings plus benefits (calculated as 1/12 of 13th and 14th month pay plus holiday allowances plus Christmas allowances) of full-time, full-year workers. Source: German Socio-Economic Panel, Waves 1–8. Calculated by Viktor Steiner, Zentrum für Europäische Wirtschaftsforschung, GmbH.

UK: gross hourly earnings of persons paid on adult rates, whose pay for the survey week was not affected by absence. Data prior to 1983 include men under 21 and women under 18. Source: New Earnings Survey.

Japan: monthly scheduled earnings of regular workers, 18–59 years old, at non-governmental establishments with at least 5–10 workers (varies by survey year), excluding agriculture, forestry and fisheries, private household services and employees of foreign governments. Source: Basic Survey of the Wage Structure. Taken from Katz, Loveman and Blanchflower (1993).

USA: gross hourly earnings, computed as annual earnings divided by annual hours worked (annual weeks worked multiplied by usual weekly hours) of wage and salary workers. Source: Current Population Survey.

[a] Ninth over fifth decile. Source: *OECD Employment Outlook*, July 1993.

[b] First over fifth decile. Source: *OECD Employment Outlook*, July 1993.

[c] Males only.

movement and the authoritarian faction of the German business class were, for different reasons, excluded from political participation.

Under these circumstances, those who wanted to turn the new Germany into a liberal market economy had to accept the revival of a variety of traditionalist status protections – for farmers, civil servants, *Mittelstand* (the class of small business owners) – as well as an extensive welfare state and established labour unions. At the same time, the old middle classes, represented especially by the Christian Democratic Party, while successfully defending some of their protective institutions – like the special status of artisanal firms – had to learn to use these under the competition regime of a market economy *and* in the presence of a safely entrenched union movement. Labour, finally, was never strong enough, as in Sweden, to rid society in the name of progress of, for example, small firms, apprenticeship or works councils. Indeed German unions were rebuilt after the war as *Einheitsgewerkschaften*, uniting previously divided socialist and Catholic movements, which contributed to the recognition by labour of the need to seek productive coexistence with non-socialist, traditional forms of social organization, as well as class compromise at the workplace and beyond.

While the result of all this was certainly a capitalist market economy, it was one that was and remains richly organized and densely regulated by

Table 2.3   *Other indicators of inequality*

	Intersectoral wage dispersion		Average earnings of workers in small enterprises, in percent of earnings of workers in large Enterprises[a]	Ratio of CEO earnings to average earnings of manual workers in manufacturing[b]
	Freeman[c]	ILO Data[d]		
Germany	17.7	14.9 (29)	90 (58)	10.2
UK	21.0	20.0 (20)	80 (40)	15.5
Japan	26.7	24.1 (20)	77 (68)	7.8
USA	27.3	24.8 (24)	57 (35)	25.8

[a] Source: Loveman and Sengenberger (1990: 34). In parentheses: employment in small manufacturing enterprises, in percent of total employment in manufacturing 1986–7. Small manufacturing enterprises are those with less than 500 workers. Sources: Acs and Audretsch (1993: 228); Statistics Bureau of Japan, Management and Coordination Agency, *Annual Report on the Labour Force Survey*.

[b] Source on CEO earnings: The Wyatt Company. German and British data relate to large companies in all industries; Japanese data, to companies of all sizes in all industries; US data, to manufacturing firms of all sizes. To increase comparability, earnings are calculated as average earnings in the upper quartile of CEO earnings. Average earnings of workers: various national sources.

[c] Freeman (1988) uses several indicators of inter-industry wage dispersion, calculated on different data as the variance of the *logarithm of earnings by industry, multiplied by 100*. The figures in the table represent the average of the three most recent indicators that include all four countries. The indicators are based on UN data from 1983, ILO data from 1984, and US Bureau of Labor Statistics data from 1986.

[d] Coefficient of variation of average wages and salaries of full-time workers at adult rates of pay between ISIC categories (industries). Source: *ILO Yearbook*, own calculations. In brackets the number of sectors over which the coefficient was calculated. Fewer categories are likely to underestimate the coefficient.

a vast variety of institutions that have sprung from sometimes incompatible sources, from *Mittelstand* traditionalism to various ideological stripes of organized labour. While this makes Germany different from the USA, it also distinguishes it from Sweden, in that Germany never became a Social-Democratic society. Although workers and unions were able gradually to build a strong position for themselves in German capitalism, stronger than in all other large capitalist countries, the German political economy continued to allow for decentralized compromise and local commitments supplementing, underpinning and sometimes superseding the high politics of class accommodation at national level. On the other hand, although its political economy is highly institutionally coordinated, and regardless of many other often striking parallels, Germany differs also from Japan, in that the institutions which embed its economy and shape its performance are politically negotiated and typically legally constitutionalized, rather than commanding compliance as a matter of informal obligation or as a result of successful conservative social engineering in a closed national or 'enterprise community'.

Compared to the other major capitalist economies, the institutional framework of the German economy can be summarily described as follows:[1]

Markets These are politically instituted and socially regulated, and regarded as creations of public policy deployed to serve public purposes. The postwar competition regime is strict, resulting in comparatively low industrial concentration in most sectors. At the same time, wide areas of social life, like healthcare, education and social insurance, are not governed by market principles, and some markets, like those for labour and capital, are less so than others. Competitive markets coexist with an extensive social welfare state, and political intervention and social regulation often interfere with the distributive outcome of markets, for example, by building a floor under them. Also, small firms are in various ways shielded from the competition of large industry, or are publicly assisted in competing with it. Reflecting a history of fragmented markets offering little space for mass production, price competition is often mitigated by product specialization.

Firms These are social institutions, not just networks of private contracts or the property of their shareholders. Their internal order is a matter of public interest and is subject to extensive social regulation, by law and industrial agreement. Also, managers of large German firms face capital and labour markets that are highly organized, enabling both capital and labour to participate directly in the everyday operation of the firm and requiring decisions to be continuously negotiated. Decisions thus take longer, but are also easier to implement once taken.

German capital markets are not 'markets for control'. Many companies continue to be privately held; only a small part of the productive capital is traded at the stock exchange; banks may hold equity; shareholding is highly concentrated; and shares and companies do not often change hands. Firms finance themselves less through equity than through long-term bank credit. Since banks can cast proxy votes on behalf of shares they hold in deposit, they can effectively monitor management performance, which allows them to give firms long-term loans and creates an incentive for them not to speculate with stock. Labour is similarly present within firms, with workforces exercising legal rights to co-determination through works councils and, where applicable, supervisory board representation. Together with collective bargaining and legal regulation, co-determination supports an employment regime that makes it difficult for employers to dismiss workers, resulting in employment spells almost as long as in Japan, and much longer than in the USA (Table 2.4). Turning labour into a more fixed production factor and making it more similar to capital than in market-driven employment, this encourages high employer investment in skills.

Table 2.4   *Employment stability*

	Median tenure in present job, in years	Average tenure in present job, in years
Germany (1990)[a]	7.5	10.4
UK (1991)	4.4	7.9
Japan (1990)[b]	8.2	10.9
USA (1991)	3.0	6.7

[a] 1990. Excluding apprentices.

[b] Regular employees (persons hired for an indefinite period); temporary workers hired for more than one month; daily workers hired for over 17 days, in private establishments with over 9 employees.

Source: OECD *Employment Outlook*, July 1993

The postwar German state   The state is neither *laissez-faire* nor *étatiste*, and is best described as an *enabling state*. Its capacity for direct intervention in the economy is curtailed by vertically and horizontally fragmented sovereignty, and by robust constitutional limitations on discretionary government action. Vertical fragmentation between the federal government and the *Länder* closely limits what political majorities at national level can do, making political change slow and policies less than immediately responsive to electoral majorities. The electoral system, which favours coalition governments, further adds to the centrist drift and the long response time of German politics.

Horizontally, sovereignty is divided between the federal government and a number of independent authorities insulated from electoral pressure, like the Bundesbank or the Federal Cartel Office. Policy objectives like monetary stability and competitive markets are in this way removed from government discretion and depoliticized. A similar effect is caused by strong constitutional protections, like the right of unions and employers associations to regulate wages and working conditions without government interference. The result is both immobility and predictability of government policies, precluding rapid political innovation and allowing economic agents to develop stable expectations, pursue long-term objectives, and build lasting relations with one another.

Constitutionally dedicated to competitive markets and a hard currency, the postwar German state lacks capacity for a selective industrial policy. In compensation, it offers firms and industries a wide range of general infrastructural supports, like high public spending on research and development. Moreover, to safeguard social cohesion, the federal government spends a considerable share of the gross domestic product on social protection. It also accepts a constitutional obligation to provide for 'equal living conditions' in all *Länder*, which has given rise to an extensive redistributive system of revenue sharing. To expand its capacities in line with its responsibilities, the German state has developed an extraordinary ability to assist groups in civil society in organizing themselves, devolving

on them governance functions that would otherwise have to be either performed by the state or left to the market. It is through state-enabled collective action and quasi-public, 'corporatist' group self-government that
the German political economy generates most of the regulations and collective goods that circumscribe, correct and underpin the instituted
markets of *soziale Marktwirtschaft* (the social market economy).

Publicly enabled associations   Widespread organized cooperation among
competitors and bargaining between organized groups, conducted through
publicly enabled associations, is probably the most distinctive feature of the
German political economy. Governance is delegated either to individual
associations or to collective negotiations between them, with the state often
awarding its outcome legally binding status. Associations performing
quasi-public functions are typically granted some form of obligatory and
quasi-obligatory membership, helping them overcome the free-rider problems associated with collective goods production and giving Germany the
most densely organized civil society among the larger countries.

   Publicly enabled associations regulate instituted markets in a variety of
ways. German business associations, prevented by law from operating as
cartels, turn price into quality competition, by promoting product
specialization and setting and enforcing high-quality standards. To the
same effect, employers associations prevent low-wage competition by
negotiating uniformly high labour standards with national industrial
unions. To make the outcome economically viable, 'dual' training, with
associatively organized cooperation between competing firms, between
government and industry, and between business and labour procures the
skill base that firms need to be competitive in quality markets. For the
same purpose, associations also organize cooperative research and technology transfer. Legally enabled associational support is especially vital
for small and medium-sized firms.

   Above all, associative regulation constitutes the single most important
source of egalitarianism in the German economy. Joint governance of
labour markets by employers associations and centralized industrial
unions is so firmly established that by the 1980s Germany had become the
only major economy in which the 'postwar settlement' between capital
and labour remained intact (Table 2.5). Although unionism has been comparatively stable, associative labour market governance in Germany is
above all accomplished through near-universal collective bargaining
coverage, due to strongly institutionalized industry-wide negotiations
and legal extension of agreements. More than anything else, it is the
German system of centralized and interconnected collective bargaining
that is responsible for the low dispersion of wages in Germany between
individuals, industrial sectors, and small and large firms.

German economic culture   This is often traditionalist; savings rates are high,
and consumer credit, although increasing, remains low by comparison.

Table 2.5   *Unions and collective bargaining*

| | Union density[a] | | | | Collective bargaining coverage[b] | | Variation in coverage rates by industries |
	1980	1985	1988	1990	1980	1990	1990[c]
Germany	37.0	37.4	33.8	32.9[d]	82	82[e]	0.14
UK	50.7	45.5	41.5	39.1	70[f]	47	0.34
Japan	31.1	28.9	26.8	25.4	28	21[g]	0.74
USA	23.0	18.0	16.4	15.6	26	18	0.61

[a] Employed members only. Sources: 1980, 1985, 1988: Visser (1991). 1990: *OECD Employment Outlook*, 1993.

[b] *OECD Employment Outlook*, 1993. The German figures are estimates supplied by the WSI, a research institute of the German Trade Union Confederation (DGB). The Bundesarbeitsministerium (Federal Ministry of Labour) reports a coverage rate of 90 and 91 per cent for the two years; the OECD source uses the government data.

[c] Coefficient of variation. Source: see *b*.

[d] West Germany.

[e] West Germany.

[f] 1978.

[g] 1989.

Price competition is mitigated by socially established preferences for quality. Markets do not *per se* confer merit: social status and solidarity interfere, and security is regarded as important. Speculation is not valued. Continuous monitoring of one's short-term balance of economic advantage is not a social norm, encouraging long-term orientations and commitments and supporting, among other things, a redistributive tax system. Professional competence is highly regarded for its own sake; German managers tend to be engineers, and authority at the workplace is based on superior technical knowledge. Collectivism and discipline have given way as core cultural values to privacy and autonomy from organizational control and market pressure, as evidenced by strong cultural support for short working hours, low participation in paid employment, and a qualification-based organization of work. Work-related knowledge is vested in an occupational qualification structure, where the distinction between knowledge and skills is conceived as gradual rather than categoric. Institutionally, this is reflected in the unique vocational training system, with its long socialization periods leading to portable certificates under national regulations negotiated between unions and employers associations.[2]

Institutional structure and economic performance

In the 1970s and 1980s, the institutional structure of the West German economy conditioned and sustained a distinctive pattern of performance that happened to be highly competitive in world markets. High costs originating in socially circumscribed labour markets ruled out price-competitive production throughout the economy and forced firms to seek survival in quality-competitive international markets. Here, the same set of German institutions that constituted a prohibitive liability in price-competitive markets served as a competitive asset – with what would be debilitating rigidities for firms trying to compete on price, offering enabling flexibilities to firms pursuing quality competitiveness through upgrading and customization of products.[3]

While imposing constraints that make low-cost production prohibitively costly, German economic institutions offer firms rich opportunities for strategic upgrading. An extended social welfare state, negotiated management under co-determination, and encompassing collective bargaining place the economy under social pressures that prevent anything beyond moderate differentiation of wages and working conditions. Unions and business associations, then, find it in their common interest to deploy their quasi-public powers to help the economy move into quality-competitive markets, through cooperative upgrading of skills, work organization, technology and products. Just as the universality of the pressure accounts for the fact that only very few German products have remained price competitive, the general availability of cooperative supports, also generated by encompassing labour-inclusive associative governance under state facilitation, explains the high general competitiveness and low sectoral specialization of the German manufacturing sector. How successful this system has been is indicated by the fact that before unification that sector was proportionally larger than in any comparable country, in spite of having to pay much higher wages. It also was and still is internationally competitive across a uniquely wide range of products, making Germany by far the world's most diversified export economy.

German industrial upgrading is typically slow and gradual but also continuous, reflecting an institutional infrastructure that makes for long decision times while fostering long-term orientations. The resulting pattern of innovation is one that is more likely to generate improvements of existing products of existing firms and sectors than to give rise to new sectors. Generally, sticky decisions, steady commitments and delayed responses in German institutions make for slow fluctuations, up or down, in economic activity and performance; for flat cyclical movements, especially compared to the USA; and for low dispersion of outcomes, all of which are conducive to stable cooperation and steady improvement across the board. Averages are typically high, coefficients of variation low, and extreme cases are rare at both ends.

The broad movement of the German economy in the 1970s and 1980s into quality-competitive markets was helped by the traditional preference of German consumers for quality. Traditionalism contributed also to a high savings rate, which helped generate the patient capital needed for continuous upgrading of products and production factors. Within firms, sticky capital and committed labour, having access to voice as an alternative to exit, enabled managements to take the long view, based on stable bargains with and between both. In politics, divided and immobile economic government enshrined a currency regime that foreclosed devaluation to restore price competitiveness, and offered investors insurance against electoral volatility.

Above all, the success of the 'German model' as long as it lasted, derived from the way in which it utilized social pressures for an egalitarian distribution of economic outcomes to generate an egalitarian distribution of productive capabilities, with the latter in turn enabling the economy to underwrite the former. Complementing social constraints on some economic strategies with productive opportunities for others, and thereby creating a pattern of production capable of sustaining a socially desirable but economically improbable pattern of distribution, the system managed to combine competitive efficiency with high economic equality and social cohesion.

Three conditions of success: a socio-economic tightrope walk

Competitive success of an institutionalized high-wage economy like Germany's is inevitably precarious and fragile, as it must simultaneously accommodate international markets and domestic pressures for equality and social cohesion. Three highly elusive conditions must be met for this to be possible.

First, worldwide product markets for quality-competitive goods must be large enough to sustain full employment in an economy that has barred itself from serving price-competitive markets. The volume of demand that a quality-competitive economy can attract depends on the historical evolution of global demand generally, the competitive capabilities of other economies, successful domestic product innovation expanding quality-competitive markets at the expense of price-competitive ones, and domestic production costs not exceeding the point where the price differential between quality-competitive and price-competitive goods becomes too large for too many customers.

Second, product innovation must proceed fast enough to give the economy a sustained edge in the quality-competitive markets in which it competes. This requires continuous high investment in research and development. Product leadership also depends on a country's culturally rooted pattern of knowledge production and diffusion, as well as of management, technology use, work organization and skill formation continuing to match changing markets and technologies.

Third, the economy's labour supply must fit the volume and character of demand in quality markets, providing the skills needed to serve such markets and allowing for a satisfactory level of employment in high-skill and high-wage jobs. The latter requires that no more than a few among a country's workforce be unable to function in high-skill jobs. Only if their numbers are small can they be taken out of the labour market and sustained by a welfare state funded from the rich proceeds of high-quality competitiveness. Employment for the others must be made possible by a labour market policy – public, private or both – that upgrades their skills to a level where they can earn the high wages mandated for them by collective bargaining and social citizenship. Moreover, to the extent that markets for high-quality products cannot be indefinitely expanded by accelerated product innovation, demand-side employment constraints must be accommodated by cutting the labour supply, through reducing working time or retiring part of the workforce, to allow for an equitable distribution of the available high-wage employment among the vast majority.

Socially acceptable redistribution of employment is possible only as long as quality-competitive product markets are large enough for institutionally mandated underemployment to be small enough to be welcomed as leisure. If underemployment incurred in defence of normalized high-wage employment exceeds the very low level that alone can be socially acceptable, thereby turning into unemployment – be it because international quality markets have become crowded; the rate of innovation in the domestic economy has slowed down in comparison to relevant competitors; labour market policy has failed, for whatever reason, to upgrade skills or retire capacity efficiently and equitably; or wage moderation, containment of social spending and process innovation fail to compensate for limited product advantage or the failures of labour market policy – the costs of social support for those outside the labour market must soar, further depressing the economy's international competitiveness, and high equality among the employed is bound to be increasingly overshadowed by deep inequality between the employed and a large number of long-term unemployed.

At this point, social institutions that rule out low-wage employment in order to generate high-wage employment become increasingly likely to be overridden by market forces. As the labour constraint that drives industrial strategy in an instituted high-wage economy is weakened, with low-wage employment becoming an option for profit-seeking employers and work-seeking workers, its virtuous supply-side effect wanes, eventually resulting in even less high-wage and high-skill employment than there might have been without deregulation. In the ensuing spiral of institutional erosion and structural downgrading, the difference in governance and performance between an instituted high-wage and a liberal market economy disappears.

Can it survive?

In 1993 the German economy moved into its worst recession in postwar history, raising the possibility that the German economic *Sonderweg* (Germany's distinctive pattern of modernization) might finally have ended. In the following I will distinguish three sources of the present malaise of German capitalism:

1 a possible secular exhaustion of its capacity to perform the complicated balancing acts required for its success;
2 the strains caused by the shock of unification;
3 the changing conditions in the global economy of which Germany is part.

My argument will be that while in normal circumstances the 'German model' may or may not once again have found a way out of its difficulties, unification may have so much exacerbated these as to make them unsurmountable. Moreover, even if East Germany could against the odds be incorporated in united Germany on West German terms, the simultaneous incorporation of Germany as a whole in a globalized world economy exposes German economic institutions to new kinds of pressure that they may be unable to withstand.

The model exhausted?

If there was one blemish on West German economic performance in the 1980s, this was persistent high unemployment. To be sure, unemployment in the much more market-driven economy of the UK was even higher throughout the period (Table 2.6). But in Germany, with its institutionalized commitment to social cohesion and its deployment of labour constraint as a supply-side stimulus, it posed more fundamental problems. This explains why German unions in the 1980s used their political and industrial clout to redistribute employment by reducing working time (Table 2.7) – foregoing economic growth by cutting labour input (Table 2.8), and trading potential increases in money income for leisure, in an effort to defend high equality. They also tried to win employers and government for a nationwide 'training offensive', aimed at raising worker skills to a level where ideally everybody could be employed at high wages in a flat wage structure, so as to avoid the need to restore full employment by wage cuts, broader wage dispersion, and a proliferation of low-wage and low-skill jobs.

This strategy was not entirely ineffective. By the end of the 1980s, unemployment was beginning to decline, and overall employment and workforce participation had slightly increased. Still, a sizeable number of unemployed, almost half of them long term, remained. Depending on the perspective, this could be blamed on the institutional rigidities of German labour markets, or alternatively on lack of effort in labour market policy and working time reduction. It could also be attributed to costs of labour or the welfare state, having crossed the threshold beyond which they begin to count again even in quality markets. But it could as well have been due to deficient product innovation failing to keep the economy quality competitive in spite of and together with its institutional rigidities

Table 2.6   *Employment and unemployment*

	Average unemployment rate[a]			Long-term unemployment[b]	
	1981–5	1986–90	1991–4	1990	1993
Germany	6.4	5.8	5.4[c]	46.3	40.3[d]
UK	11.3	8.8	9.7	36.0	42.5
Japan	2.5	2.5	2.4	19.1	17.2
USA	8.2	5.8	6.7	5.6	11.7

[a] OECD standardized unemployment rates, defined as the number of persons unemployed as a percentage of the total labour force (including the self-employed and the armed forces). Unemployed persons are persons aged 15 and over who (1) are without work; (2) are available to start work within the next two weeks; (3) have actively sought employment at some time during the previous four weeks (definition adopted from ILO and used by both EUROSTAT and OECD to calculate standardized rates). *OECD Employment Outlook*, various issues.

[b] From survey-based data. Long-term unemployment is defined as the percentage of the unemployed that have been out of employment for 12 months or more. Source: *OECD Employment Outlook*, 1992.

[c] West Germany only. According to EUROSTAT, the rate for united Germany was 7.1 per cent.

[d] Data refer to united Germany.

and high social costs. As high unemployment became increasingly entrenched, the question for those trying to save the system became whether there were possibilities for speeding up innovation and improving labour market, training and working time policies that, if inevitable together with some negotiated cost cutting, could restore high-wage full employment, thereby pre-empting pressures for more markets, more managerial prerogative, and a liberal *Ordnungspolitik* (policies for sustaining a particular pattern of rules) of deregulation. Conversely, arguments for such changes came to be based on claims that improved product innovation alone would not win back a sufficiently large market share; that labour market, training and working time policies had reached their

Table 2.7   *Working time*

	Average hours worked per person and year[a]		
	1973	1983	1993
Germany	1,804	1,668	1,534[b]
Japan	2,185	2,095	1,965[c]
USA	1,831	1,754	1,743

[a] Source: *OECD Employment Outlook*, July 1993. Data includes part-time work. Germany and USA: dependent employment only; Japan: total employment.

[b] West Germany only. No data for united Germany available.

[c] 1992.

Table 2.8 *Labour input*

	Labour force participation total (females)[a]		Average yearly rate of change in employment, 1983–90[b]		Percent change in resident population 1970–88[c]
	1979	1992	Males	Females	
Germany	68.3 (52.2)	69.8 (59.0)	0.9	1.7	0.8
UK	74.3 (58.0)	75.1 (64.5)	1.2	2.9	2.6
Japan	71.8 (54.7)	75.5 (61.7)	1.0	1.6	18.6
USA	72.1 (58.8)	76.9 (68.9)	1.7	2.8	20.1

[a] Total labour force, divided by the population of working age (15–64) at mid-year. Source: *OECD Employment Outlook*, July 1993.
[b] Source: *OECD Employment Outlook*, July 1993.
[c] Source: *The Economist Book of Vital Statistics*, 1990: 18.

financial, social or other limits; and that effective cost reduction was achievable only by deregulation returning allocational decisions to 'market forces'.

To many, the collapse of employment in the 1993 recession confirmed earlier diagnoses of endemic weaknesses. Japanese advances in traditionally German quality markets suggested that the era of undisputed German product leadership had ended, and with it the capacity of German industry to evade price competition. Also, growing pressures on German firms to cut costs confirmed suspicions that in times of assured product advantage, German managements had neglected process innovation, especially the introduction of 'lean' production methods, not least in response to powerful works councils defending jobs under endemic high unemployment. Mounting mass dismissals and rapidly rising unemployment rates, not just in East Germany but also in the West, seemed to show that the possibilities for working time reduction and early retirement had been exhausted. The limitations of skill upgrading as a means of full employment policy seemed to be indicated, among other things, by a higher than ever number of young people dropping out of the apprenticeship system, due apparently to its significantly raised intellectual demands.

Perhaps most disturbing were concerns, also older than the crisis but dramatized by it, that the German system of knowledge production and diffusion might have structurally and, barring major institutional adjustments, irreversibly lost touch with changing markets. With the Japanese successes of the late 1980s, competitive advantage in quality markets appeared to derive increasingly from fast product turnover rather than slow product refinement. The German system of innovation, management and 'organizational culture' – with applied research conducted by research institutes and associations close to industrial users linking up with widely available shopfloor-generated worker skills vested in long-term commitments to quasi-professional occupational identities, and governed by consensus building institutions like co-determination – seemed far better suited to the former than to the latter, and unlikely to be able to move from the one to the other on short notice.

Already before unification, German capitalism may thus have hit its limits with respect to the size of its possible product markets, its capacity to maintain product leadership, its ability to manage its labour market, or more than one of these at the same time. Indications were that in response, it had slowly begun to deteriorate into a pattern where socially instituted markets, negotiated management, structurally conservative politics, quasi-public associational governance and cultural traditionalism resulted no longer in industrial upgrading, but in an ever-expanding number of people being relegated to an ever more expensive and, ultimately, unsustainable social safety net in the widest sense, being kept out of employment at public expense, or in employment at private expense.

Whether or not these tendencies could have been corrected in normal conditions is a moot question. Experience suggests that prospects for consensual cost cutting were not entirely bleak. German collective bargaining, together with the institutionalized monetarism of the Bundesbank, has always been remarkably good at keeping unit labour costs under control, without deregulation and indeed in order to prevent it (Streeck, 1994b). Unification, however, and the boom and bust that followed it did nothing to resolve whatever structural problems may have existed at the time. Instead it imparted an historical shock to the 'German model' that may well have been powerful enough to throw it off course once and for all.

The shock of unification

The crisis of the early 1990s might have come even without unification, because of a secular exhaustion of the 'German model'. But it could also have been caused by unification alone, since rebuilding a country as large as East Germany would have been demanding even on the strongest economy. Sorting out the two explanations is further complicated by the possibility that the inherent institutional logic of the (West) German political economy may have forced it to define the problems of unification in a way that made them even more difficult to resolve than they would otherwise have been.

The West German response to unification was above all designed to protect the West German social order from being modified by the event. Unification was conceived and executed as a giant exercise in *Institutionentransfer*: a wholesale transplantation of the entire array of West German institutions to the former East Germany. This approach was supported by all major West German players, including business, labour, the conservative government, and the Social-Democratic opposition. With respect to the economy, unification involved the immediate expansion to the East of socially circumscribed markets, negotiated firms, enabling state intervention and market-regulating associations. Immediately thereafter, national unions and employers associations formally committed themselves to raising East German wages to West German levels within the next half decade, explicitly ruling out the establishment of a low-wage area in the East. In part this reflected a shared belief that however low East German wages might be, German industry could never be price competitive. But there was clearly also a fear that a low-wage regime in the East might erode the high-wage and high-skill regime in the West by opening up opportunities for low-wage production that might lure German firms away from the upgrading path of industrial virtue.

While its wages were being raised far beyond its productivity, East German industry was included in the rigorous competition regime West German firms had had four decades to learn to live with. Nobody can have been in doubt that this was bound to place the East German economy under potentially destructive adjustment pressures, with the likely outcome of prolonged mass unemployment. This, in turn, inevitably triggered massive financial transfers from West to East, given that among the institutions that had been transplanted wholesale with unification was the West German welfare state. While it has been argued that these risks were difficult to gauge at the time of unification, it is questionable whether more realistic forecasts would have made much of a difference. Bent on protecting West German institutions, all relevant parties more or less consciously opted for a policy of trying to buy the East German economy into the West German high-wage system, at whatever cost to East German workers or West German taxpayers, in the hope that somehow the price would be less than catastrophic.

That hope may well be disappointed. By the mid-1990s united Germany was engaged in the largest wealth transfer in economic history, having committed itself for at least a decade to subsidize the *neue Länder* at a level of about $100 billion a year, to cover all manner of expenses, from public infrastructural investment to pension supplements and, not least, unemployment benefit. Still, there is no guarantee that this extraordinary redistributive effort will not in the end be self-defeating. Public debt has exploded since 1989, and may not be reined in for a long time – or only by cuts in the welfare state or in research and development effort that would in more than one way be obstructive of a quality-competitive 'social market economy'. Also, world markets for German products, hardly large enough to provide full employment for West Germany and perhaps shrinking anyway for reasons of their own, may prove too small for Germany as a whole. The training costs of continued industrial upgrading, even if they might have been manageable for the West, may be too high for West and East together, especially as the latter has to be subsidized by the former. The capacity of the West German economy for industrial innovation, perhaps already in decline, may not suffice to restore competitiveness to West and East Germany at the same time.

Eastern unemployment and, compared to the Western part of the country, regional impoverishment may thus become a lasting condition, owing in a paradoxical sense to the excessively ambitious targets imposed on the *neue Länder* as part and parcel of *Institutionentransfer*. At the same time, abiding efforts to subsidize internal inequality down to a level compatible with institutional continuity may cause constant financial bleeding. Protracted economic stagnation and declining competitiveness may then unleash market forces strong enough to erode, gradually and under a growing risk of divisive political conflict, the very same institutions, and make impossible the kind of economic performance, that unification by *Institutionentransfer* was intended to preserve.

The challenge of globalization

On the surface, it would seem hard to understand why a set of economic institutions as successful in world markets as the German one should be threatened by further economic internationalization. But while the free trade regime of the postwar period left national boundaries intact – although allowing them to be crossed – globalization abolishes them. Competitive performance of German high-wage capitalism requires continuous supportive as well as directive public or quasi-public intervention, inevitably organized at national level and dependent on a capacity, vested in the nation-state, to police the boundaries between the national economy and its environment. While versions of capitalism that require less state capacity for their governance may hope that the attrition of national boundaries under globalization will leave them intact, this is quite different for a nationally organized economy like Germany.

The postwar German compromise between labour and capital, or between German society and its capitalist economy, was conditional on limited mobility of production factors across national borders. At its core was an institutionalized mutual accommodation of capital and labour markets – both themselves highly organized by government intervention and associative self-regulation – that turned less than perfectly mobile capital into a societal resource, and the financial sector into an economic infrastructure, for a pattern of production compatible with social objectives like low inequality. In exchange, society provided a labour supply willing and able to satisfy economic requirements of high competitiveness in international quality markets. Globalization, by increasing the mobility of capital and labour across national borders, extricates the labour supply from national control and enables the financial sector to refuse doing service as a national utility. By internationalizing, and thereby disorganizing, capital and labour markets, globalization dissolves whatever negotiated coordination may have been nationally accomplished between them and replaces it with global hierarchical dominance of the former over the latter.

The West German labour market has long attracted foreign workers, so much so that by the late 1980s the number of foreigners living in West Germany had become far higher than in any other Western European country. Still, the German mixture of immigration controls, effective enforcement of labour standards, full extension to immigrants of union representation and social rights and partial integration of foreign workers in training and retraining kept the supply of unskilled labour to domestic employers low enough to sustain labour market pressures for upward restructuring. The breakdown of communism in Eastern Europe, however, has unleashed an inflow of immigrants of a dimension that in the long term seems incompatible with high labour standards, an extended welfare state, and a normalized pattern of high-wage and high-skill employment.

Unemployment in Eastern Europe will change German labour markets even without direct immigration, much more so than the completion of the European Community's Internal Market in 1992. It has always been part of the German model that low-skill jobs were to be allowed to move to low-wage countries, with job outflow ideally balanced by growth of, and training for, high-skill and high-wage employment. High long-term unemployment in the 1980s showed that achieving this balance was becoming difficult even when the Iron Curtain was still in place. Today the Czech Republic in particular has become a vast low-wage labour pool for German firms – and, unlike classical low-wage countries such as Portugal, one with a skilled workforce geographically close enough to Germany even to be included in just-in-time production.

Accession of Eastern Europe to the European Union, which Germany cannot resist because it must be vitally interested in political stability behind its eastern borders, will remove the last remaining uncertainties for Western investors, most of whom will be German. It will also make construction of a social dimension of the European Internal Market, one that might protect German labour markets from the deregulating effects of internationalization, even more difficult than it already is. The consequence will be a further increase in the availability to German employers of cheap and sometimes not even unskilled labour, undermining the German high-wage system by encouraging outflow of jobs at a time of growing inflow of workers.

As the German labour market is dissolving into its international environment, so is the German capital market. Financial capital was always more internationally mobile than labour, and West Germany was one of the first countries after the war formally to dispense with capital controls. But for a long time there was a number of effective impediments to capital mobility sufficient to allow for a meaningful distinction between German and non-German capital, and for the former to be governed by national institutions. For reasons related to national history and international politics, German finance capital was historically less cosmopolitan in outlook and enjoyed less international market access than British capital. Also, German banks' *Hausbank* mode of operation was and is hard to apply outside Germany. Different national regulatory regimes made international operations costly to enter; and communication technology before the micro-electronic revolution slowed international capital flows, thereby limiting the size of the international capital market. As to German industrial capital, general logistical, organizational and political uncertainties combined with cultural idiosyncrasies of management and work organization – as well as with the specific incentives offered by *Standort Deutschland* (Germany as an investment location), such as high-skilled labour and social peace – to keep the outflow of investment and jobs limited.

Globalization has removed most of these constraints and turned formal into de facto liberalization of capital markets. Financial internationalization weakens the hold that German banks have over the credit supply to German firms, which in turn weakens the banks' capacity and motivation to monitor company performance and promote prudent long termism in company strategy. Large German firms seem to have for some time been making efforts to extricate themselves from the tutelage of their *Hausbanken* (banks which take a close long-term in a company's affairs), in part because with globalization their credit needs are beginning to outgrow the German market. Simultaneously, attracted by burgeoning international opportunities, the German financial sector is becoming more internationally minded, with even *Sparkassen* (savings banks) and *Genossenschaftsbanken* (mutual banks) taking a keen interest in the global casino. As national boundaries wither away, and the German financial sector dissolves into a globally integrated financial services industry, the special relationship between German banks and German firms may increasingly become less 'relational' and more market-like.

The parochialism of nationally organized capitalism

If national boundaries are doomed to fall in the course of globalization, making it impossible for nationally distinct versions of capitalism to remain discernible from their environment, could the German model not survive by being extended to the emerging global economy? Indeed as the capitalist economy internationalizes, some of the institutions that govern its German version are being adopted by other countries and international organizations. Unlike the *Institutionentransfer* of German unification, however, this process is highly selective, being strictly limited to institutions that make or accommodate markets at the exclusion of others, equally central to German capitalism, which socially embed and correct such markets.

The market   International markets are constructed through diplomacy, not through the complex domestic class politics that gave rise to *soziale Marktwirtschaft*. They are therefore not likely ever to become embedded in similar protective-redistributive arrangements as German markets. It should be noted that Germany, in coalition with the British and against the French, succeeded in extending its competition regime to the European Community, whereas its efforts to endow the Internal Market with a 'social dimension', in alliance with the French and against the British, came to naught.

The firm   The German firm cannot serve as a model for corporate reorganization in other countries. Co-determination is not based in the individual firm and its competitive interests, but in the broader German political and institutional context. It cannot therefore be internationally extended. This holds even within the European Community, where efforts to export German company law, and with it the characteristic balance between capital and labour in the governance of large firms, were defeated by resistance not just from European capital, but also from most non-German trade unions. Moreover, German management practices, unlike Japanese ones, have never been successfully reproduced outside Germany, reflecting the dependence of German firms for crucial governance functions on a – national – exoskeleton of rule-setting institutions that an individual firm cannot and will not build on its own.

The state   Even more than in Germany, what state capacity there is in the international economy is weak and fragmented. International efforts to mobilize state-like forms of public power for purposes of economic governance never got very far, not even in the European Community, which historically represents the most ambitious attempt at state-building above the nation-state. If monetary union is ever realized, the European Central Bank will be as insulated from political pressure as the German Bundesbank, and will operate under the same monetarist principles. Unlike the German state, however, the European quasi-state has no capacity to provide for equalization of living conditions in its territorial subunits. Even more importantly, the German state's quintessential ability to replace direct state intervention and provision with assistance to organized social groups regulating themselves in the pursuit of collective goods – such as the infrastructural conditions of international competitiveness under high labour standards and a hard currency regime – cannot be replicated at the international level. Just as German *Marktwirtschaft* is being internationalized without its social correctives, German institutionalized monetarism is about to be transferred to the European Community without the associative self-governance that makes it *sozialverträglich* (enabling it to work with other institutions in society) in Germany.

Associations   German associations prosper because of their close relationship to a facilitating state. No such state exists, nor can one exist, in the international economy. To the extent that the latter is a negotiated economy, it is negotiated between states, not between associations. Beyond the nation-state there are no organized social groups with the capacity to build and maintain a floor under international markets, or correct international market outcomes by negotiated redistribution. Other than states, the only major actors in the international arena are large firms, increasingly institutional in character, with ample resources to pursue their interests individually, unconstrained by union or government pressure forcing them into international class solidarity, and indeed with a growing capacity to extricate themselves from associative governance at national level, very likely increasingly also in Germany.

Culture German traditionalist culture would seem to be even less suitable for internationalization. As Michel Albert (1993) has pointed out, Germans are as susceptible as anybody else to the attractions of non-traditional, 'American' economic culture. Compared to these, the slow-moving, conservative, collectivistic and all-too-prudent German system must inevitably seem boring and utterly devoid of 'fun'. In fact there are many ways in which cultural internationalization may disrupt the standard operating procedures of a densely organized society like Germany that thrives on long-term incremental improvement and requires stable commitments and suppression of opportunism. Just as German savers and investors may grow more *rechenhaft*, German managers, increasingly trained at American business schools, may want to be allowed to 'make decisions' like their American role models. There are indications that the German vocational training system is about to be dramatically transformed by internationalization, among other things by European Community 'harmonization' of skill profiles in the unified European labour market.

Market-modifying and market-correcting political intervention in the economy, including publicly enabled associational self-regulation, can take place only within nation-states, because it is only here that the public power necessary for the purpose can be mobilized. Economic globalization therefore erodes the conditions for such intervention and, by default but also by design, leaves only de-politicized, privatized and market-driven forms of economic order. It is above all for this reason that the German version of capitalism cannot be exported. Globalization discriminates against modes of economic governance that require public intervention associated with a sort of state capacity that is unavailable in the anarchic world of international politics. It favours national systems like those of the USA and Britain that have historically relied less on public–political and more on private–contractual economic governance, making them structurally more compatible with the emerging global system, and in fact enabling them to regard the latter as an extension of themselves. It is this deregulatory bias of globalization that seems to be at the bottom of Albert's (1993) pessimistic prediction that global competition will result in the perverse outcome of the less well-performing Anglo-American model of capitalism outcompeting the better performing 'Rhine model'.

Notes

I am indebted to Jonathan Zeitlin for critical comments. Most of the tables draw on data assembled by Greg Jackson, under the auspices of joint work with Ronald Dore.

1   The following stylized account draws on the typology developed in Hollingsworth et al. (1994).

2   It is not intended to suggest that the institutional configuration that made up the 'German system' in the 1970s and 1980s was created in one piece, or created for the economic purposes that it came to serve. Some of its elements were pre-Wilhelminian, others were introduced by the Allies after 1945, and still others originated in the politics of the Federal Republic, sometimes drawing on and modifying older arrangements, and sometimes not. Moreover, each element, for example, the banking system, was subject to its own historical dynamic. All were and continue to be changing, for their own reasons as well as in reaction to each other, and certainly there can be no presumption of a pre-established fit between them, even though one might want to allow for some reinforcement effects of the 'model's' historically contingent, social and economic success. That its parts happened to perform together so well during the period in question must be attributed at least as much to *fortuna* as to *virtu*.

3   For more detail see my chapter on 'diversified quality production' (Streeck, 1992). Quality competition can be described as the pursuit of monopoly rents through product diversification. The latter can, within limits, expand quality-competitive markets by breaking up existing mass markets. Within quality markets, price competition is suspended as long as the price differential to less customized, substitute products is not excessive.

3

BETWEEN NEO-LIBERALISM AND THE GERMAN MODEL: SWEDISH CAPITALISM IN TRANSITION

Jonas Pontusson

In the course of 44 years of uninterrupted social-democratic government, from 1932 to 1976, Sweden came to be viewed by Swedes and foreigners alike as a model of 'welfare capitalism'. Enabling the country to achieve the highest level of employment and the lowest level of income inequality in the OECD, the Swedish model combined an export-oriented private sector with extensive public provision of social services, wage compression through economy-wide collective bargaining, selective state intervention in the labour market, and a system of taxation that encouraged productive domestic reinvestment of corporate profits.

Most observers agree that the Swedish model died in the 1980s, or at the latest in the early 1990s. Political actors in other countries no longer look to Sweden as a model of economic management, and Swedish political actors increasingly look abroad for models of how to promote competitiveness and growth. In the Swedish debate, it is now commonplace that the egalitarianism of the 1970s was not sustainable, and that equality must, to some degree, be sacrificed at the altar of efficiency. Even those who resist the notion of a necessary trade-off between efficiency and equality concede that the polities and institutions of the postwar regime no longer represent a viable means to reconcile these imperatives. As we shall see, Swedish governments have responded to economic difficulties and associated political pressures by reversing traditional policy commitments, and this policy realignment has been accompanied by important changes in the institutional arrangements of the Swedish political economy. Along with Britain, Sweden stands out as one of the most clear-cut cases of 'regime change' in advanced capitalism.

Albert (1993) conceives the crisis of Swedish social democracy in terms of a grand conflict between the 'Anglo-Saxon model' of free-market capitalism and the 'Rhine model' of organized capitalism, predicting that 'in the battle of capitalism against capitalism, the first casualty in the ranks of the Rhine model will be Sweden' (p.174). In my view, this interpretation conceals as much as it reveals, for Albert's conception of the 'Rhine model' encompasses capitalist political economies with very different character-istics, and hence different prospects of economic success and political stab-ility. The following analysis will contrast Sweden's postwar regime to that of Germany, the largest of the Rhine countries apart from Japan.

In terms of the standard categories of the literature on comparative capitalism, the Swedish and German cases share many features: both are characterized by a high degree of business coordination, encompassing trade unions, institutionalized bargaining between labour and capital, well-developed mechanisms of social compensation for economic restruc-turing, and an 'enabling state' that has shied away from heavy-handed selective intervention to steer economic development. However, there are also major differences between the Swedish and German models – differ-ences which are related, as both cause and effect, to the political hegemony of social democracy in Sweden, and the absence of such hegemony in Germany.

Three contrasts stand out. First, the German economy is characterized by greater regional differentiation and a larger small-firm sector than the Swedish economy. Second, the politics of class compromise in Germany revolves around firm-level co-determination and industry-level collective bargaining, whereas in Sweden, institutionalized class compromise came about through a national political settlement, and bargaining between labour and capital has assumed more centralized forms, linking govern-ment policy more directly and explicitly to wage formation. Third, the public sector is much larger in Sweden, and the Swedish welfare state is more universalistic than its German counterpart.

On these grounds, I conceive the Swedish case as representing a pro-gressive, social-democratic variant of the Rhine model, and the German case as representing a traditionalist variant, blending elements of Social Democracy and Christian Democracy (see Streeck, this volume). While few would contest these differences, the literature on comparative capital-ism rarely pursues their significance. Arguably, the Swedish and German variants of organized capitalism looked similar and tended to produce similar political and economic outcomes during the Golden Age of postwar expansion, especially during the ascendancy of German social democracy between 1965 and 1975, but their trajectories diverged from the mid-1970s onwards.

The institutional stability of Germany in the 1980s, prior to unification, stands in marked contrast to the far-reaching changes that have occurred in Sweden since the 1970s. This invites exploration of how different politi-cal systems facilitate or constrain innovation, but also of the fit between existing institutions and new challenges emanating from the changing dynamics of the world economy. The argument that I shall develop pro-ceeds from the notion that the long-term viability of high-wage economies, such as Sweden and Germany, depends on their ability to shift into high value added product markets and to adopt some form of 'diversified quality production' (Streeck, 1992). Simply put, my argument is that the German model was more conducive to this shift than the Swedish model, and that institutional change in Sweden should be seen as a product of firms and business organizations seeking to overcome obstacles to their pursuit of new production strategies, and of governments responding to the macro-economic consequences of inadequate industrial adjustment.

In what follows, I shall first describe the major policy and institutional changes that have occurred in Sweden since the early 1980s. I will then elaborate on the differences between the Swedish and German postwar regimes, and develop my argument about their implications for industrial adjustment. By way of conclusion, I will return to the politics of institutional change in Sweden.

Regime change in Sweden

The notion of 'regime change' implies an enduring change in the parameters of government policy or collective bargaining, and a certain coherence of change across policies or policy arenas. As far as government policy is concerned, we might say that regime change has occurred when new policies endure from one government to another, and from one phase of the business cycle to another. In other words, regime change involves a lasting reorientation of overall policy priorities and, most likely, a reconfiguration of the institutional arrangements that make up the political economy.

In Sweden, the policies of the Centre-Right coalition governments between 1976 and 1982 essentially conformed to the postwar regime. In 1991, the non-socialist parties returned to power promising fundamental reform of the Swedish political economy – a 'change of system' – and this time did introduce major changes. However, they deserve only part of the credit or blame for the break with the postwar regime, as the Social Democrats had already begun to dismantle some of its key components in the 1980s, and the most important changes introduced between 1991 and 1994 were crisis measures supported by the social-democratic opposition. The new social-democratic government elected in 1994 was able to adjust, but not reverse the new course of policy.

The most obvious change in the ongoing transformation of the Swedish political economy is the decentralization of wage bargaining. In the course of the 1970s, private employers, especially export-oriented engineering employers, became increasingly disgruntled with the compression of inter-occupational wage differentials and the rise of public-sector relative to private-sector wages. In their view, reversing these trends required the abandonment of the system of peak-level bargaining that had been established in the 1950s (Pontusson and Swenson, 1996). Though resisted by the government, the unions and some private employers, the campaign to decentralize wage bargaining launched by the engineering employers in

Table 3.1   *Earnings dispersion, 1981 and 1990*

	1981		1990	
	Sweden	Germany	Sweden	Germany
Ratio of top decile to median	1.54	1.63	1.54	1.64
Ratio of bottom decile to median	0.77	0.61	0.74	0.65

Source: OECD Employment Outlook, July 1993

the early 1980s ultimately prevailed. In the most recent wage rounds, the unions no longer demanded a return to peak-level bargaining: now the issue of contention between unions and employers is the extent to which industry-level agreements should constrain wage bargaining at the firm level. As one might expect, the decentralization of wage bargaining has been accompanied by a noticeable increase of wage differentials (Table 3.1).

In the wake of the successful campaign to impose new wage-bargaining arrangements, the Swedish Employers Association (SAF) announced in 1991 that it would immediately withdraw its representatives from tripartite boards of state agencies and other government bodies. The Centre-Right government of 1991 followed up on this by eliminating formal interest group representation on the decision-making boards of several major state agencies. The significance of such representation is debatable, and so is that of its abandonment. The decision-making body of the Labour Market Board (*Arbetsmarknadsstyrelsen*) is still composed primarily of union officials and employers, now directly appointed by the government rather than nominated by their respective organizations, but the Labour Market Board was always unique. Overall, the role of the 'social partners' in the formulation and implementation of public policy has clearly been curtailed (Ahrne and Clement, 1994).

The economic recovery strategy pursued by social-democratic governments in the 1980s sought to curtail public spending to allow the private sector to expand. As a percentage of GDP, current government expenditures declined from an all-time high of 61.1 per cent in 1982 to 57.2 per cent in 1989 (OECD, 1992). The Social Democrats reduced government spending by cutting industrial and agricultural subsidies, introducing user fees for certain public services, and rationalizing the public sector. They did, however, avoid cuts in basic welfare entitlements. These were implemented in the early 1990s, under the pressure of a most severe recession and a soaring deficit. Most notably, the replacement rates of public sick pay and unemployment insurance were reduced from 90 per cent to 80 per cent, and one waiting day for sick pay insurance benefits was introduced. Before and after 1991, these and other social spending cuts were the product of agreements between government and opposition.

The tax reform of 1990 represents another major policy reorientation. Explicitly modelled on the US tax reform of 1986, it sharply reduced marginal income tax rates and created a single income tax bracket for most wage earners, while eliminating many deductions and extending the VAT base. Also, the reform eliminated the possibility for firms to avoid taxation of profits by setting aside funds for future investment, the release of which required government approval.

The Swedish welfare state remains distinguished by its universalism, but it has become less redistributive as a result of higher user fees for public services, entitlement cuts, and tax reform. Government policy has thus reinforced labour market trends towards greater inequality. It should be noted that recent reforms have been designed to link welfare benefits more directly to income from employment, and to create incentives to work more. The 'decommodification of labor power' (Esping-Andersen, 1990) has become a less prominent feature of the Swedish welfare state.

The deregulation of financial markets constitutes yet another area where social-democratic initiatives in the 1980s anticipated the neo-liberal policy thrust of the Centre-Right government of 1991–4. Having deregulated domestic markets in 1985–6, the Social Democrats phased out all exchange controls in the late 1980s. In 1992, the government eliminated all restrictions on foreign ownership of corporate equity.

Finally, and closely related to the last point, Swedish membership in the European Union represents a major change in the parameters of economic policy and wage bargaining. In itself, EU membership does not bring any significant policy change, but it locks in the market-oriented domestic reforms of the past decade. Again, this has occurred under bipartisan auspices: the decision to apply for membership was made by a social-democratic government, while the terms of membership were negotiated by its Centre-Right successor. The EU debate also illustrates the prominent role played by business in Swedish politics since the early 1980s.

Active labour market policy would seem to be the only component of the Swedish model that has not been abandoned or fundamentally altered in the last decade. How, then, can we explain the many changes that the Swedish political economy has undergone? What is the impetus behind them, and how should we conceive the new Swedish political economy? As indicated at the outset, I propose to address these questions by way of a comparison of the Swedish and German models of postwar capitalism.

Sweden and Germany compared

The social-democratic regime of capitalist regulation, as it existed in Sweden during the era of postwar expansion, differed from the standard 'Rhine model' as typified by Germany. Some of the differences can be directly attributed to the reformist initiatives of social-democratic governments, but others predate the era of social-democratic rule in Sweden, and may be invoked to explain why the Swedish labour movement has been more powerful and has pursued more egalitarian policies than its German counterpart. The causal relationships between, on the one hand, the power and goals of social-democratic labour movements and, on the other, the institutional structure of the political economy are complex, and cannot be fully sorted out in this chapter.

The welfare state provides the most obvious entry point for a discussion of the impact of social-democratic political hegemony on the structure and dynamics of the Swedish economy. Esping-Andersen (1990) argues persuasively that Sweden and Germany typify different patterns of welfare state development. What sets Sweden's 'social-democratic welfare state' apart from Germany's 'conservative welfare state', according to Esping-Andersen, is not so much the level of welfare spending, but rather the types of benefits and the criteria whereby they are distributed. Specifically, the Swedish welfare state differs from its German counterpart by a strong commitment to universalism, and a strong preference for services over transfer payments. More than in Sweden, the public provision of social welfare in Germany is based on occupational stratification, with benefits linked to employment and work performance, and the administration of social insurance schemes is delegated to occupational associations and other organizations that are neither strictly public nor private. Whereas public employment accounted for 32.5 per cent of total Swedish employment in 1985, the corresponding German figure was only 15.5 per cent (OECD, 1992).

For Swedish social democracy, the pursuit of a distinctive path of welfare state development was facilitated by the underdevelopment of public welfare prior to the 1930s, the relatively egalitarian cast of pre-industrial Swedish society, and the centralized nature of the Swedish state. In Germany, by contrast, social-democratic governments always had to contend with the institutional legacies of conservative welfare policy, and the federal structure of the republic reinforced this constraint by rendering comprehensive reforms more difficult (Katzenstein, 1987).

As Scharpf (1991) points out, the growth of public-sector employment served as a means to maintain full employment in Sweden during the economic downturns between 1974 and 1983. While Germany learned to live with mass unemployment, the Swedish rate of unemployment never exceeded 3.5 per cent in the 1980s – indeed, it fell below 2 per cent in the latter half of the decade. Scharpf also notes that Sweden achieved this at a remarkably high level of employment. Already in 1960, Swedish labour force participation, at 74.3 per cent, was higher than in Germany (70.3 per cent), and while the Swedish rate increased steadily over the ensuing thirty years, to reach an all-time high of 83.2 per cent in 1990, the German rate had declined to 68.8 per cent by 1990 (OECD, 1992).

The achievement and maintenance of full employment can be characterized as the linchpin of social-democratic hegemony in postwar Sweden. Two points of contrast with the German case seem particularly pertinent in this context. First, German economic policy did not assume a Keynesian orientation until the late 1960s, and German policy-makers never fully embraced the Keynesian paradigm (Allen, 1989). While the postwar strategy of the Swedish labour movement, the famous 'Rehn-Meidner model', emphasized supply-side measures and thus went beyond conventional Keynesianism, it was based on the political consensus around active fiscal policy that was forged in the 1930s and 1940s. Second, cross-national variations in labour force participation are to a very large extent a function of variations in the rate of labour force participation of women, especially mothers. In family as well as macro-economic policy, goals and arguments originating within Christian Democracy have had a pervasive influence in Germany.

The achievement of full employment must not be conceived simply as a matter of political will, or as an expression of the balance of political forces. As the Swedes have recently learned, there are clearly external, balance-of-payments constraints on the ability of governments to maintain full employment.[1] While Germany enjoyed a substantial trade surplus for most of the 1970s and 1980s, the Sweden–Germany comparison highlights the fact that full employment also depends on institutionalized government capacities. Scharpf's (1991) analysis brings out three key institutional differences between Sweden and Germany:

1 the separation of fiscal and monetary policy in Germany, that is, the existence of an autonomous central bank with a consistent policy bias towards disinflation;
2 the constraints that federalism imposes on the ability of the German government to pursue an active fiscal policy;
3 the deeper institutionalization of active labour market policy in Sweden.

The structure and dynamics of wage bargaining provide another point of contrast between Sweden and Germany (Swenson, 1989; Thelen 1993). In Sweden, industry-level bargaining has occurred on an economy-wide basis since the first decade of the century, and LO and SAF became directly involved in wage bargaining in the postwar period, negotiating wage ceilings and distributional provisions that were de facto binding on the parties of industry-level bargaining. In Germany, by contrast, industry-level bargaining takes place on a regional basis, and there is no peak-level bargaining.

Soskice (1990b) argues that it is coordination rather than centralization which matters, and that Sweden and Germany are both cases of highly coordinated wage bargaining. While Germany's industrial unions and cohesive employer organizations have coordinated regional bargaining within sectors, wage leadership by the IG Metall has provided an informal mechanism of union coordination, and the employers' federation (BDA) has played an important role in coordinating wage bargaining across sectors (Thelen, 1991). Soskice's emphasis on coordination is well taken so long as the aim is to understand the politics of the trade-off between inflation and unemployment. As Table 3.1 illustrates, however, the Swedish and German systems of wage bargaining are associated with different distributive outcomes. For reasons indicated above, the dispersion of earnings increased in Sweden in the course of the 1980s, but even at the end of this decade, wage differentials were considerably more compressed than in Germany.

It is commonplace in the literature on the Swedish model that centralized wage bargaining enabled the unions to implement a solidaristic wage policy. Swenson (1993) rightly questions the premise that Swedish unions had to impose wage compression on resistant employers. Initially at least, employers went along without major objections, viewing wage compression as assisting them in their efforts to manage inter-firm and intersectoral competition for labour in tight labour markets. The strengthening of the market power of unskilled and semi-skilled labour that resulted from full employment constituted a key ingredient of the dynamics of Swedish wage bargaining in the postwar era, together with importance of public-sector employment. For political reasons, public-sector employers were especially willing to raise the relative wages of the least well paid, which put pressure on private employers to do the same. Public provision of social services, government efforts to promote employment growth, and solidaristic wage bargaining were thus mutually reinforcing components of the Swedish model.

Turning to conditions of production, or the micro-economic side of the postwar regulatory regime, Sweden and Germany differ markedly in the distribution of private-sector employment by establishment size (Table 3.2). Industrial structure is more bifurcated in Germany than in Sweden, and small business occupies a far more prominent place in the German economy. This is related to the fact that the Swedish labour movement conceived wage solidarity not only as a goal in itself, but also as a means to promote productivity growth and economic restructuring by squeezing the profit margins of inefficient firms. Insofar as corporate profitability during the era of postwar expansion was determined by economies of

Table 3.2   *Employment by establishment size*

Number of employees	Manufacturing		Manufacturing and services	
	Sweden %	Germany %	Sweden %	Germany %
1–49	17.3	28.2	NA	47.8
50–199	45.8	33.8	NA	31.4
200–	36.9	38.1	NA	20.8

Germany: 1987. Sweden: 1989.
Sources: = *Statistical Abstract of Sweden*, Sweden, 1991; *Statistisches Jahrbuch für die Bundesrepublik Deutschland*, Federal Republic of Germany, 1991

scale, wage compression and other features of the Swedish model favoured large firms over small firms (Pontusson, 1992a). The greater strength of Swedish unions and their increased capacity to adopt egalitarian goals thus help explain the differences in the distribution of employment by establishment size.

At the same time, the greater importance of small business might be invoked to explain the fact that the German rate of unionization (37 per cent in 1985) is much lower than the Swedish rate (84 per cent), and one might also argue that the homogeneity of Swedish industrial structure facilitated the compression of wage differentials. The kind of time-series data required to sort the causal interaction between these variables are not available. Suffice it to note here that, for Germany, government regulation and protection of small business, especially of the *Handwerk* sector (Streeck, 1992), can be traced back to the *Mittelstandspolitik* pursued by conservative governments prior to World War I.

While recognizing that small manufacturing firms tend to be less unionized than large firms, Herrigel (1989) argues persuasively that local community solidarity strengthens labour's bargaining power in small-firm regions. Relying on skilled workers, small firms in these regions often pay above average wage rates. In any case, they must abide by the minimum wage rates stipulated by collective agreements. In Loveman and Sengenberger's (1990: 35) data set, which does not include Sweden, Germany stands out as the country with the narrowest wage gap between small and large manufacturing firms. The key to the viability of small manufacturing firms in Germany would seem to be high rates of investment and innovation rather than low wage costs, and virtually all the existing literature attributes this dynamism to local and regional level institutional arrangements that serve to coordinate business activities and pool resources for worker and management training, R&D and marketing.

Business coordination at regional level is far less developed in Sweden. To the extent that we can speak of regional manufacturing networks in the Swedish case, these tend to be organized around large firms subcontracting to small firms. Together with country size and geography, the federal structure of the postwar German political system helps to explain the greater importance of economic regionalism. According to Vitols (1994), banks owned by state governments (*Landesbanken*) play a crucial role in the supply of long-term finance to small business, by providing refinancing facilities and technical expertise to semi-public local savings banks.

Related to the role of small business and regional institutional infrastructures, vocational training is commonly viewed as a crucial component of the German model. One line of argument in the literature holds that the German system of vocational training socializes some of the costs of training, and yields a more highly skilled workforce than the profit calculations of individual firms would justify. Another emphasizes the way in which apprenticeships – the core of the system – combine formal training in vocational schools with on-the-job training to produce the kind of polyvalent workers required by new production strategies geared towards enhanced flexibility.

German vocational training should not be confused with Swedish active labour market policy. The ideology of active labour market policy has emphasized labour mobility rather than commitment to a particular trade, and the training efforts of the Labour Market Board have focused on retraining workers who have lost their jobs. At the same time, and more importantly for our purposes, educational reforms introduced by the Swedish Social Democrats in the postwar period created a vocational training system that is very different from the German one and covers a much smaller portion of the secondary-school population.

Swedish educational reformers generally eschewed apprenticeships and preferred a school-based approach to vocational training in the 1940s and 1950s. Vocational schools were eliminated altogether as vocational training was brought into comprehensive secondary schools in the 1960s. During the process, the emphasis of the educational system shifted steadily to more academic subjects (Hadenius, 1990). Arguably, the social-democratic goal of providing educational opportunities for children of all classes within integrated secondary schools was at odds with a German-style approach to vocational training. It is noteworthy that the German Social Democrats, when they took control of the government in 1969, launched an ambitious effort to combine general and vocational training within comprehensive secondary schools, but achieved only token success as 'federalism, interest groups and sharply divided opinion . . . conspired to block the implementation of any uniform system' (Kommers, 1993: 234).

Again, the features that distinguish the Swedish from the German model are closely related, but cannot be reduced to the political hegemony of social democracy in Sweden. The German system of vocational training has always depended heavily on apprenticeships within the *Handwerk* sector, and has catered primarily, though by no means exclusively, to the needs of small and medium-sized business (Herrigel, 1989; Streeck, 1992). Because in Sweden the *Handwerk* sector was much smaller, a German approach to vocational training was less viable, and political resistance to social-democratic reforms was less strong in the Swedish case.

To conclude, Sweden and Germany typify two different forms of institutionalized class compromise. Both cases are characterized by collective bargaining at the sectoral level; what distinguishes them is how sectoral bargaining fits into the overall configuration of the political economy. In Germany, co-determination at firm level emerged in the 1950s as a second pillar of the institutionalization of class compromise, and political bargaining at the national level assumed a subordinate role. In Sweden, by contrast, the class compromise forged in the 1930s was first and foremost a national political settlement, and firm-level cooperation between employers and unions played a subordinate role until the 1970s.

Patterns of economic growth and restructuring

How did the differences between the Swedish and German regimes of capitalist regulation affect industrial development, in the era of postwar expansion and, in particular, in response to the new world market conditions of the 1980s? My discussion proceeds from the proposition that the long-term viability of high-wage economies, such as Sweden and Germany, has increasingly come to depend on their ability to move into high value-added product markets and to adopt to some form of 'diversified quality production' (DQP).

Streeck (1992) argues persuasively that capitalists operating in an unregulated economy are unlikely to pursue DQP strategies, even if these represent the most rational solution to the problems of high-cost producers, and that the development of DQP presupposes an institutionally dense economy. Specifically, Streeck identifies three mechanisms whereby the institutional framework of the German economy has promoted the development of DQP: first, German institutions restrict the ability of firms to meet competitive challenges by cutting wages or shedding labour through automation; second, they require firms to include unions in the process of industrial innovation; third, they provide for public investment in infrastructure, skills and other necessary 'collective factor inputs'.

As Sweden and Germany are both institutionally dense political economies, characterized by cooperative relations between labour and capital, these arguments might lead one to expect DQP development to be the dominant pattern of industrial adjustment in both countries. I want to suggest that the Swedish case does not bear out this expectation, and that Streeck's general argument needs to be amended to take into account the affinity between Social Democracy and Fordist mass production brought out by Swedish and German experiences alike.

Plant size is hardly a satisfactory measure of Fordism, but the data on the distribution of employment by plant size (Table 3.1) is consistent with the proposition that the pattern of postwar growth was more Fordist in Sweden than in Germany. Despite the much smaller size of the economy, Sweden's postwar boom depended on domestic demand to just about the same extent as Germany's.[2] While wage compression and other supply-side features of the Swedish model squeezed the profit margins of small firms, and encouraged firms to substitute capital for labour, the redistributive effects of Swedish welfare reforms and centralized wage bargaining promoted mass consumption of standardized goods and services. In important respects, the postwar Swedish welfare state partook in the Fordist paradigm – delivering standardized services, and reducing costs through economies of scale.

Different patterns of postwar growth are related to historical variations in industrial structures and the sectoral composition of exports as well as the politics of class compromise. Customized, batch-produced machine tools and other capital equipment always accounted for a larger share of

German than Swedish exports. For Sweden, processed raw materials and a limited range of consumer goods – cars and household appliances – remained or became major export items. As a consequence, the Swedish economy was more exposed to international market pressures for product standardization and large-scale production.

With mass production industries gaining in relative importance and unions becoming stronger, the German political economy moved in a Swedish direction in the late 1960s and early 1970s. However, the social-democratic experiment under Willy Brandt was short-lived with respect to economic policy as well as educational reform. While institutional features of the political system constrained policy change, the dynamics of world market competition in the 1970s turned against Fordist mass production. In Sweden and German alike, manufacturing firms have responded to new market pressures and technological opportunities by seeking to reorganize production in ways that would enhance flexibility and product quality as well as productivity. Volvo and other large Swedish firms engaged in radical innovations, and the rhetoric of the 'new workplace' became a prominent feature of Swedish political debate in the 1980s. Though major changes have indeed occurred at Swedish workplaces, German industry appears to have moved further in the direction of diversified quality production. Following Boyer (1991a), the Swedish pattern of industrial adjustment might rather be characterized as a shift towards 'flexible mass production'.

Three pieces of quantitative evidence support this proposition. First, the average annual rate of productivity growth in Swedish manufacturing industry fell behind the German rate in the 1970s, and continued to be lower through the 1980s.[3] Second, Sweden stands out as a rare case in which average plant size, measured as the average number of employees per manufacturing establishment, continued to increase through the 1970s and held steady in the 1980s. Whereas average Swedish plant size increased by 23 per cent from 1971 to 1988, average German plant size declined by 17 per cent over the same time period (Pontusson, 1995).

The third piece of evidence concerns worker skills. Kern and Schumann (1989) report significant increases of 'skilled production workers' as a proportion of blue-collar labour in the three major sectors of German industry – autos, machine tools and chemicals – from 1973 to 1983, and project increases of similar if not greater magnitude for the 1983–93 period. By contrast, a survey by the Swedish Metalworkers' Union (1989: 67–83) shows that the proportion of engineering jobs requiring few skills and involving physically arduous work actually increased from 1977 to 1987, as a result of changes in the sectoral composition of employment within the engineering industry. Machine tools and other engineering sectors employing skilled production workers lost ground, both to mass producers of consumer durables and to high-tech sectors distinguished by their disproportionate employment of unskilled blue-collar workers as well as well-educated white-collar workers. Although these observations are not strictly comparable to Kern and Schumann's, they do suggest that the reskilling thesis does not hold as readily for the Swedish as it does for the German case.

Two other features of divergent economic development in the 1980s deserve to be noted. First, OECD (1992) data show that while real hourly earnings in manufacturing grew at a much slower annual rate in Sweden than in Germany (0.3 per cent as compared to 1.4 per cent for the period 1979–90), the unit labour costs of Swedish manufacturing industry grew much faster (7.0 per cent as compared to 3.3 per cent). This asymmetry can be attributed to slower productivity growth, but also to tax increases and a more rapid increase in wages outside the manufacturing sector in the Swedish case. Second, the two cases diverge most strikingly with respect to direct investment abroad. In 1981, direct investment abroad corresponded to 7.6 per cent of domestic gross fixed capital formation (excluding the public sector) in Sweden, and 3.1 per cent in Germany. By 1990, the Swedish figure was 36.1 per cent, and the German 7.6 per cent (calculated from data in UN 1993a, b). Investment abroad by Swedish firms was largely motivated by a perceived need to get inside the Single Market, but this remarkable outflow of productive capital is also indicative of business dissatisfaction with domestic policies and institutions. It would appear that existing domestic arrangements suited the adjustment strategies of German firms much better.

If it is indeed the case that Swedish industry has not embraced DQP to the same extent as Germany, there are at least four factors that might account for this. First, the Swedish Social Democrats opted for an export-led recovery strategy based on currency devaluation in the 1980s, which boosted the cost competitiveness of Swedish mass producers, especially auto producers, and their share of manufacturing employment (Pontusson, 1992b). In view of the huge government deficit accumulated during the period of bourgeois government (1976–82), this was arguably the only viable strategy to maintain full employment. In any case, it also relieved the pressure on Swedish industry for product and process innovation.

Second, centralized wage bargaining with wage solidarity may be viewed as an obstacle to the development of DQP. This is certainly the view of Swedish employers, who have come to regard decentralized bargaining and individualized wage incentives as prerequisites for successful adjustment to new world market conditions. Employers typically argue that individualized wage incentives are needed to encourage workers to assume greater responsibilities at work, and to engage in further training. Also, corporate investment in training increases the costs of labour turnover, and employers need to restructure pay systems in order to retain trained workers (Pontusson and Swenson, 1996).

Third, the relative sluggishness of DQP development in Sweden might be attributed to the absence, or underdevelopment, of appropriate institutional arrangements for socializing the costs of worker training, and supplying small business with long-term finance at competitive interests rates.

Fourth and finally, one might perhaps argue that mass unemployment facilitated the development of DQP practices in Germany in the 1980s. As the American and British experiences amply demonstrate, mass unemployment alone is certainly not enough to bring about DQP, but its beneficial effects may be conditional on an appropriate institutional infrastructure. More immediately threatened by unemployment, German workers and unions may have been keener to cooperate with management initiatives than their Swedish counterparts. Certainly, full employment contributed, along with the compression of wage differentials, to very high rates of labour turnover in Swedish industry in the 1980s. In several ways, the development of DQP would seem to depend on a stable labour force.

Where is Sweden heading?

The changes that the Swedish political economy has undergone over the last decade involve a greater emphasis on market mechanisms to allocate productive resources, income and consumption. What remains to be determined is how far Sweden will move in this direction. Do recent changes represent a full-scale abandonment of the social-democratic features assumed by organized capitalism in postwar Sweden, or even of the 'Rhine model'?

The Swedish welfare state has yet to be dismantled. So far all that has happened is a curtailment of public spending and employment and a series of efforts to render the provision of welfare benefits, services as well as transfer payments, more market conforming. In this, the Swedish welfare state is to some degree being brought into line with the continental pattern, typified by Germany. Similarly, the crisis of the Swedish model has not had any major impact on union density and, as long as that remains high, coordinated sectoral wage bargaining is likely to prevail. In conjunction with subsequent management efforts to reorganize workplace industrial relations, the Swedish co-determination reforms of the 1970s can be said to have contributed to a shift towards firm-level mechanisms of integrating labour into advanced capitalism. On both scores, wage bargaining and co-determination, the emergent system of industrial relations resembles the German one.

Two other elements of this rapprochement with the German model should be noted. First, the major Swedish parties all agree on the need for greater autonomy for the central bank. Although its constitutional status has yet to be changed, the bank has already assumed a more prominent and more autonomous role. Second, the German model has figured prominently in recent Swedish debates about vocational training. Legislation introduced by the Social Democrats before they lost power in 1991 created the possibility, on an experimental basis, for firms to establish vocational training programmes in cooperation with public schools.

On the other hand, the radical deregulation of financial markets that has occurred over the last decade has been inspired by Anglo-Saxon examples, and has had the effect of exposing policy-makers to speculative pressures, and Swedish firms to the threat of hostile takeovers by foreign interests. Over the long run, this component of the Swedish search for a new model may be antithetical to any form of organized capitalism, be it social-democratic or more conservative.

In view of the strong performance of German industry in the 1980s, and the similarities between the two organized capitalisms, one might well ask why Swedish efforts to emulate the German model have not been more consistent and self-conscious. However, there are strong reasons to expect that the pressures of German unification, European integration, and econ-omic globalization will bring about major changes in the German politi-cal economy (see Streeck, this volume). If the German model is no longer viable for Germany, why would the Swedes want to adopt it? Of course, 'Sweden' is not a unitary actor, looking around for a new regime to adopt. Insofar as the Swedish political economy has become more like the German political economy over the last decade, this is not the product of anyone choosing the 'German model', but the product of a compromise, or even stalemate, between political forces associated with business inter-ests and pushing for market solutions, and forces associated with labour, which seek to preserve key elements of the old model.

From a political point of view, the neo-liberal temptation is strong, since it is easier to destroy institutions or remove institutional constraints than to construct or impose new ones. Moreover, the neo-liberal approach to institutional reform appears to resonate more powerfully with popular culture than the Germanic approach. As Albert (1993) suggests, the German model may be more efficient than the American model, but the American model is more popular.

The Swedish labour movement's traditional commitments to full employment and wage solidarity, and more recently to gender equality, limit the attraction of the German model. But the Social Democrats and their union allies are no longer in a position to deliver on their traditional goals. The post-1994 government clearly indicated its desire to cooperate with the business community in solving Sweden's competitiveness problem. For better or worse, the German model provides a potential con-ceptual framework for what is in effect an effort to forge a new class com-promise. While membership in the European Union will probably reinforce the political influence of business, it may also draw Swedish Social Democrats towards the German model or, more broadly, the politi-cal discourse of defending organized capitalism against neo-liberalism.

The crucial question is whether the emerging new class compromise can be economically viable. Streeck's pessimistic assessment of the prospects of the German model may be more relevant for Germany than for Sweden. Obviously, the pressures associated with unification are unique to the German case. In addition, Streeck's suggestion that worldwide product markets for quality-competitive goods may not be large enough to sustain full employment would seem to represent a more serious problem for a large economy like Germany. There are at least some reasons to hope that Sweden will find a swimmable eddy of the Rhine rather than drown in mid-Atlantic.

Notes

For comments on previous drafts of this chapter, I wish to thank Peter Auer, Ann-Britt Hellmark, Peter Katzenstein, Wolfgang Streeck, Kathleen Thelen, and Lowell Turner.

1   Incredibly, the Swedish rate of open unemployment has recently risen above 8 per cent, with an additional 6 to 7 per cent of the labour force in government programmes, while labour force participation has declined to 77 per cent (late 1994 figures supplied by the Swedish Information Service). Altogether, some 500,000 jobs have been lost since 1990, an employment contraction of about 20 per cent.

2   Exports accounted for an average of 21.8 per cent of Swedish GDP in 1960–67, and 33 per cent in 1980–89, as compared to 18.5 per cent and 29.7 per cent for Germany (OECD, 1992). Throughout this period, Sweden was much less export dependent than most small countries on the European continent, and Germany much more than other large countries.

3   The average annual growth of productivity in Swedish manufacturing industry, measured in terms of value added, was 6 per cent in 1963–75, 2.5 per cent in 1975–83, and 2 per cent in 1983–8. The corresponding German figures were 5.5 per cent, 3.5 per cent and 2.5 per cent (Swedish Ministry of Industry, 1990: 66).

4

FRENCH STATISM AT THE CROSSROADS

Robert Boyer

The silence of economic theories

Economists' theories of capitalism have failed to analyse the origins of capitalist diversity. If one defines the capitalist mode of production as combining very generally the logic of the market and the dominance of private property, it is unnecessary to specify the extent and nature of market adjustments: at the very most, possible variants of capitalism may be characterized by reference to the development of forms of public property, such as state capitalism or a mixed economy. Such treatment of capitalism originates in the emergence of political economy itself.

Classical British economists proposed laying the foundations for market economy analysis in the broadest possible terms. The better to respond to the physiocrats, they examined the relations between industry and agriculture, the saturation of output in agriculture accounting for the convergence on a stationary economy. Marxist theories renewed the same point of view when they showed on the contrary that the spread of industrial wage labour ushers in a new phase of market capitalism, thus introducing economic and social history in the full meaning of the term. Those who succeeded Marx completed his analysis and brought it up to date in particular by introducing a problematic element in terms of stages in capitalism: commercial, industrial, then financial, competitive, monopolistic, tending towards state monopoly. For each major historical epoch there corresponds a dominant form of capitalism on the basis of which the unequal pattern and development of international relations is organized. But national differences count for little, being no more than the projection of a central mechanism – imperialism, for instance, for Lenin and his successors.

Neo-classical theory which was developed gradually from the end of the nineteenth century was first systematized by Walras, who reduced the capitalist economy to a series of markets for products, factors of production and shares. This genesis of pure economics dispenses with the particular features of the social and political environment, restricting itself to the problems of production and allocation of resources. That being the case, distinctive national features could only find expression by way of the variation of some of the parameters in regard to consumer preference or technological potential. These are secondary in relation to a universally valid general model, so long as one accepts the epistemological rift that the concept of pure economics represents. However, the reality of capitalism in its manifold forms shows its imperfections in relation to the Walrasian ideal.

This representation, which was more prescriptive than positive, proved incapable of accounting for developments in the interwar period, whether financial instability, the tendency towards stagnation or the persistence of

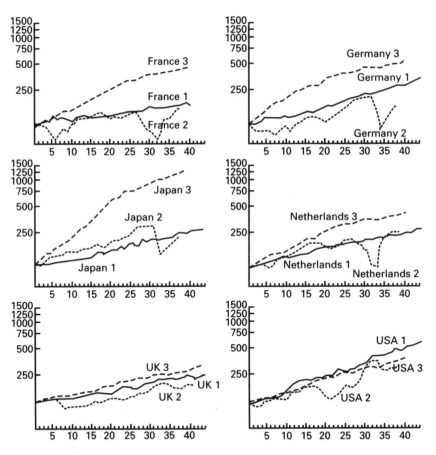

Figure 4.1   *Comparison between national trajectories of growth*
Maddison (1982: 90–91) has devised a series of retrospective statistics describing the development in volume of GDP in France, Japan, Germany, the Netherlands, UK and USA, comparing three major periods: 1870–1913; 1913–50; 1950–82. An index of 100 is taken as the basis for each period.

mass unemployment. The merit of the Keynesian general theory lay in amending the neo-classical theory of its day so as to take account, first of the appearance, then of the permanence, of imbalance in the markets for both goods and labour. After World War II a new conception of political economy was called for. The state had a duty to offset budgetary expenditure and taxation, and the tendency to stagnation and unemployment, by the expansion of the money supply. For Keynes's successors, contemporary capitalism was essentially institutional control of the private economy. Industrialized countries were differentiated by the extent to which they adhered to Keynesian principles of adjustment required by circumstances. In fact, the degree of difference is slight insofar as the model Keynes conceived applied by and large to virtually all industrialized countries, with the notable exception of Germany. Again, national trajectories, whatever their dissimilarities after World War II (Figure 4.1), found few or no structural explanations.

Keynesian theory which had been very widely adopted as a basis for macro-economic analysis and inspiration in governmental policies for short-term fine tuning then experienced a decline, due in particular to its inability to account for accelerating inflation, rising unemployment and the ineffectiveness of measures to boost the economy, features that marked the 1970s. Monetarist theories returned to favour, before being superseded by supply side, then by an updated version of classical, economics. In this debate that has dominated macro-economic analysis in the 1980s and 1990s a return to full market rationality and equilibrium tends to assimilate micro- and macro-economics. Aside from its analytical complexities, it marks a return to pre-Keynesian theories, where national characteristics have no place since the principle of methodological individualism derives from the preferences shown by agents and not by economic institutions that characterize contemporary economies. In other words, capitalist economies are classed as a group of integral markets that function on the principle of pure and perfect competition.

The improbable effect of the collapse of Soviet-type systems

Moreover, it is this view that seems to have influenced a number of Western advisers in analysing the possibilities of and conditions for transfer to a market economy in the former 'socialist' countries of Eastern Europe. All that was required was to dismantle the centralized planning system and the monopoly of the Communist Party and, behold, a market economy was in place. In fact, such a hope, already particularly naive by the middle of the 1980s, has become still more so with the experience of these countries between 1989 and today. Markets may be efficient once constituted, but they do not possess the property of setting themselves up; on the contrary, the organization of transactions on the basis of market exchange requires a legal, accounting, monetary and financial system to be in place. So theorists came to realize that they have no cast-iron answers to the nonetheless fundamental question: What is capitalism? Having promoted capitalism as being one and unique, they are nonplussed by the variety of forms that capitalism by way of transition adopts. It is in this context that the work of researchers, who are not economists in the strict sense, comes into its own. Thus Andrew Shonfield (1967) endeavoured to show the variability of capitalism in time and in space, his purpose being to grasp the extent to which the remarkable growth observed after 1945 derived from major changes in the relations between market and government. At the same time, he laid stress on how the basic institutions of capitalism differed when comparing Britain, France, Germany and the USA.

Furthermore, comparison between the economic systems of East and West had convinced certain analysts of a tendency towards convergence. On one side, free market economies registered increasing intervention by government, including the planning of strategic decisions. On the other, centrally planned economies implemented reforms whose aims were to introduce greater flexibility by encouraging greater recourse to market mechanisms. The dramatic events that brought about the collapse of Soviet-type societies discredited the assumption that growing uniformity would develop between different economic systems.

Yet, with customary historical irony, it was just when capitalism appeared to have triumphed over the socialist system that was supposed to transplant it, and when the political elites of Eastern Europe dreamt of once and for all attaining the level of performance and living standards of 'capitalism' (American capitalism implied), that attentive observers noted the emergence of a new phase in the international system. Capitalism, far from being a completely homogeneous system, offers a variety of patterns which are far from being equivalent and which, that being the case, are in competition on two counts. In the world market, the development of relative positions confirms the degree of greater or lesser effectiveness of different forms of organization. In the former socialist countries, the question has arisen as to the models it would be desirable and possible to acclimatize and adapt to situations inherited from the disintegration of the previous political and economic systems. Here themes developed by Michel Albert (1991) will be recognized.

Capitalist diversity defined in terms of mode of regulation

On reflection, it is something of a paradox that these notions tend to emanate from experts in international relations, political pundits and industrial leaders, too seldom from economists, though there are notable exceptions (Rowthorn, 1992; Soskice, 1990a). The theory of 'regulation' (Aglietta, 1997) developed by French economists over the past twenty years has sought precisely to account for the variability of forms of capitalism in space and time. There is not one but a multiplicity of types of accumulation in accordance with the consequences of political conflict and the processes of institutionalization which develop in particular out of major structural crises (Boyer, 1990). In a sense, such studies propose an analysis of the economic consequences of institutionalized compromises (Delorme and André, 1983), whose emergence is signalled by political specialists and historians. Hence an interdisciplinary approach is required, indispensable in order properly to characterize capitalist diversity (Boyer and Saillard, 1995).

The starting point is none other than the Marxist theory of modes of production: capitalism is defined by the conjunction of two principles of economic organization. A market relationship, horizontal in type, organizes exchange relations between economic agents, while the vertical capital – labour relationship codifies the subordination of wage earners to a rationale set by the firm. However, in theory there is not just a single way of organizing these two fundamental relationships but a degree of variety. On the one hand, market exchange has a greater or lesser degree of development, from the market for certain products to that for labour, capital, credit or for certain derivative rights (intellectual property, law, pollution, etc.), whereas in addition competition may occur between a host of producers and buyers/product-seekers or on the contrary bring into play the dominant position of a small group of agents, whether suppliers or buyers. Here, in the nature and extent of market relationships, is an initial and highly significant source of capitalist differentiation. On the other hand, a no less marked diversity governs the pattern of capital/labour relationship, in line with the nature of the principles of the division of labour (degrees of skilled labour, job organization, the internal market peculiar to major firms, etc.) and the various forms of wage remuneration (whether fixed locally, on the professional market or on the basis of collective negotiations at different levels, both by sectors and nationally, with more or less complete recognition for collective rights through social security cover). Thus from a strictly theoretical point of view diverse forms of capitalism can coexist and succeed one another in an historical perspective.

But a *régulationiste* interpretation broadens the analysis by specifying some of the reasons for national forms of capitalism and their stages of development. The institutionalization of one form of market relation and of one type of wage relation is not simply the result of selection in terms of criteria of economic efficiency. Long-term historical research suggests that the process takes place by way of reaction to structural crises that have developed in a previous system, that it essentially activates political conflict and, further, that wars have frequently played an important part in the synchronization and legitimization of change wrought in an economic order previously reputed to be immutable (Figure 4.2(a)). This justifies the identification of national forms of capitalism, since the process of institutionalization reflects the social and political conflict particular to each

(a) New economic institutions may emerge from a major crisis

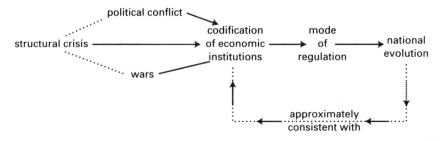

(b) The success of a mode of regulation strengthens the possibility of
unprecedented structural crises

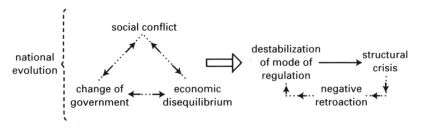

Figure 4.2   *Stages of development in different forms of capitalism: a*
régulationiste *interpretation*

country. Hence a process of path dependence is set in motion, since an
institutional framework is constructed on the basis of an architecture that
is more or less specific to each social pattern, even though of course the
analyst's task is to isolate classic forms, some examples of which are given
in what follows (see Figure 4.4 and Table 4.6).

But no economic system is capable of reproducing itself identically over
a very long period. This is contrary to the assumptions of most contemporary economic theories, obsessed as they are by the hypothesis of
rational anticipation on the part of agents optimizing their decisions
across the entire horizon of their lifecycle in a stationary environment. A
body of institutional forms may at first promote a mode of regulation that
is initially viable and more or less coherent. But as economic cycles
succeed one another, miscellaneous sources of destabilization make their
appearance. Social conflicts, articulated through politics, may cast doubt
upon key institutions, even while in general new forms for economic disequilibrium come into being. For instance, cumulative inflation was
associated with post-war Fordist growth, and this eventually brought
about the destabilization of the national and international monetary
system. A new episode in structural crisis in the precise sense of the term
may now emerge: economic adjustments actuated by the mode of regulation destabilize the underlying institutional forms (Figure 4.2(b)).

France, a double paradox

We may now turn to France as an illustration of these processes. If one seeks a perspective beyond the short-term politico-financial context, the French economy provides an illustration of three contrasting phases that succeeded one another in contradictory sequence. In the 1930s France displayed a number of political and economic weaknesses which are frequently attributed to its Malthusian traditions (Boyer, 1991b). Few expected the catharsis inflicted by World War II to be superseded by an economic miracle which would be the subject of analysis and often admiration on the part of foreign observers, surprised by the speed and stamina of the recovery that took place between 1954 and 1973.

In 1995 it is the reverse paradox. In an ageing and somewhat ossified Europe, French capitalism for some typifies excessive government regulation and intervention and the harm caused by a set of 'social oligopolies'. Thirty years of economic expansion have given way to a climate of lethargy and renewed apprehension of impending decline. In fact, the sequence of events is neither accidental nor mysterious but the expression of an abiding French particularity. Beyond technological and economic modernization, lately and so successfully achieved, French society still shows a distressing inability to come to terms with institutionalized innovation, which it needs to do in view of changes in the principles of productive organization, the intensification of global competition and attrition of growth.

The source of postwar expansion: a model Fordist approach

Over and above a number of constants within the political sphere, the major role of government in technological innovation and the postwar settlement marked a new turn, ending the destructive spiral of the 1930s and continuing to exert its influence in France on the eve of the millennium. First and foremost, renewal of the political and economic elites gave power to a generation determined to apply the lessons of past errors and create a climate for the most modern technology and appropriate social and economic concepts (Gruson, 1968; Fourquet, 1980). Engineers and administrators took the place of the cautious entrepreneurs and all-powerful financiers of the interwar period in a transition that had its parallel in Germany and Japan.

Thereupon an unprecedented settlement between capital and labour came into being. Heads of firms were given a free hand to organize production and implement modernization so long as the workforce profited from the outcome in terms of payment and social benefits. Productivity and wages soon registered swift and steady growth, testifying to the transition to a new form of development. Mass production, the potentialities of which were demonstrated during World War I, flourished with the majority of wage earners enjoying mass consumption, as represented in particular by cars, housing and consumer durables. The Fordist model of material affluence originating in the USA was adapted with considerable success, since it was novel and distinctive to France.

Hence the establishment of a comprehensive system of social security and the adoption of Keynesian precepts of direct intervention in investment and countercyclical policies had the effect of regularizing and 'lubricating' the Fordist model. Last but not least, the lifting of trade restrictions and exposure to international competition was gradual and cautious, in the context of significant global growth given stability by the all-pervading technological, financial, diplomatic and military superiority of the USA. The Treaty of Rome was well timed to boost modernization, once the process of decolonization – and the consequent dismantling of captive markets enjoyed by a number of French industrialists – was underway.

The state as central to the 'modernization' of French capitalism

If then the blueprint for the model was substantially the same in most major European countries and in Japan, its realization varied with the traditions, constraints and possibilities particular to each society (Table 4.1). Where the USA invoked the market and constitutional and civil law, the tendency in France was to give greater importance to parliamentary law and regulations and to administrative law. Where in Germany trust was placed in intermediary bodies, affording equal representation (for instance, between unions and management and *Länder*), the social and economic system in France favoured direct action on the part of government. This frequently sought to break across the rooted opposition to change, bred of confrontational attitudes between management and labour that had been so marked throughout the 1950s and 1960s. Besides, the weak legitimacy of employers as a body, or of the firm even, stood in the way of a Fordist form of microcorporatism, as in Japan.

Yet the situation was more favourable than in Britain, where the domination of industry by a highly internationalized financial sector and restrictiveness in trade practice and wage negotiation was for long a factor that retarded growth. Further, Italy provided evidence that government can be essentially clientelistic rather than a catalyst for a Fordist solution as it was in France. Even then, through a kind of reaction, the paralysis of government fostered local initiative – the industrial districts – and stimulated innovation on the part of the leading captains of industry.

Clearly, the distinguishing mark of the French model has to do with the intervention of central government exercising, first, a strategic, then a permanent, function with the object of piloting a modernization programme which seldom reflected compromise actually achieved between management and unions. In the matter of wage relations, one only need call to mind the part played by the 1950 Act extending collective agreements,

Table 4.1 *Originality of French model of development, 1945–73*

Country	Wage relation	Competition	Money	Government	International penetration	Mode of regulation
USA	Role of collective agreements	Quasi-oligopolistic practice of mark-up	Dollar's international status favours growth	Minimal welfare system	Dominant, hence favourable	Fordist model promoted by major firms and market
Japan	Microcorporatism and wage synchronization	Intense between major groups competing	Monetary policy aimed at stimulating growth	Reduced social welfare; motivating role of government	Protectionism for nascent industries	From hybrid Fordist model to Toyotist model
France	Highly institutionalized and codified by government	Government-controlled with price regulation	Monetary policy applied to stimulate growth	Fully developed welfare system; institutional initiative by government	Specialized intermediary role, and that of former colonies	Fordist model promoted by government
Germany	Strength of compacts between management and labour	Controlled by alliance between banks and industry	Initial underestimation boosts growth	Upholder of market economy	Favoured by specialization; control over export prices	Late adoption of flexible Fordist model; production differentiated and centred on quality
UK	Fragmentation of wage negotiations	Quasi-oligopolistic	Sterling against industry	Early established and developed welfare system	Financial more than industrial	Fordist model under constraint
Italy	North/South divide	Oligopolistic	Money and exchange favoured growth	Owing more to clientelism than to Beveridge	Complementary role in specialization	Part delayed Fordist model, part flexible specialization

Source: Boyer, 1990

then the transition from a minimum wage to a share in the benefits of growth. Competition between firms was closely monitored. Over forty years the now defunct office of prices in the Ministry of Finance super-vised and regulated price setting, in a manner that was virtually unique among the major industrialized countries. Similarly, the Bank of France, in effect subservient to government and its priorities, conducted an accommodating monetary policy, favouring investment and growth and, intermittently, restoring competitiveness by means of devaluation, when inflation became too marked in relation to France's trading partners. The welfare state underwent development that was closer to social-democratic countries than to the American ideal favouring the market and dogged, individualized, self-confidence. Finally, the government was concerned to filter international relations as best it could, so as to stimulate industrial expansion and preclude more advanced economies from gaining a foothold too soon and so blighting whole areas of industry.

The major transformation following World War II

In the years between 1945 and 1978, the omnipresence of government was far from having had the adverse effects that both a naive and extreme con-ception of economic liberalism might imply. On the contrary, social relations and the economy underwent greater transformation between 1950 and 1973 than between 1870 and 1950 (Table 4.2). For the first time, France became a fully industrialized nation with the manufacturing sector counting for 38.4 per cent of employment in 1973 as compared with 34.8 per cent in 1950 and 27.8 per cent in 1913. Agriculture registered an extremely rapid transformation which certainly provoked a revolt on the part of farmers but not the stalemate that was feared, thanks to national and subsequently European price support policies. At the same time, the services sector took off after 1950, evidence in itself of the feminization of the workforce. Between 1913 and 1950 France was no match for the USA in terms of productivity, but thereafter it made up lost ground in a spec-tacular effort that lasted till 1990.

Education was given a shot in the arm with the extension of secondary schooling; the degree of competence and qualification of the workforce came to be more relevant than lengthening working hours, promoting as it did productivity and sometimes product quality – intensive rather than extensive growth. The Fordist model called for a higher level of education for the broad mass of the working population, apart from the unskilled or semi-skilled, though vocational training remained the weak point in the system. Nor was government any longer merely the upholder of law and formal agreements, the vector of diplomacy and the pillar of national defence. Its unequivocal integration in the new system involved both mul-tiple intervention in the economy – sector by sector, with transport, housing and so on; and in a general way, through subsidies, government

Table 4.2 *The major transformation of the French economy*

	1870	1913	1950	1973	1990
Proportion of employment (as %)					
In agriculture	49.2	37.4	28.5	11.0	6.1
In industry	27.8	33.8	34.8	38.4	29.9
In services	23.0	28.0	36.7	50.6	64.0
Living and working conditions					
Waged labour: proportion of women in employment (as %)		35.6	36.0	37.1	41.2
Mean number of years in full-time education for age groups 15–64		6.18	8.18	9.58	10.79
Hours worked per year	2,945	2,588	1,989	1,785	1,554
Role of government					
Proportion of welfare expenditure in GDP (as %)	0.3	1.2	3.7	9.3	18.1
Total public expenditure in GDP (as %)	8.2	8.8	28.9	26.7	28.4
Productivity (GDP per hour) compared to USA (= 100)	54.7	49.2	41.5	74.7	97.5

Sources: Delorme and André, 1983; Maddison, 1987: 689, 688, 690, 1991; OECD, *France* various numbers

bids and credit – and the construction of a system of social security which sustained an ever-growing source of redistribution in terms of social welfare.

After 1973, these factors were effective in cushioning the economic and social consequences of rising unemployment noticeable from 1967 on, while at the same time they gave food for thought to advocates of neo-liberalism who were concerned about the extent of government borrowing and the trade deficit. Further, the pattern of regulation and government intervention soon turned out to be incapable of correcting the pace of growth, still less of curbing the virtually inescapable escalation in underemployment and job vulnerability. Conversely, and at the same time, growth in real wages was virtually arrested.

Success of the Fordist concept delayed perception that times had changed

Between 1973 and 1978, the government vaunted French economic performance on the grounds of avoidance of the blunders that affected other economies. Certainly the apparently orderly and regular character of short-term adjustments contrasted with the brusque switches in policy conducted by Margaret Thatcher in Britain and to a lesser extent by Ronald Reagan in the USA, or indeed with the state of affairs in Italy, characterized by earlier awareness on the part of employers of the gravity and extent of the Fordist crisis, both nationally and internationally. In France, when the left arrived in government in 1981, they even reckoned on being able to rid themselves of the deflationary bias of conservative policies, which militated in favour of sound money to the detriment of employment.

After 1984, it became clear that government-inspired policies in pursuit of Fordist-type growth had their limits. The quality of short-term economic management, in effect the reduction in fluctuating economic activity, finally squeezed profits and firms' finances to a point where investment, hence modernization and product innovation, including quality, were effectively inhibited. Even so, the implementation of a policy of wage and budgetary restraint, in itself a courageous choice for a socialist government, was insufficient to restore viable competitiveness, depending as it did not merely on prices but also on quality, on new market lines and the ability to introduce them.

Here is probably one explanation for the deterioration in French macro-economic performance (Table 4.3). Growth, which had customarily been above OECD average, became significantly weaker after 1979. The decline showed itself even more clearly in the level of unemployment, which from having been 18 per cent below the average in the OECD in 1973, rose to 42 per cent above in 1993. Inflation, always a vulnerable point, certainly moderated and this was an achievement, but most other indicators bore witness to the decline. The foreign trade balance which had tended to improve in relative terms between 1973 and 1979 deteriorated subsequently. Mediocre structural competitiveness led to a lower rate of growth than among trading partners (Figure 4.3). In the 1990s trading figures improved and inflation was markedly down, but unemployment was well above the OECD average.

In effect, the French economy had far more trouble adapting in conditions of recession, when the gap widened in relation to economies considered by politicians as being close to France. After 1973 Japan succeeded in accelerating the pace of innovation, eventually establishing an original model that continued and outstripped the Fordist one, thanks to the mass production of differentiated quality products. Germany found benefit in its technical prowess, its experience in producing capital goods and its skill in managing periods of recession no less well than periods of expansion. In some respects, Italian industry, considering the failings of the political system, showed remarkable powers of adaptation, insofar as obdurate specialization produced a response to the uncertain climate of the 1980s. Goaded on by the Iron Lady, Britain showed signs of a possible if not definite reversal of the unpromising pattern that had prevailed. Japanese multinationals injected a new vitality into the British motor and electronics industries, in spite of this occurring against a background of deindustrialization and the growing importance of financial priorities.

In contrast, France was afflicted by the growing inefficacy of her mode of regulation, previously so impressive. It required nearly ten years for the

Table 4.3 *French macro-economic performance: from miracle to normalization*

Country	Growth			Level of unemployment			Trade balance foreign GDP			Rate of inflation		
	1962–73	1973–9	1979–93	1973	1979	1993	1973	1979	1993	1973	1979	1993
USA	4.1	2.4	2.4	4.8	5.8	6.8	0.5	0	-1.7	6.1	9.2	3.0
Japan	10.4	3.6	3.7	1.3	2.1	2.5	0	-0.9	3.1	10.8	3.6	1.3
EEC (mean)	4.6	2.5	1.9	2.9	5.7	12.0	0.4	-0.2	0.1	9.0	10.0	3.3
France	5.5 110	2.8 104	1.8 75	2.7 82	5.9 116	11.7 142	0.6 150	0.9 300	0.9 300	7.4 89	10.7 123	2.1 58
Germany	4.5	2.3	2.0	0.8	3.2	8.9	1.5	-0.7	-1.1	6.4	4.2	4.1
UK	3.3	1.5	1.7	3.0	5.0	10.3	-1.5	-0.2	-1.7	8.6	13.6	1.6
Italy	4.8	3.7	2.0	6.2	7.6	10.4	-1.5	1.6	1.3	9.0	10.2	4.2
OECD (mean)	5.0 100	2.7 100	2.4 100	3.3 100	5.1 100	8.2 100	0.4 100	-0.6 100	0.1 100	8.3 100	8.7 100	3.6 100

Source: Computed from OECD national accounts, various years

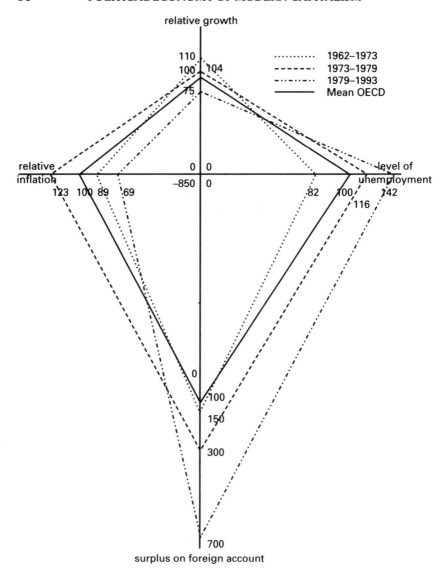

Figure 4.3   *Over a twenty-year period, inflation reduced and competitiveness restored at the cost of low growth and high unemployment (France in relation to OECD mean)*

diagnosis to be made and recognized (Table 4.4). Indeed, between 1973 and 1982, successive governments simply applied an extension of the Fordist model *à la française*. For instance, the first oil crisis produced an intensification of the policy of protecting employment, while devaluation continued to be a preferred method for adjusting internal disequilibrium. In 1981 a new left-wing government again attempted a Keynesian bout of reflation against a background of international recession (Ross et al., 1987)

Table 4.4 1973–83: Extension of a state-driven variant of the Fordist model until its rejection in 1983

	Wage relation	Competition	Money	Government	International penetration
1974	Increased protection for employment	Oligopolistic competition led to a marked rise in prices	Franc floated	Slowdown in growth implying a recurring social security deficit	Decreasing French share in world economy
1976	First questioning of Fordist wage setting	Price freeze to combat inflation	Re-entry into EMS (1975)		
1978			Credit squeeze applied by Central Bank	Growth in government taxation and social security deductions as a proportion of GDP	Erosion of French industrial competitiveness (prices, quality, innovation)
1981	Significant increase in minimum wage	Nationalization of industry (25%) and banking (97%)	Franc devaluations		Temptation of taking specific protectionist measures
1982				Acts of devolution	
1983	Backtracking on inflation linking of wages	Price freeze; recognition of French industry's loss of competitiveness	Major financial crisis; adoption of financial orthodoxy; priority given to fight against inflation	Reversal of budgetary policy: reduction in the proportion of compulsory contributions	Active European integration strategy

and extended the field of nationalization. Throughout the entire period the French economy was losing its competitiveness, as revealed as much by the growth in relative costs as by a falling-off in inventiveness. It almost appeared that the representations and anticipations of virtually all participants in the French economy had assumed the continuity of the postwar expansion at the very time when in most other countries political and economic elites had realized that a major change had occurred in the conditions of international competition. Optimism crumbled in 1983, when French politicians rejected the option of global protectionism and resolved on a strategy of European integration, albeit at the cost of opposing the expectations of the electorate.

The turning-point of 1983: renouncing a purely French approach

It would be misleading to speak of 'immobilism' with the number of reforms launched between 1983 and 1994; however, most of them foundered or have still to yield their results. Policies pursued were initially clearly interventionist, then market driven but tempered by the promise to uphold a fundamental welfare provision. To begin with, an intensive legislative programme aimed at reforming the structures of industry and the institutional organization of the French economy. The so-called Auroux Acts sought to bring industrial negotiations up to date, but their effect was to worsen a decline and crisis in union strategy. Nationalization of a number of major firms produced an initial injection of capital and modernization of production, but without resolving the problem of how to take on board the newly emergent principles of global competition or to tap the financial market more successfully. Legislation for devolution gave wider powers to regional and local authorities, and was timely insofar as it did something to offset the over-centralization of administration in France, but without the prospect of enabling the regions to be as effective and autonomous as their counterparts in Germany, Italy or Spain.

This phase of Keynesianism in one country revealed its limitations during 1982–3. The left once in power appeared to forget its own analyses exposing the structural crisis affecting the Fordist model, since reflation by way of public spending and wages had a damaging effect on the trade balance, leading to speculation that the franc would depreciate, rather than, as in the 1960s, having a beneficial effect on growth and employment. Even before the period of cohabitation during Chirac's premiership, there was a radical change in economic policy to give priority to a strong franc, thereby controlling inflation and eschewing protectionism. Still more significantly, the rationale of the market underwent a surprising rehabilitation with a series of reforms effecting denationalization, financial deregulation, tax exemption for reinvested profits and a far more rigorous management of public finances (Table 4.5).

Table 4.5   1984–94: Recalibration of institutional forms, but no new viable pattern

	Wage relation	Competition	Money	Government	International penetration
1984	Act decentralizing negotiations between management and labour	Reorganization and rationalization of the nationalized sector	Strong franc policy, maintenance of exchange rate with DM	Policy to reduce government deficit	
1986	Promotion of profit-sharing	Complete removal of price controls	Adoption of policy of competitive disinflation	Reform of unemployment	Financial liberalization
	Withdrawal of administrative authorization to make redundant	Start of denationalization	Monetary policy directed towards price stability and maintenance of parity	Privatizations	More appreciation of the economic situation pertaining in Germany
				Rationalization of health insurance.	
1989	Establishment of income support (RMI)	Resumption of denationalizations	Monetary policy – no longer instrument of government policy	Government deficit increased by recession	Implementation of single European market
	Persistence of unemployment and gradual erosion of status of wage-earner				Increasing pressure by financial markets upon economic policy
1994	Continuing erosion of the the postwar wage compromise	Competition law at European level; loss of autonomy	Independence of the Banque de France	Incompatibility between low growth and past institutional compromises	Acceptance of Maastricht Treaty; aim for pace of growth to be an objective for Europe

With a view to curbing the rise in unemployment, government and industry gave serious attention to the progress of job creation in the USA, attributable to the benefits of labour market flexibility, the absence of an active minimum wage policy and restricted employment protection. Throughout the 1980s, American and British free market experience was followed with interest, and sometimes with envy, resulting in an easing of regulations regarding working agreements, hiring labour, minimum wages and welfare contributions. This initiated a somewhat defensive approach to flexibility in the sense that it meant going back on concessions long won by unions yet without any alternative social pact to propose. Nor did these initiatives adumbrate a new employment relationship that might successfully get to grips with unemployment by means of fuller functional flexibility. Indeed, ten years after this attempt at 'rationalizing' the labour law, the expected beneficial effects on employment are still awaited. Hence the pursuit of a policy of wage restraint and a stable franc have been influential in curbing inflation and stimulating competition, but have not clearly formulated a viable medium-term strategy. Indeed, none of the measures taken has succeeded in reducing the unemployment level, which remains one of the highest in Europe; and this in spite of numerous employment schemes that combine tax exemption with incentives for traineeship schemes. It has to be said that the continuance of unemployment over so long a period puts the cohesion of French society at risk and is likely to add to the lure of xenophobia.

More generally, it is hardly going too far to claim that a structural crisis persists; the pattern of institutions has not yet been reconstructed to ensure stability. Yearly the postwar wages compromise is being eroded, frittered away across a series of decrees that afford less and less protection. Similarly, the claims of competition are finding ever greater acceptance at a European level, which wrongfoots the relationship that previously existed between French firms and their supervisory authorities (Dumez and Jeunemaître, 1991). In 1994 the transition that made the Bank of France independent of government constituted major change with likely repercussions on most other areas of economic policy. Furthermore, the unusual length of the 1990s' recession has served to emphasize anew the incompatibility of the legacy of the institutionalized trade-offs following World War II and the prospect of slow growth, if only because in the short-term German reunification is having somewhat negative effects on European growth potential. Last, there is no evidence to show that acceptance of the clauses of the Maastricht Treaty will guarantee growth within the momentum of European integration at a pace sufficient to curb unemployment and make the pattern of French capitalism again viable.

The seductions of Rhineland capitalism

For a long time the debate was between French-type interventionism and the market-driven policies favoured in Britain and the USA. The parallel problems and/or setbacks on each side led at the start of the 1990s to a quite different view, pointing up the virtues of an alternative approach in which market forces and institutional sophistication combine to realize the competitiveness and potential instanced by Japan and Germany or within regions like the Rhineland and Piedmont. The concept of organized capitalism has re-emerged following observation of strongly contrasting national performance curves during the 1980s. The Anglo-American countries which had adopted the rationale of the market and placed their trust in entrepreneurial initiative, however speculative, had to face a renewal of inflation, rapidly rising unemployment (Britain) and further a loss of competitiveness, in part caused by the shortfall in public expenditure on infrastructure, education and training (USA). On the other hand, countries where government has played a central role in socio-economic regulation encountered major problems at the end of the 1980s, for example, the collapse of the Soviet system, the overt crisis of social democracy in Sweden, or doubts raised concerning the pattern of state interventionism in France.

Conversely, countries such as Japan or Germany that had taken action to discipline competition and develop a nexus of institutionalized compromise within the firm and between firms, both regionally and nationally, manifested undoubted economic drive, which sprang from an aptitude for assimilating new technology and constantly reaffirming their competitive advantages. At the very moment when 'communism' collapsed, so sealing the apparent triumph of undiluted capitalism, practitioners and experts discovered how various were its forms, combining in differing degrees, markets, associations, networks, hierarchies and government, existing side by side and performing with differing degrees of success according to context. A current of opinion formed to point to the superiority, in many respects, of Rhineland capitalism that brought together a close relationship between banks and industry, an ongoing and many-sided process of negotiation between management and unions and a major delegation of economic as well as political responsibility (Streeck, 1994b).

In fact, since the break-up of the Bretton Woods system, there have been four major versions of capitalism in competition (Table 4.6), each with its advantages and disadvantages, which in a given situation can benefit or penalize a given geographical area.

First, the Rhineland model (with an important variant which is Japanese microcorporatism) depends on a dense network of intermediary institutions between central government and individual economic agents (professional associations, strong unions, large firms and financial groups). The chief advantage of this type of capitalism is that it is built upon a highly versatile workforce, an enormous asset when competition involving quality and service is superimposed upon competition of a more traditional kind based on production costs for mass production goods. Further, the German and Japanese models, though not conforming to exactly the same pattern, are functionally equivalent in regard to the skills they display (Boyer and Durand, 1997).

Table 4.6 *The four types of capitalism: distinctive forms of labour market*

Capitalism	Market-oriented	Rhineland or corporatist	Statist	Social democrat
Institutional characteristics	• Decentralization • External mobility • Role of market • Little mediation with trade unions	• Role of occupational labour market or trade-off within the firm • External or internal mobility • Significant trade union intermediation, whether explicit or implicit	• Central role of government • Strong internal labour markets, weaker external markets • Several labour unions divided by political affiliation	• Tripartite agreements between trade unions, management and government • Mobility organized by government and regions • Major role for a strong union
Variables for adjustment	• Reduction of workforce • Variation in mean wage • Variability of wage spread • Regional mobility	• Transfer from firm to firm or post to post • Versatility • Role of wage adjustments • Pressure for product innovation	• Reduction of workforce • Rigidity of real wages • Slight variation in wage spread • Youth unemployment	• Industrial restructuring • Possibility of wage flexibility • Narrow wage differentials • Training and qualification
Advantages	• Rapid response to recession • Adjustment to structural changes	• Short-term reaction: hours and wages • In the long term: productivity and product innovation	• Maintenance of a welfare state • Boosting productivity	• Maintenance of wage comparability • Assertion of principle of full employment
Disadvantages	• Inadequacy of training and social investment • Marked and/or increasing inequality • Possible disincentives against technological change	• Hoarding of labour • Compartmentalization of labour (major firms/subcontractors) • Inappropriate for low-skill, labour-intensive industries	• Arbitration in favour of those who are actively employed • Erosion of the wage relation • Youth unemployment; pressure to reduce employment rates	• Strain on the trade-off between labour and management • Strain on public finances • Adverse effect of narrow wage differentials on incentive
Examples	USA, Canada, Britain	Germany, Japan	France, Italy	Sweden, Austria

A second variant combines types of capitalism in which the market plays a decisive if not exclusive role in regard to other forms of coordination. It is the model observed in most Anglo-American countries and one that allows a rapid response in economic uncertainty and to the emergence of new industries. This aptitude for inventiveness has as its corollary a poor level of public investment, the likelihood that inequalities persist, if not increase. There is sometimes a loss of productive drive, given the absence of union representation that is able to impose real wage increases and a degree of control over the organization of labour.

Third, over almost half a century the social-democratic variant showed that it could combine technological drive with the fight against social inequality. Its very success led to contrary tendencies stemming from too narrow pay differentials, increasing importance of public employment, a tendency for inflation to grow, and then a transnationalization of major firms. Since the mid-1980s the Swedish economy has undergone an institutional crisis, a crisis that Austria has so far escaped, probably because outside conditions and the institutional pattern itself are different.

The fourth model involves robust and multiform interventionism on the part of government. Government has a central role to play within the institutional pattern in the fields of labour, competition and integration at international level. Furthermore, the budget and the social security system accumulate every distortion, whether general, sectorial or even local. France and the southern European countries belong to this category. This form of capitalism has proved highly effective in keeping pace with the USA, but reveals its limitations when prospects for both technology and demand become uncertain.

As a model it has been particularly tested over the last twenty years, and this may help to explain the current notion that variants of capitalism are becoming normalized on the Anglo-American model. Yet developments are not as simple as this, since in France there is more frequent reference to the Rhineland model than to market forms of capitalism. Such reference has in fact increased to the extent of initiating a measure of reform in connection with training schemes or the marriage between banks and insurance firms with a view to acquiring the means of promoting industrial restructuring and efficiency (Albert, 1991; Pastré, 1992; Morin and Dupuy, 1993). Where the Japanese system is perceived as being particularly difficult to implement on account of its cultural distinctiveness, the German model is closer and of special interest in that it gives a key role to training in respect of competitiveness. Besides, initially, German reunification sustained European, but also French, growth with the result that at the end of 1991 bilateral trade between France and Germany was at par for the first time in almost twenty years. Moreover, whatever the destiny of the Maastricht agreement, the mark of German ideas and institutions is already present in the reform of the statutes of the Banque de France on the model of the Bundesbank.

However, this major institutional change has occurred in the context of the long European recession of the 1990s, linked in part to the difficulties encountered in the modernization and assimilation of the eastern *Länder*. One may suggest in passing that the mere transfer of an institutional system, by no means incompatible in itself, may well precipitate unfavourable economic adjustments to the extent that it is at odds with the technological, industrial and social background of the country concerned.

Types of capitalism cannot be imported like merchandise

But to recognize the superiority of one organizational mode of capitalism is not to say that it is an easy task to import, copy or assimilate its rationale and its institutions, by the very fact of their being specific to a society and the products of one particular history. For instance, time and time again both Britain and France have sought to set up schemes for training modelled on the German, so far however without success. Similarly, the constitution of powerful financial groups is a necessary, but doubtless insufficient, condition wherewith to prompt an industrial revival, which after all depends both on the quality of organization and those who administer it, and on the soundness of industrial relations and their ability to confront constant technological change. One is therefore entitled to question the chances of success for a strategy of acclimatizing the Rhineland model within a French social context that is so marked by interventionism. Certainly, the strategy of constituting 'financial cores' may create one of the enabling conditions for a German form of capitalism, but on its own it is insufficient (Figure 4.4).

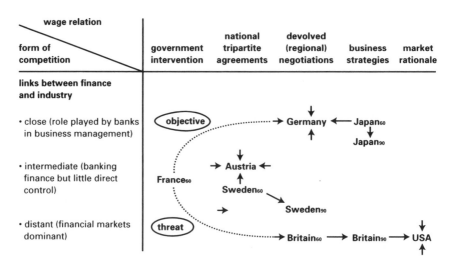

Figure 4.4   *A typology of capitalism: nature of the wage relation and form of control of capital*

Further, the scope of activities involved in negotiations between professional bodies, unions, the authorities of the *Länder* and the federal ministries would have to be generalized. Here there is a major distinction vis-à-vis the decisive role of government in France. In spite of the reforms of the last ten years, central government continues to administer education and occupational training, and one may wonder whether this does not constitute one of the obstacles in the way of adhering to a new productive model centred upon quality-led competitiveness (Boyer and Dore, 1994). If one looks to find both diversity of competition and the assembly of skills, over the last thirty years only two types of capitalism have maintained a degree of stability – the Rhineland and the market economy models. The other models have sometimes been affected by fairly rapid change (as in the case of Sweden, moving from national tripartite agreements to devolved negotiations), while in Japan close relations between banks have been put to the test by the internationalization of finance.

This being so, the present strategy of French elites could face an anomaly: given the dearth of institutions sufficiently fertile to allow adoption of the Rhineland model, is there not a risk of Anglo-American capitalism selecting itself by default (Figure 4.4). Indeed it is a great deal easier to let markets have their way than to channel their development, precisely at a time when financial innovation is multiplying and when the vigorous control exercised by markets upon the economic policy of governments is becoming more marked. In fact there are three series of obstacles which militate against the ready institutional convergence of capitalisms on both sides of the Rhine. First, the very interdependence of economic institutions which provides the strength and stability of the Rhine model itself explains the structural difficulty of its adoption by other countries. This is a very general property of models which function in a highly path-dependent way. In the German case this applies in particular to vocational training (Boyer and Dore, 1994).

It is also difficult to synchronize changes in forms of competition, wage relationship and monetary system outside periods of major recession or war (Chartres, 1995). Last, analysis of debate in France shows the extreme difficulty that government encounters in settling upon the new compromises necessary if the Rhineland model is to be adopted. Firms and social groups speak and act on the basis of the negotiating power given them by the previous Fordist model centred upon government and the resulting status quo.

Innovating on the basis of a strong tradition of government impetus

Hence one should be wary of recklessly duplicating a model that is thought of as superior; rather one should emphasize the advantages associated with the existing social and political inclination of each country.

This is also a problem for the USA, where it is no longer certain that 'Japanization' holds the key to the future, any more than 'Rhinelandization' does for French society. As an alternative, what is there to prevent the abundance of means of intervention available to French government from being redeployed to obtain the functional equivalent of what German (or Japanese) institutions are able to do? By way of example, the corps of telecommunications engineers that came to the fore with Minitel might be considered as the equivalent of the pioneers in Silicon Valley or the major electronics groups in Japan.

The direction adopted by a particular country hence needs to be recognized (Figure 4.5). The precedent of the Fordist model is illuminating in this respect since it might be thought that the fact of importing American methods of production and an accompanying lifestyle carried with it ready acceptance of the rationale of the market. On the contrary, the economic advantages that accrued were due to an application and adaptation of these methods within a French context, that is within the tradition of government interventionism. The modernization of French capitalism was effected through the adoption of Fordist concepts, not with their market ethos, but in a highly institutionalized form and under the impetus of government. Allowing for the different context, it is legitimate to ask oneself whether similar hybridization is not likely to occur in the 1990s.

(a) The precedent of the Fordist model

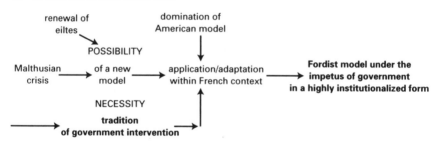

(b) The 1990s

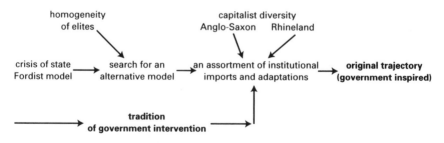

Figure 4.5   *The influence of national trajectories – to imitate one form of capitalism is always to adapt it*

Admittedly the crisis is no longer Malthusian, since it also has to do with a style of government interventionism. In seeking alternative solutions, whether Anglo-Saxon or Rhineland, it is beyond doubt that impetus from government remains essential. There is also a lack of social partners at once autonomous, dynamic and able to negotiate concessions independently of such interventionism. Indeed recourse to government is the traditional French means of resolving conflict and initiating possible institutional innovation. In France (as also in Russia) even strategies that resort to the market are imposed by government, in the absence of a powerful entrepreneurial group behind such a strategy. These elements encourage one to anticipate that such tenacious characteristics of French capitalism will be maintained.

Certain weaknesses are also strengths

In times of structural crisis, confidence in national institutions is severely shaken, with the result that the governing class frequently searches for solutions from elsewhere, such are its misgivings as to the adaptability of inherited forms of organization. This may lead it to underestimate the problems of transposing alien institutions. Alternatively, it may search some mythic golden age, long past, for the sources of a different strategy, forgetting that the context is new and changed conditions make the past relatively irretrievable. Perhaps there is a method to be followed in this mistaken dilemma, which is to allow that the new too is constructed by recombining familiar forms to face the major challenges of the moment. Tradition is frequently just the – forgotten – result of past innovation. But it is also the seed bed of future innovation.

The whole art would seem to lie in turning the limits of the previous form of organization into so many assets with a view to recomposing them in an arrangement appropriate to the new context (Table 4.7). Here are a few examples among others.

In regard to wage relations, the persistence of a marked contrast between manual and non-manual work, between work that is of its nature 'noble' and work that is not, is frequently denounced as one of the defects of French capitalism (d'Iribarne, 1989, 1994). This has certainly had an unfavourable effect on competitiveness over the last twenty years. However, if in a newly emerging productive paradigm the intellectual factor in the productive process is acquiring greater significance, the stress given to a general education may become a strength, as illustrated in an indirect way by Japanese achievement. Similarly, union weaknesses and divisions make it uncertain that a national agreement to renew the Fordist compromise can be negotiated. However, this is also the seed bed which nurtured the strategies of human resource management in major firms, with an ever larger fraction of opinion recognizing the legitimacy of the firm, a circumstance new to France (Hatchuel, 1993). Also it might be said

Table 4.7   *Strengths and weaknesses of French state driven capitalism in the 1990s: an analysis in terms of institutional forms*

Institutional forms	Limitations and weaknesses	Strengths and ability to evolve
Wage relation	1 Persistence of divide between manual and non-manual work.	1 Intellectual factor acquiring increasing significance.
	2 Inadequacy of training for those with low skills.	2 Stress given to general education with an increasing number of each cohort.
	3 Loss of union influence in industry with union representation weak or divided.	3 Recognition given to the legitimacy and rationale of the firm.
	4 Multiplication and disintegration of wage-earning status.	4 Maintenance of general social welfare cover.
Forms of competition	1 'National champions' no longer suffice in order to compete internationally.	1 Setting up of 'financial cores' to pilot industrial reconstruction.
	2 European construction puts a question mark over French-style industrial policy.	2 Sectors such as armaments, infrastructure and heavy engineering that benefit from government orders are innovative.
	3 Lack of cooperation between large and small firms.	3 Some small and medium-sized firms display drive in developing new technologies.
Monetary system	1 Financial innovations destabilize traditional instruments of monetary policy.	1 Ambition for Paris to become a major financial centre.
	2 Credit policy constrained by external situation.	2 Acceptance of necessity to be competitive.
	3 Adherence to monetary integration eliminates an instrument of economic policy.	3 Acceptance of the need for DM/ franc stability has been built into industrial strategy.
Government	1 The selectiveness of industrial policies faces challenge in the European Union.	1 Government continues to prompt innovation.
	2 Delay in the process of devolution by government.	2 Relative legitimacy of centralized government effective in crisis-solving policies.
	3 Difficulty of fiscal reform and of financing social security.	3 Presidential system advantageous in effecting 'top-down' reforms.
International penetration	1 Erosion of specialization in typically Fordist industries.	1 Specialization increasingly complementary to that in other European countries.
	2 Slow response in adapting to geographical and sectorial shifts in demand.	2 Past success in redirecting specialized production from the ex-colonial to the new European market.
	3 Serious problems in adaptation during periods of slow and/or unstable growth.	3 Swift move to internalization in terms of direct investment, partnership, etc.

that government, through its encouragement of profit sharing, has promoted the emergence of a type of microcorporatism which in certain respects is reminiscent of Japanese capitalism.

In the matter of forms of competition, first the success and then the erosion of the policy of support for 'national champions' gave rise to the complementary strategy of 'financial cores', piloting an industrial reconstruction which now goes beyond national frontiers. The construction of Europe calls characteristic French industrial policies clearly into question, at the very moment when the competitive position of firms that have long benefited from government orders in telecommunications, high-speed trains and major infrastructural undertakings is becoming more pronounced. Similarly, the new generation of heads of small businesses and the burgeoning of new technology are surely signs that the unfavourable developments accentuated by the Fordist ethos of the 1960s can be righted (Lane, 1991).

The financial and monetary system is also permeated by contradictory tendencies. The new financial instruments and the globalization of markets have to a large degree destabilized traditional monetary policy which for a long time maintained a strict control over credit. Even if one rules out the fugitive hope of making Paris a major international financial centre, tough financial constraints and the adoption of a strong franc policy have given general credence to the necessity of being competitive in manufacturing industry and internationally traded services. Occasionally employment has declined, but these sectors have performed fairly impressively, according to a 1994 report in the *Financial Times*. One need only measure the difference with performance in Britain to appreciate the relevance as well as the limits of the French strategy.

As has been several times pointed out, government, even when it has adopted market-driven policies, continues to play a decisive role in policy for both innovation and competitive infrastructure, including sociopolitical stability. It may be a matter of regret that French capitalism is in a minority by not yet having profited from sweeping fiscal reform, while the recurring imbalance in financing social security has so far not led to a comprehensive redefinition of objectives, means and results that might be expected of an alternative system of social redistribution and insurance. Yet the presidential system of the Fifth Republic confers a degree of power on the executive which few governments in other countries enjoy. This puts it in the position of being able to effect reform of the country's economic institutions from the top down should it be so inclined. However undemocratic such a move might appear, there is ample precedent for it in French tradition.

Finally, France's penetration of the international market is not as catastrophic as predictions on the basis of the situation at the start of the 1980s might have suggested. Certainly, its influence and rank in world production has fallen, largely because of the upsurge of new industrial nations, but the foreign trade balance is no longer in deficit but of course the rate of growth is lower than in the past. It should not be forgotten that previously specialized French production was redirected from the former colonial empire towards the European market, a transition that was accomplished with surprising swiftness (Marseille, 1984). Further as historical studies have shown, it would be a mistake to relate the problems of the 1980s to the twenty-first century since in the past this type of halt to progress never lasted so long (Bouvier, 1987; Bloch-Lainé and Bouvier, 1986).

There is a final relatively optimistic factor. Within the context of the increasing consolidation of Europe, each of the national or regional economies has to specialize in order to ensure comparative advantage. For example, Italian or Spanish industrial structures are not the same as their German counterparts, but build their competitive advantages upon their own institutional endowments. Thus, through the fact of competition strengthening at European level, it could well be that the French economy cannot – and is not required to – follow the Rhineland pattern, but explores a path which in one sense is complementary, playing on a mobilization of resources inherited from state-driven capitalism. Here is an invitation for a more systematic analysis of some pathways relating to the future.

Some possible reassembling – four scenarios

The uncertainties of the 1990s have much to do also with the ultimately hybrid character of contemporary French capitalism. In an earlier study an attempt was made to formulate a typology between inventiveness and economic performance by means of an analysis of data from twelve OECD member countries, taking as a basis more than 180 characteristic variables (Amable et al., 1997). On the one hand, profiles studied involving science, technology and industry put France in the company of Anglo-American countries where technological change depends on a clear scientific bent as well as on programmes – in aerospace, pharmaceuticals and life sciences – that are more or less linked to government. By contrast, Japan and Germany have a more technological orientation, specializing in capital goods and active research in natural sciences (Figure 4.6). On the other hand, macro-economic performance produces a different pattern, where France, Germany, Italy and the Netherlands combine a concern to restructure productive output and pursue efficiency alongside persisting high unemployment and low growth (Figure 4.7). Meanwhile, Anglo-Saxon countries display greater inequalities but higher levels of employment, whereas Scandinavian countries and Japan until 1990 shared a healthy model for growth that combined efficiency with relatively full employment and only slight inequalities.

French capitalism is now immersed in the European situation, which is largely determined by Germany. Even so, the two countries do not share the same systems for innovation and this may explain the recurring problems encountered by the ongoing movement for European integration,

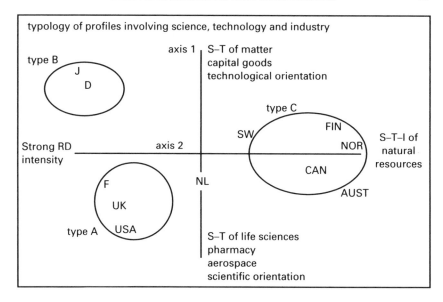

Figure 4.6 *France in the company of Anglo-Saxon countries*

which itself may lead to the erosion of France's particular potential for technological inventiveness, unless innate technological drive manages sooner or later to revive French macro-economic performance. In this respect, one may set out some of the courses available the better to high-

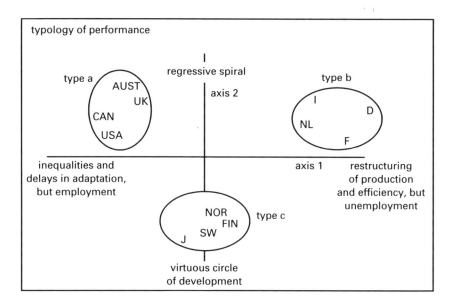

Figure 4.7 *France following the European model (Amable et al., 1997)*

light the consequences of the preceding historical analysis (Table 4.8).

Nostalgia for a government-led Fordist policy is still to be reckoned with since it was the course taken in the wake of the two oil crises. In this scenario, the previous institutional compromises would continue to be defended by the best-placed social groupings, even if this means that, within a context of ongoing internationalization, the corresponding loss of competitiveness shows itself in a relative – perhaps absolute – decline in the international position of French capitalism. A variant of this scenario would allow for the increased probability of a programme of state-driven capitalism, marked by technological, though not necessarily social, modernization, if a major crisis in the construction of Europe were to occur.

A slow transition towards a form of Rhineland capitalism is possible, though on the face of it unlikely, judging by historical precedents. Previous developments have pointed up the difficulties of making such a transition. Conceivably, the nationalized sector might be reconstructed round a financial core operating at European level and maintaining a degree of coherence and perspective in the medium term. But it would be harder to develop German-style industrial relations, which would presuppose a quite exceptional infusion of vitality into management and labour relations and negotiating bodies, of which there has been little sign over the last twenty years.

Transforming government-led capitalism into another form corresponds to a third scenario which has been explored in outline in some of the preceding analyses. If new organizational principles become more evident, ensuring competitiveness not only in terms of price but of quality, service and innovation, the economic administration could well conduct

Table 4.8 *Some scenarios for French capitalism*

Scenario	Strength	Weakness	Probability
1 Nostalgia for a state-driven Fordist model	In line with and continuing previous institutional compromises	Endorses relative – or absolute – decline if global growth is slight	Relatively strong
2 Transition towards a form of Rhineland capitalism	Possible reconstruction of banking sector and nationalized industry	Difficulty in developing German-style industrial relations	Fairly, perhaps very, slight in view of historical precedent
3 Government-led transformation to another form of French-type capitalism	In keeping with lessons learnt from history	Pays scant account to the decline of the nation-state with growing internationalization and European construction	Significant, stronger if a new international system ensured strong growth
4 Gradual 'normalization' and convergence on an Anglo-Saxon type of capitalism	Corresponds to what has occurred over last twenty years (market revival, growth of inequality, etc.)	Breaks with traditional factors of cohesion in French society	Might well result from failure of preceding strategies

this transformation, as has been the case on previous occasions. The probability of such a course is heightened by the fact that the international system would ensure strong growth, since in view of the myriad institutionalized trade-offs and the fixed costs that result French capitalism is traditionally better fitted to modernize in periods when the international system is stable than in periods of crisis. Yet the probability of a 'happy ending' on these lines is questionable to the extent that internationalization and the goal of European integration involve the nation-state in a loss of autonomy.

An end to French exceptionalism and, willy nilly, a movement towards market-driven capitalism might well result from abortive strategies in respect of the above three scenarios. Certainly one may have misgivings in regard to a theory of convergence built on the assumption that globalization implies eventual erosion of all national specificity and the increasing resemblance of all forms of capitalism to the Anglo-American form. Even so, the degree of parallelism between the French and American trajectories, over and above the political agenda, is striking: the renewed vigour of market ideologies, pre-eminence of the principle of the individual firm over that of solidarity, growth of inequality, under the constraints of a high level of unemployment (though considerably attenuated in its French form). It would constitute a major break with the ideals that brought about the cohesion of French society (liberty, equality, fraternity); also French political institutions and concepts have little in common with those that characterize the USA.

One must leave it to the future to deal with these predictions, bearing in mind how in the inter-war period most observers were incapable of foreseeing the miracle of Fordist modernization that came in the aftermath of World War II. An optimistic view would stress that French capitalism has never been in a position of stalemate for long without a political crisis – or a war – occurring, to set off a series of ambitious reforms. To this the pessimist would rightly respond that history only ever repeats itself in a stumbling way, and that the untried conditions of the 1990s invalidate the predictions that hold good for a scenario where national forms of capitalism are autonomous, itself an inevitably dated assumption.

Be that as it may, a certain erosion of what constituted French particularity is taking place, yet it would be imprudent thereby to surmise that complete and definitive convergence on a single model will result, if only because the period ahead will probably be marked by competition and very probably the co-existence of types of capitalism whose divergence will remain.

5

SOCIAL INSTITUTIONS AND PRODUCTION STRUCTURE: THE ITALIAN VARIETY OF CAPITALISM IN THE 1980S

Marino Regini

In the literature of political economy, description of the relationships between the economy and institutions in Italy from a comparative perspective centres around two principal questions. The first is whether the Italian case represents a particular mix among the various forms of regulation of the economy (Lange and Regini, 1989) or, to use more recent formulations, between the Anglo-Saxon and the Rhenish types of capitalism – or whether it is a distinct type that falls outside this conceptualization. The second question is whether Italy can be treated as a national whole or only as an amalgam of subnational patterns, each characterized by its own relationships between economy and institutions (Trigilia, 1986; Bagnasco, 1988; Locke, 1994).

Although this chapter will occasionally address the second of these questions, it will concentrate mainly on providing new answers to the first, by relating the configuration of the Italian production system – namely, the mix of organizational models adopted by Italian firms – to the features of the institutional environment.

The configuration of the Italian production system

The basic premise of this section is that 'post-Fordist' firms are able to choose from a wider range of organizational and market strategies than most literature would have us believe. For instance, to view them – as is often the case – as enterprises which equip themselves to compete not on price but on quality, is rather simplistic and basically misleading. In fact, the industrial adjustment processes which took place in Italy in the late 1970s and 1980s showed the emergence of several types of innovative market strategies. While price constraints remained important to all of them, some firms were able to compete chiefly on quality or design, others on product diversification, and others still on flexibility, in the sense of versatility and rapid adjustment to changing demand. For the purposes of this discussion, I shall call the first of these innovative market strategies 'diversified quality production' (DQP), thus borrowing Streeck's (1991) term while giving a somewhat different meaning to it. The second I shall call 'flexible mass production' (FMP), thereby taking up the distinctions made by Boyer (1987). The third is 'flexible specialization' (FS), although this concept in its original formulations (Piore and Sabel, 1984) was somewhat wider in scope than will be used here.[1]

Of course, these three innovative market strategies do not cover the entire universe of companies in a country like Italy, where both Fordist firms and – especially – traditional small firms competing mainly on price remain a sizeable reality. However, my analysis on the role of institutions deals primarily with companies adopting one of the three abovementioned more innovative market strategies, or post-Fordist trajectories. While the overall production structure of a country is, in fact, the outcome of long and complex processes rooted in its history, the opportunities for innovation within this structure are to a greater extent influenced by the institutional environment, which opens up some possibilities while foreclosing others. The innovative market strategies mentioned above imply different organizational solutions as well as different patterns of human resource utilization; solutions and patterns whose viability is deeply affected, as we shall see, by the prevailing institutional environment.

In the terminology used here, a DQP strategy is adopted by firms seeking to compete on the quality – and to a lesser extent on the diversification – of their products, rather than solely on their price. The aim is to avoid competition from the low-wage economies by concentrating on higher segments of the market, and by responding to the greater sophistication and volatility of demand with semi-customized products, etc. Quality thus defined is determined by various factors, such as organizational and coordination skills. But it depends crucially on the degree of skill of the workforce at all levels, on its ability to switch among a variety of tasks, as well as rapidly to learn new ones, and on its involvement in company goals of constant improvement and incremental innovation.

This gives rise to a pattern of human resource management based on a large proportion of the workforce receiving extended training – both basic and company specific – and being encouraged to develop social skills such as initiative, a problem-solving attitude and the ability to work with others, as well as close identification with the corporate culture. Also required of the workforce is high internal or functional flexibility, which is matched by low levels of the other types of labour flexibility (external or numerical, wage, and working time flexibility).

The FMP strategy is instead based on the mass production of a variety of goods (rather than the standard goods of classic Fordism) in order to respond to changing demand while keeping prices low. The ability to compete simultaneously on price and product diversification is made possible by programmable automation, which enables the mass production of a broad range of goods and which drastically reduces demand for both medium and low skilled workers (especially production blue collar and 'back-office' white collar) and technical skills in many other roles, for which adaptability to change and cooperation are instead increasingly required. The demand for high skills concentrates on three crucial groups: middle management, technicians and commercial staff (sales, marketing, customer relations).

The pattern of human resource management that stems from these features is based on a polarization between highly skilled personnel belonging to these occupational groups and personnel with low or obsolete skills. Required of the entire workforce is high flexibility, mainly functional (polyvalence) and wage flexibility (incentives) for the crucial occupational groups, and mainly numerical (temporary work, training and work contracts, possibility to lay-off) for the marginal groups.

The FS strategy, in which the principal weapon in the competition's armoury is the company's versatility and rapid adjustment to changes in demand – which we may call 'firm flexibility' to distinguish it from the forms of labour flexibility discussed so far – is particularly common among small firms, although not exclusive to them. In fact the small-firm systems, typified by low costs for entry into the market and exit from it, extremely low organizational costs, and low costs for production plan selection and errors, are best equipped to respond rapidly to quantitative and qualitative changes in demand, or even to anticipate them. Diffuse production systems, in fact, enable a wide range of products to be placed on the market, leaving to it the task of selecting the 'fittest'.

The crucial human resource in this kind of firm is the entrepreneur, who must be able to perform a plurality of functions – productive, commercial, administrative, etc. – calling on outside consultants but often with very few employees. In medium-sized enterprises, on the other hand, this role is often performed by technical–commercial experts, namely by employees with a variety of abilities who assist the entrepreneur and may sometimes take his/her place. The entrepreneur and these assistants must possess broad and varied technical and social skills. These are rarely imparted by formal training programmes or by higher education; they may instead be provided by learning acquired as employees of large firms who 'set up on their own' (if they become entrepreneurs) or simply move to jobs with higher responsibilities (in the cases of assistants), after accumulating long and varied professional experience. For the small number of employees in these firms, the crucial requisites are extreme temporal and functional flexibility, pragmatic adaptability, and a general willingness to cooperate.

Having outlined the different types of innovative market and organizational strategies adopted by Italian firms in the 1980s, we may now raise the difficult question of their relative success. The available data do not allow one to prove definitively that the FS-based firms were more successful than the others. Yet the bulk of the literature (Barca and Magnani, 1989; Regini and Sabel, 1989), as well as much indirect evidence, suggests this conclusion as highly plausible. During the 1980s in Italy it was the small firms that prospered best and, among them, those that adopted a FS-type strategy, rather than the traditional small firms, were especially successful. The large firms – both those which restructured along FMP lines and those which adopted a DQP model – instead ran into major difficulties. They performed well only in the second half of the decade, to fall again into a state of crisis in the early 1990s.

The ample literature on the industrial districts of the Third Italy (for example, Piore and Sabel, 1984; Trigilia, 1986; Bagnasco, 1988) testifies indirectly to the outstanding performance of these small-firm areas, where the FS model is especially widespread. Equally indirect but more significant is the evidence on the international specialization of Italian industry and the composition of Italy's share of international trade (see Table 5.1). These data show that, in the 1980s, Italian industry improved its share in both 'traditional' sectors – particularly in certain niche productions in clothing and textiles – and the 'specialized supplier' sectors such as the machine tools industry, but its position worsened in 'scale intensive' and 'science based' ones, to use Pavitt's (1984) taxonomy. The former two sectors, however, are those in which Italian small firms are most widespread – both the traditional small firms and, especially, those based on FS – while the 'scale intensive' sector includes most large FMP firms, such as those in the chemical, food, steel and auto industries.

In the 1980s, Italian small firms proved to be not only internationally more vital, as the data above have shown; they reproduced themselves better as well. Firms with less than 100 employees increased their share of Italian industry, while those with over 500 decreased significantly (see Table 5.2). Therefore attention is now turned to the Italian institutional environment.

Table 5.1 *Major balances within industrial sectors contributing to the Italian trade balance (in billions of lira)*

Industrial sectors	1980	1989
Machinery and equipment (machine tools, equipment for textile industry, etc.)	5,248	16,139
Clothing, footwear, furniture	4,726	11,722
Textiles	2,525	7,812
Various engineering products	2,514	6,140
Chemical and pharmaceutical products	–2,596	–12,534
Foodstuffs	–3,013	–6,982
Steel and metals	–2,311	–6,876
Cars and spare parts	–223	–4,857

Table 5.2   *Share of firms and employees in Italian industry according to size of firm (as %)*

Size of firm (number of employees)	Firms (as %)		Employees (as %)	
	1984	1991	1984	1991
0–19	89.89	89.46	28.90	32.13
20–99	8.45	9.04	24.10	26.55
100–499	1.44	1.32	20.17	19.53
>500	0.21	0.18	26.83	21.79
Total	100	100	100	100

The Italian institutional environment and its relationship to the production system

The institutional environment within which Italian firms prosper or struggle to survive is often described as a mix of modes of regulation. The evolution of various public policies – from welfare to labour to industrial policies – can apparently be interpreted as the changing predominance of one or other combination of state, market, community, and associational forms of regulation (Lange and Regini, 1989). However, the 1980s displayed a relationship between institutions and firms which is much more intricate and interesting than a straightforward mix. It has been widely observed that even when public policies apparently assign a leading role to state regulation, as is the case, for example, with fiscal policies or labour market policies (Paci, 1989; Reyneri, 1989), mechanisms for circumventing them are often set in motion; or else the state rules are only weakly and inefficiently implemented, with the consequence that even the opposite result may be achieved. From this point of view, Italy is therefore a case of weak institutional regulation deriving from the duality between what can be called the 'overt' aspect of the Italian institutional environment – the existence of apparently tough constraining mechanisms – and the more 'covert' aspect of their inadequacy which enables constraints to be circumvented.

However, institutional regulation, whether public or associational, may be facilitative rather than restrictive in character. That is to say, the role of the institutions vis-à-vis firms does not stop at the simple imposition of constraints. They may also fulfil the crucial function of providing firms with resources, advantages and opportunities, so that they structure, as it were, the economy in which the firms operate. Although I will still call this a regulatory function, it should be clear that this type of regulation is quite different from the simple setting of constraints.

Consider the role in human resources development performed by the public vocational training system, or the coordination of activities and stabilization of employment relations performed, respectively, by interest associations and by the industrial relations system. From this point of view also, that is, the provision of resources to firms, institutional regulation in Italy is weak, flimsy and inadequate. But, once again, closer analysis reveals two levels, one 'overt' and represented in this case by the weakness and scarcity of institutional resources, and the other more 'covert' or hidden, consisting of compensatory processes of negotiation or of communitarian mechanisms. I shall call these mechanisms a voluntaristic ad hoc regulation by subjects of civil society in order to fill the gaps created by the weakness of the institutions. It is a type of regulation largely based on implicit and case-by-case negotiation, which may be very effective in coping with problems as and when they arise but – as we shall see – is necessarily more laborious, diversified, and above all uncertain and unstable than institutional regulation.

The two levels of regulation – institutional and voluntaristic – are linked together not only by the fact that the latter seeks to compensate for the weakness or the harmful effects of the former, but also because universalistic though weak institutional regulation can act as a point of reference for the voluntaristic one. That is to say, it provides a benchmark against which, or a framework within which, different voluntaristic solutions can be attempted. However, voluntaristic regulation also has the somewhat paradoxical effect of sustaining weak institutional regulation. The fact that ad hoc solutions are found for problems as and when they arise by relying on implicit negotiation processes serves to divert attention from the shortcomings of the institutions and postpones action to reform them.

Hence, weak institutional regulation and voluntaristic ad hoc regulation are not simply two co-existing features of the Italian situation; they are closely interwoven. Italian institutional mechanisms suffer from a chronic inability – which dates back to the beginning of industrialization – to contain and regulate economic interests and civil society (Cassese, 1987); a civil society, moreover, which although historically fragmented is also unusually dynamic. The Italian public apparatus has always been able to enact a plethora of laws and norms but less able to enforce them. Moreover, the associational system has proved largely unable to impose consistent and universalistic rules on the pronounced sectoralism of Italian society; a feature which also has profound historical roots and hampers collective action in pursuit of common goals.

My central tenet is that the interweaving between these two levels of regulation is crucial for an understanding of the Italian institutional environment and its influence on the configuration assumed by the production system. In other words, this interweaving between weak institutional regulation and effective but unstable voluntaristic regulation explains why certain types of firm continue to prosper and reproduce themselves in Italy while others run into greater difficulties.

Broadly speaking, this institutional environment has more favourable consequences for small firms and especially for production systems based on FS than for large firms, whether based on DQP or FMP. On the one hand the possibility of circumventing the constraints imposed by regulatory public policies – which in principle is of interest both to companies competing on price (such as the FMP-based) and companies competing on flexibility (such as the FS-based) – is greater for small firms than for large ones, which have higher social visibility. On the other, while the combination of weak institutional regulation with voluntaristic ad hoc regulation may provide flexibility to the production system, it also creates considerable uncertainty and instability, a lack of clearcut and universalistic rules. This means that the Italian institutional environment is generally unsuitable for large firms, especially the DQP-based that are competing on product quality and crucially require the certain and stable provision of such goods as cooperation and skills. Uncertainty and instability are instead less serious for small firms, which are used to striving in an unstable environment and may indeed draw advantage from the malleability of the sales, so they have to adjust quickly to changing demand. Very often, the two levels – the formal overt level and the informal covert one – correspond respectively to the centre and the periphery of the institutional system. From this derives the widespread view of the Italian political economy as characterized by an inefficient and lethargic centre and a dynamic periphery comprising firms, decentralized administrative bodies, and the lower and intermediate levels of the associations. Yet the interweaving between institutional regulation and voluntaristic regulation is a phenomenon broader in scope and weightier in consequences than the simple centre–periphery dualism.

I now propose to examine some of the institutions which the literature on the different forms of capitalism considers to be important (Soskice, 1990a, b). I shall seek to show how each of them, in Italy during the 1980s, displayed the two levels described above, and how each thus helped to create an institutional environment favourable to small firms based on FS but less favourable to large firms based on FMP and DQP. As well as public policies, I shall briefly discuss the features of the interest associations, of the industrial relations system, and of the training-educational system, and their influence on the configuration of the Italian production system.

Public policies

A wide variety of public policies influences the production system. I shall here discuss only two examples of the areas in which public policies display that constraining character which is then more or less easily circumvented, as well as one area in which they have a facilitative or supportive nature.

Both state regulation and that produced by inter-industry or industry-level collective bargaining are particularly wide-ranging in their effect on the labour market. For most of the 1980s they were designed to set close constraints not only on worker dismissals but also on recruitment and the duration of employment. The rigidity produced by these rules – especially before their partial deregulation from the mid-1980s onwards – was frequently circumvented by firms, which used various expedients; for example, the law was interpreted so that firms could hire whom they wanted rather than abide by the criteria established (Reyneri, 1989). In various cases, state regulations were replaced by more flexible rules, that is rules agreed by the parties concerned and adapted to local circumstances; for example, rules on the use of the Wages Guarantee Fund, early retirement, or other measures addressing the problem of labour market exit.

The possibility of using this type of voluntaristic ad hoc regulation to avoid constraints was crucial to both FS-based small firms, which needed flexible adjustment to change, and price-sensitive, FMP-based large companies, which saw these constraints as just additional costs to bear. However, small firms found it easier to circumvent state regulations than the large ones, given the visibility of the latter and therefore the greater likelihood of public and central trade union control. Moreover, although the voluntaristic creation of new ad hoc rules adapted to local circumstances may work to the advantage of all firms, it does not eliminate the problem of uncertainty and instability, which affects large firms to a much greater extent than small ones; uncertainty over the likelihood of reaching effective agreement; instability due to the revocability of any informal or weakly institutionalized pact.

Fiscal and welfare policies are another area of major difference between the constraints on large and small firms. On paper, all Italian firms are subject to a strict tax regime and to particularly onerous welfare contributions (for pensions, health care, etc.) which raise labour costs more in Italy than in most competitor countries. It is common knowledge, however, that tax evasion is rife in Italy and there has been significant evasion of welfare contributions (Paci, 1989). Although firms of various kinds, as well as professionals and self-employed workers, have distinguished themselves in what amounts to a national sport, small firms have been able to evade taxes and contributions to a much greater extent than large ones, for the reasons of visibility and control mentioned above.

However, distributive public policies do not usually work selectively against large companies in the same way as regulatory policies. In some cases they may even benefit them more than small ones. For instance, industrial policy, which in Italy has a predominantly distributive character, has mostly aimed at providing all types of firms with various subsidies. Furthermore, it has greatly facilitated their restructuring through the Wages Guarantee Fund and early retirement plans, which are naturally targeted on large firms. Only by taking into account the other institutions which are expected to play a supportive role for firms can one fully appreciate the overall consequences of the institutional environment in Italy, namely the relative bias in favour of FS-based small firms and against FMP and DQP large companies.

The interest associations

In the literature on the different forms of capitalism, the contributions by Soskice (1990b, and this volume) have placed the most insistent emphasis on the role of associations – trade unions and especially employers' associations – in inducing workers and firms to coordinate their actions in order to produce collective goods, such as control over the wages dynamic or the development of training. The more that the regulation – whether legislative or associational – of intra-organizational relationships or those with members renders this influence broad and stable, the better they are able to perform this role. Highly comprehensive and centralized associations with monopoly of representation, as neo-corporatist theory would have them, or those simply equipped with institutionalized sanctions and incentives are naturally more powerful and better able to perform this coordinating role.

From this point of view, Italian interest associations suffer from what one could call a 'constitutional weakness'. Membership bonds are weak and voluntarist. Associative pluralism and therefore competition for representation are high as regards both trade unions and employers' associations, and intra-organizational relationships are poorly institutionalized. The picture that emerges is therefore consistent with the image of weak institutional regulation. The institutional resources available for collective action taken by both firms and workers are scanty, so that such activity is severely restricted and unable to fulfil the functions that the literature assigns to it.

Yet the history of associative action in the 1970s and 1980s, as well as the relative ability to coordinate the wage dynamics which was shown during the same period (Regini, 1995), presents a somewhat different picture. Quite considerable influence or de facto control, if rather discontinuous and uneven, was exercised by the associations over those they represented (members and non-members), and by the top organizational levels over the bottom and intermediate ones. This control, or de facto influence, stems from a number of factors which cannot be discussed at length here. Suffice it to point out that the trade unions long relied on identity incentives of an ideological character. Moreover, the associations considered here have often utilized their mutual recognition not only to exclude or delegitimate their competitors but also and especially to 'bargain' implicitly with their rank and file over the value to assign to their role. The top leadership has behaved in the same way with the intermediate organizational levels, using for this purpose its privileged access to state decisions. Finally, the weakness of formal membership bonds and the scant institutionalization of relationships have often been offset by the use of resources deriving from the participation – and this is indeed highly institutionalized – of associations in the myriad bodies which manage public policies (Regalia and Regini, 1995).

This interweaving between constitutional weakness and the de facto relevant but institutionally non-consolidated influence of the interest associations has had numerous consequences. From the point of view of interest to us here, the chief of them is the rather unstable behaviour of the Italian associations as they constantly shift between actions instrumental to their own long-term organizational interests and those symbolic actions periodically necessary to reconstitute or reaffirm their representation relationship (Regini, 1981). This instability and uncertainty of associative behaviour, combined with substantial de facto influence, has hindered Italian firms from pursuing what must have appeared to many as the only two alternative roads ahead. Most of them repeatedly attempted either the 'Anglo-Saxon road' of full decentralization and conflict accommodation through bargaining in a deregulated market, or the 'German road' of stable and institutionalized in-company cooperation, in a context regulated at a relatively centralized level by associations functioning as private governments.

The first road, which is more congenial to FMP firms, was attempted by Fiat and a few other companies at the beginning of the 1980s. The second road, which is the environment in which DQP firms seem to prosper best, was followed in different ways, most notably by companies belonging to the IRI state holding, which enacted a set of rules known as 'Protocollo IRI' to try and institutionalize cooperative relations with the unions. Both attempts had scant success, and this probably further constricted the space available for these two kinds of firm – the FMP- and the DQP-based – by rendering the Italian institutional environment more asphyxiating. Conversely, the relatively incoherent behaviour of the associations and the unpredictable use of their influence was not a major problem for the heterogeneous and continuously changing system of small firms, which is used to growing within and taking advantage of an environment characterized by the uncertainty and malleability of rules.

The industrial relations system

The opinion is widely shared that the Italian industrial relations system is poorly institutionalized (Cella, 1989; see also Regalia and Regini, 1995). Not even the Workers' Statute of 1970 managed to remedy this, causing the Italian case often to be coupled with the British one as a polar model in comparative studies of European systems. In fact, it was not until the tripartite agreement of 1993 that collective bargaining was first regulated in terms of which issues were negotiable and which actors were entitled to conduct such negotiations.

Attempts at concertation – which took concrete form in the 'negotiated laws' (*leggi contrattate*) of the period of 'national solidarity' (1977–9) and then in the two tripartite agreements on labour costs reached in 1983 and 1984 – may with hindsight be viewed as the most significant efforts to institutionalize Italian industrial relations by means of a mix of associational and public regulation. In fact, although they explicitly addressed problems of unemployment and then of inflation, the more general goal was to replace the adversarialism and informality prevalent in the relationships between the social partners with rules that imposed stable and institutionalized cooperation at the central level, thereby creating a model which would be reproduced as a knock-on effect at the more decentralized ones. But these attempts failed even more signally from this point of view than they did in terms of the goals explicitly pursued, thus confirming that the weakness of institutional regulation in Italy also has deep and stubborn roots in the field of industrial relations (Cella, 1989).

However, while a sense of paralysis and diffuse adversarialism continued to permeate industrial relations at the central level, a practice of 'secluded micro-concertation' began to spread through the periphery of the system, especially in large companies trying to reorganize on a DQP basis, as well as small firm areas where an FS model prevailed (Regini and Sabel, 1989). A voluntaristic and negotiated approach was taken to the problem of making more flexible the rules governing the employment relationship and the involvement of employees in the organization of production. This amounted to the genuine de facto joint management – albeit covert, peripheral and informal – of industrial adjustment that distinguished the Italian economy in the 1980s. In many large firms the industrial restructuring of the 1980s was carried forward not in open conflict with the trade unions, but with constant consultation over possible solutions to emerging problems: whether to use the Wages Guarantee Fund, early retirement or other similar measures; how to keep the effects of technological innovation under control; whether overtime should be paid or a system of compensatory rest days adopted.

As regards the small firm districts based on FS, what had been their traditional characteristics were simply accentuated: the tendency to define problems jointly; to adapt pragmatically to the needs of the opposite party; to search for mutually advantageous solutions. These solutions were often informally negotiated. However, in these areas flexibility and cooperation were so deeply embedded in the social fabric and so strongly sustained by community trust relationships that they often seemed to be naturally part of the employment relationships, and therefore in no need of institutional mediation by the representative institutions (Bagnasco, 1988).

Hence, what emerged in the 1980s was the tacit acceptance of the existence of two distinct spheres of action: one at the central and official level, which was still dominated by difficult and often adversarial formal relationships; and the other at the local and informal level of the firm or the district, where the search for an informal voluntaristic joint regulation of flexibility predominated. This non-institutionalized nature of union involvement was in many respects an advantage for firms, because it could be terminated at any time and the cost it represented could therefore be seen as transitory. However, it also meant instability in relationships, and above all uncertainty over the rules and outcomes. As was suggested in the previous section, these were more damaging for large firms than for small ones. Moreover, employees' cooperation was more effectively secured though the trust relationship prevailing in FS-based small firms than by the voluntaristic arrangements and informal negotiation taking place in large firms.

This limited, non-institutionalized provision of cooperation in production especially hindered the full development of DQP-based firms, which require high functional flexibility as well as innovative forms of work organization such as teamwork. However, both are based on cooperation. The persistence of egalitarian values in both the unions' ideology and bargaining practice heavily constrained the FMP-based firms in their search for a dualistic management of human resources; namely, the use of functional flexibility for the key occupational groups and of external flexibility for the others.

One might argue, on the contrary, that in emergencies or crises large firms were favoured since they could take advantage of their greater social visibility compared with small ones; a visibility that enabled them to have recourse to 'political exchange' (Pizzorno, 1978), that is, by involving in the negotiation the public authorities most sensitive to the problem of consensus.[2] However, precisely the fact that political exchange did not consolidate itself, that it was unable to transfer from ad hoc and prevalently informal exchange into institutionalized exchange, prevented industrial relations from providing the certainty and stability that large firms, especially the DQP-based ones, needed. Indeed, it is possible to argue that, by failing to institutionalize itself into stable concertation capable of producing policies and rules of a general character, the political exchange practised by large firms degenerated into the simple exchange of favours, the political trade-offs and corruption whose perverse effects have become so apparent in the 1990s.

The vocational training system

Finally, the distinctive features of the institutional system of vocational training in Italy are territorial dualism, profound inefficiency and the inadequacy not only of resources and programmes but also of public attention. First, vocational training in Italy is institutionally separate from the general educational system. Whereas the latter is under the jurisdiction of the Ministry of Education, the former is the responsibility of the regional administrations, which organize courses on their own account or, more frequently, contract them out to private bodies. This gives rise not only to substantial differences in the effectiveness and quality of vocational training between one region and another, but also and especially to a serious lack of coordination between the educational and vocational training channels. Thus, while part of post-compulsory education consists of technical and professional schools, which attract increasing numbers of students and enjoy a certain prestige, the vocational training organized by the regions, which in theory should provide not basic education but preparation for entry into the labour market, has with time turned into an inferior copy, thereby justifying the assessment as 'second-rate education' for those expelled from the school system and with low expectations (ISFOL, 1989).

Second, firms have no obligation, legal or contractual, to invest in training – whether initial training as in Germany or further training as in France. Italian trade unions, for their part, have for a long time viewed training as the right of workers to increase their economic and political culture, rather than as a means to acquire professional skills, which have been seen as necessarily underutilized in the present system of work organization (CEDEFOP, 1987). Associational regulation of training has therefore remained weak and inadequate.

Throughout the 1980s, employers' associations and trade unions undertook only two types of initiative concerning training, and these constituted improper usage. Employers' associations placed great emphasis on 'training and work contracts' which, although they offered young people up to the age of 29 opportunities to acquire on-the-job training, had the main aim of giving firms greater flexibility in their management of entrants to the labour market. The trade unions, for their part, looked on retraining courses as a temporary solution for the many redundancies created by company restructurings. Institutional regulation of training is still inadequate in the 1990s, despite signature of several protocols of intent by the three major union confederations (CGIL, CISL, UIL) and the major private employers' association (Confindustria). These protocols set up joint committees for the promotion of training and contain a set of proposals and mutual commitments, but firms still have complete freedom to decide whether or not to provide in-house training.

However, despite these shortcomings of inefficiency and voluntarism in the institutional supply of initial training, and the absence of legal or trade union constraints on the investment decisions for further training by firms, there is ample evidence that the average level of skills has risen in several sectors of the Italian economy (Regalia and Regini, 1995). On the one hand, this has been the outcome of the acceptable performance by Italian technical schools in providing a broad-based theoretical preparation, and of the recent tendency for firms to recruit diploma holders, even for low-level jobs. On the other, it results from the relative efficiency of on-the-job training in organizational contexts made comparatively open by the restricted growth and weakness of the occupational hierarchy in Italian firms. In other words, the absence of a powerful professional group with certified formal skills – like the *Meister* in Germany, who may tend to block innovation and the transmission of knowledge in order to protect their professional status (Sabel, 1994) – has made internal training possible through the implicit negotiation of flanking tasks and career paths, or through the explicit negotiation of team work. Deficiency in the planning of training needs has made the informal negotiation of selective, reactive and ad hoc schemes both necessary and possible; training which is addressed specifically to certain occupational groups affected by techno-logical or organizational change, as has happened in the majority of large Italian firms.

However, for the large and medium DQP firms that require a highly and broadly skilled workforce, this voluntaristic ad hoc regulation of training, which produces what one could call a 'lean' system, incurs major costs. The absence of a system of efficient public training would require these firms to undertake substantial financial and organizational investments in company schools or further training courses. If they do not, they will be unable to draw on the broad reservoir of skilled labour that is such a crucial resource for innovation and an important competitive advantage for this kind of firm (Streeck, 1989). If they do, they will not only incur high costs, but may also be confronted with the 'free-rider' problem, namely their competitors poaching their skilled labour.

In small FS firms, training revolves around the entrepreneurs them-selves. They are the crucial human resource and must be able to perform a plurality of functions, usually learned in previous careers as skilled workers in large firms. The small entrepreneurs are also directly inter-ested in transmitting the knowledge that they have to their assistants and few employees. This is normally conditional on striking an implicit pact of stability in the employment relationship – as usually occurs in FS-based firms. All this amounts to a voluntaristic ad hoc regulation of train-ing that in small firms compensates, at least in part, for the weakness of institutional regulation, and at lower costs than those incurred by DQP firms.

Conclusions

The analysis conducted so far leads to rather unequivocal conclusions on the relationship between the configuration of the Italian production system and the features of its institutional environment. Let me briefly restate the main points. By focusing on the mix of organizational models adopted by Italian firms, I have argued that in Italy during the 1980s it was especially the innovative small enterprises based on FS that prospered, whereas large firms performed less well, irrespective of the organizational model adopted and in spite of major adjustment processes carried on early in that decade.

I then examined the main features of the institutional environment in which Italian firms operate, my aim being to identify which of these fea-tures may help account for both the good health enjoyed by the more inno-vative small enterprises during the 1980s and the greater difficulties encountered by large firms. The general feature that I have suggested as decisive for understanding the Italian institutional environment, and its influence on the configuration assumed by the production system, is what

I have called 'the interweaving between weak institutional regulation and effective but unstable voluntaristic regulation'.

I then went on to show that the consequences of this interweaving are generally more unfavourable to large firms than to the innovative small ones, because it entails uncertainty and instability, while also allowing adaptability to change and giving malleability to rules. I then examined not only the workings of public policies in Italy but also of some of the institutions deemed most important by the literature: interest associations, the industrial relations system, and the vocational training system.

My conclusion is that the Italian case of the 1980s cannot be described in terms of a simple mix of regulative forms, or as an intermediate case between Rhenish and Anglo-Saxon capitalism. It is instead a distinct model, one not reducible to presumed anomalies with respect to the better known ideal types. It should be stressed, however, that the analysis proposed in this chapter concerns the relationship between firms and institutions in the 1980s, and that it deliberately goes no further than the beginning of the new decade. Much has changed in more recent years in both the institutional environment and the production system, probably to the disadvantage of small firms though not necessarily to the advantage of the largest ones.

Notes

1   The analysis in this section has benefited greatly from long discussions with Sandro Arrighetti.

2   I am indebted to Ida Regalia for this point.

6

THE UK 1979–95: MYTHS AND REALITIES OF CONSERVATIVE CAPITALISM

Andrew Graham

The UK in the 1980s and 1990s was a test case for modern Conservative capitalism. Indeed, the British model, despite some of its apparent failures in the early 1990s, is still frequently held up in international discussions as an example for other countries to follow. One reason for this is that the Conservatives were in power for so long, and this dominance was particularly important because it was combined with a strong ideology and with an institutional and constitutional structure that gives an unusual degree of power to the executive (and especially to the Prime Minister if s/he chooses to use it). What happened in the UK is therefore unusually interesting and important to any judgement about contemporary capitalism.

Five factors create the strength of executive power. First, almost all appointments to executive positions rest with the Prime Minister. In addition there is no route to executive power except through the two main political parties. As a result there is exceptionally strong party discipline and the executive totally dominates the legislature (Parliament). Second, within Parliament a majority in the Commons is usually sufficient (the Lords being constitutionally weak). Third, the UK is a unitary, rather than a federal, state so there are few constraints on the power of Parliament. Fourth, there is a strong, permanent and relatively efficient civil service. In theoretical discussions the position of the British civil service is sometimes represented as a constraint on the power of the executive on the grounds that it provides continuity of policy. The reality is the opposite. Combined with a strong executive, the British civil service increases the power of government. It becomes a government service not a service to civil society. Last, but not least, while there is an independent judiciary, there is no written constitution.

The sources of opposition during the Conservative years prove the point. It came from a handful of MPs unwilling on grounds of principle to toe the party line; from civil servants choosing to leak material to the press (much increased compared to the past); from the occasional defeat in the House of Lords; and as much from appeals to European as to British courts (though latterly the British judiciary has also been exerting its muscle). But beyond this, what the Cabinet wanted it mostly got.

As a reflection of the unusual sweep of British power the discussion in this chapter has a different focus from some others in this volume. Much of the modern literature in political economy emphasizes the institutional structure and, in particular, the structure of capital markets and the organization of firms and the effects of these institutions on competitive or cooperative behaviour. However, in the UK it is necessary to look wider (one important aspect of the UK experiment has been the attempt to export the managerial practices of the market to sectors traditionally thought of as non-market) and to go deeper (the changes attempted were not limited to transfers of ownership, but also tried to shift the culture of the society and how individuals perceived themselves in relation to that society).

Given these broader objectives, this chapter will first establish the goals of Conservative capitalism. It will then assess the results; in particular, it argues that the Conservative experiment became increasingly to be seen as a failure (even in terms of its own core goals). Explanation of this failure is the subject of the following section. In summary, the argument is that Conservative capitalism failed in the UK, not through want of trying, but because it was attempting to impose a model of capitalism that does not and could not exist. Finally, the chapter concludes by discussing what the UK might learn from this experience.

The goals of Conservative capitalism

Political parties never operate in a green field site. They are always inheriting traditions and responding to the mistakes of the past, especially to the mistakes of their own party. Margaret Thatcher was no exception. Her election as Leader of the Conservative Party had been a revolution against her predecessor, Edward Heath. Corporatist capitalism, tried by Heath in the 1970s and widely regarded as a failure, was therefore not an option. Similarly she reacted against the mixed economy of welfare capitalism and 'Butskellism' pursued by the Conservative Party in the 1950s and 1960s. The main option remaining was a return to free market capitalism. Clearly this coincided with Mrs Thatcher's own instincts and with the views of her closest advisors, but neither this nor the rejection of the alternatives can explain her phenomenal political impact and political success.

The ideological impact of modern British Conservatism was large because it captured a contemporary mood and because it tapped into a much more deep-seated tradition in British society. It did so by making the liberty of the individual a central plank of its policy and by linking this to the ideological claim that society could and should be driven by the free choices of individual consumers operating competitively in the market.

This central belief was, moreover, surrounded by a set of subsidiary propositions playing a dual role – partly supportive of the central belief and partly derivative from it. Four arguments were especially important:

1 Taxes should be minimized. This was regarded by Conservatives as both morally right and economically efficient (both for incentive and informational reasons consumers know best).
2 Government should be kept to a minimum (because, not being responsive to the market, it is subject to 'government failure').
3 Production should be for profit (because, it was argued, pursuing profits achieves efficiency on three fronts simultaneously: costs are minimized, resources are guided to where returns are highest and, through a process of Darwinian selection, only the most efficient firms survive).
4 Any inequality in society was seen as a necessary result of market forces (any attempt to impose social justice being seen as inconsistent with personal liberties and as a distortion of the free market).

Of course these ideas have a long history and have influenced many other countries. But this was part of their attraction. Moreover, they had a special resonance in the UK, where many of them had originated or acquired special prominence – more important, their rise had coincided with British supremacy in the nineteenth century. As a result, even now, many in the UK (especially in the upper and middle classes and among the business and financial communities) hark back, sometimes unconsciously, to the 'golden period' of the British Industrial Revolution and the years that followed, carrying in their minds lessons from the school of British greatness constructed from the efforts of a few brilliant entrepreneurs.

The effects are profound. In the UK successful economic growth is associated not with mass production (as in the USA) nor with the application of education, science and technology (as in Germany) nor with reconstruction behind tariff barriers (as in Japan), but with small firms, free trade and free markets. In the UK, more than anywhere else in the world, apologists for economic liberalism have been heard when they have maintained that, at least in the eighteenth and nineteenth centuries, the system delivered the goods. This was the ideology adopted by the modern British Conservative Party and, with some important exceptions, the policies adopted followed from it.

At the micro-economic level marginal rates of direct taxation, especially at the top end, were dramatically reduced and the freedom of private markets was encouraged. The labour market, the financial markets and the housing market were all deregulated. Buses were privatized and deregulated. Council houses and a whole range of public utilities (telephones, gas, electricity and water) were sold, generating a new set of private property rights.

The state was also rolled back in a range of other ways. Local authority powers were curtailed, competitive tendering by the private sector for services formerly provided by local councils was made compulsory for many activities, and the Greater London Council was abolished. Private health insurance and private pension provision were expanded. Schools and hospitals were encouraged to move away from local state control and to form self-managing trusts. Even much of central government was hived off into executive agencies. Markets or quasi-markets were established in much of the public sector and managers were imported from the private sector to run the public sector as much like the private sector as possible. Systems of profits-related pay were encouraged by tax concessions in the private sector and performance-related pay promoted throughout the public sector.

Moreover, in macro-economic policy the government eschewed all concern throughout most of the 1980s with demand management. Keynesianism was abandoned and the economy left (supposedly) on autopilot, operating only within the constraints first of a monetary target and later of an exchange rate target. Borrowing from the monetarists and the rational expectations revolution, it was assumed that the Invisible Hand was not only invisible, but also all powerful.

Most important of all, after 1979 there was a major transformation in the fundamental principles intended to guide all aspects of British society. Weber (1970: 17) had defined a capitalist economic system as one in which all decisions are matters of accountancy and 'everything is done in terms of balances'. By the late 1980s this was the UK. Health, education, community care and even the civil service were to be guided by money and by competitive private sector market principles.

An assessment

Any assessment of such a contentious period in British history is inevitably partly subjective and highly debatable. In addition, statistical averages are even more misleading than normal as one feature of the years after 1979 was the spread of outcomes. Some firms did very well, others disappeared. Individuals at the top end of the income distribution also did spectacularly well, with growth rates of income more than double that of the average. The shape of the economy was also changed dramatically. Manufacturing contracted; services expanded. The financial sector in particular grew rapidly following financial deregulation and the 'Big Bang' reorganization of the stock market in 1986. The shift in the wage and salary distribution was, in part, a reflection of this structural change. People moved out of middle-income jobs in manufacturing, but their exits were of two kinds. Some were pulled into high-income jobs in financial services (extra demand in that sector pulling wages up); others were pushed into low-paid and casualized jobs in other services (where extra supply pushed wages down).

Within the industrial sector, large firms were particularly adversely affected by the 1979–82 recession (Oulton, 1987); and, at the same time, the

UK trade balance in 'medium' technology goods worsened dramatically (before recovering slightly in the late 1980s and early 1990s (Boltho, 1995). This suggests that the firms which survived best were at either end of the technology spectrum (either being high-tech and specialized or being low-tech, paying low wages and concentrating on standardized production).

Nevertheless, within this diverse picture there is general agreement that credit should be given to the first Thatcher government in reducing inflation and in revitalizing British management. This was, however at a very high cost in unemployment. Some increase was inevitable, given the high level of inflation inherited in 1979, the second oil shock and the subsequent world recession, but how much remains highly controversial. However, from the second election victory of 1982 until the late 1980s, many considered Conservative capitalism vindicated more generally by the results it appeared to achieve. Growth improved, inflation remained low, unemployment began to fall (though from a high level) and, most impressively of all, productivity in manufacturing grew faster than in any previous period (see Table 6.1). So successful did the experiment seem that the Chancellor of the Exchequer proclaimed that a British economic miracle had occurred.

Conservative capitalism might also be regarded as successful by a range of intermediate indicators. The property owning democracy was substantially extended (the proportion of houses privately owned rose from just over half in 1979 to more than two-thirds by 1991). In addition, the number of adults holding shares increased from one in twelve in 1981 to no less than one in four by 1990. Equally important was the dramatic collapse of strikes, the restoration of profitability and the return of the managerial prerogative. These last three factors were especially important. Occurring alongside rapid increases in output per person in the late 1980s, they appeared to show the return of successful free market capitalism.

However, seen in a longer term perspective and examined against ultimate objectives, the picture changes significantly. The only two achievements to persist into the 1990s have been low inflation and good productivity growth in manufacturing, and the former was only attained at the cost of the longest and deepest recession since the 1930s. Moreover, the total level of output has been both far more unstable and has grown less rapidly than before 1979.

Four other factors must also be weighed in the balance. First, the inequality of wages in the UK, which had been declining up to 1979, rose sharply thereafter and more so than in any other major country. The picture presented after taking account of the impact of tax and benefits was even more dramatic. The income share of the poorest tenth of society fell by more than a quarter from 1961 to 1991 (from 4.2 per cent to 3 per cent) with most of the fall occurring during the 1980s (Goodman and Webb, 1994).

Second, besides the growth in inequality there has been a rise in absolute poverty. Taking account of housing costs, the real income of the poorest tenth of society fell by more than 14 per cent from 1979 to 1991 (Goodman and Webb, 1994). This clearly denies the efficacy of the 'trickle down' mechanism claimed by some Conservatives. The sharp rise in homelessness alongside the increase in home ownership demonstrates the same point.

Third, difficult to quantify but well documented, is the obvious loss of morale in extensive parts of the public sector and, related to this, the combination of rising levels of expenditure in real terms on health and education alongside a rising sense by many that the real level of services has not increased proportionately.

Fourth, Conservative capitalism began to fail even in terms of its own core values and its own core supporters. Home ownership had risen, but so had the number of properties repossessed. During the recession of 1981 only 21,000 mortgages were in arrears and only 5,000 houses were repossessed. In contrast in 1991, 275,000 mortgages were in arrears and no less than 75,000 houses were repossessed. Many more people found themselves owning 'negative equity'.

In addition the party of law and order found itself with record crime rates (despite nearly doubling the proportion of government expenditure intended to stop crime), with the largest proportion of the population in prison in the European Community (apart from Luxembourg); and the party of business, especially of small business, faced a near sixfold increase in bankruptcy and insolvency. Unemployment and the threat of unemployment became a reality for the middle class.

Over the longer term there was also an increasing gap between the rhetoric and the reality. Public expenditure expanded as did the power of the state. Expenditure was increasingly centrally controlled and the number of unelected bodies appointed by central government grew rapidly, accompanied by accusations of corruption (Stewart, 1992; Davis and Stewart, 1993; Straw, 1993, 1994). Last, but hardly least, the party of stable money was forced into an ignominious devaluation, the party of low borrowing presided over one of the largest budget deficits in the UK's history and the party of tax cuts had to introduce (in the two Budgets of 1993) the biggest tax increases in the UK's peacetime history (with the effect that by the end of the period the share of GDP taken by taxation was actually higher than in 1979).

The Conservatives, however, would argue that such comments are over-influenced by the performance of the UK economy during the recession of 1989–92 and that since 1992 the behaviour of the UK economy has been displaying the full benefits of Conservative policy. At the time of writing, real output has risen by 3.2 per cent per annum since the bottom of the recession, unemployment has fallen by more than 600,000, the balance of payments has improved sharply and, despite the devaluation, inflation has remained at a low level. In addition, inward investment continues to rise – proof, it would be said, of the UK's cost competitiveness. Moreover, all of this, it could be argued, would be consistent with long lags before the beneficial effects of policy (both on inflation and in the labour market) become apparent. In particular, the rise in the inequality of wages is seen as the necessary price for raising employment and it is this factor, so the argument goes, which now distinguishes the UK from the rest of the European Union.

The problem with this account is that it does not accord well with a dispassionate analysis of the facts nor with the results of recent research. Consider first, the record on output and growth. The recent increase is no more than the above-trend increase that always occurs after an exceptionally severe recession. What matters is the performance of the economy over the longer term. Here there is already strong evidence that by 1995 the UK economy had returned close to full capacity. Barrell and Sefton (1995), the CBI survey (1995), Goldman Sachs (1995) and Walton (1995) all confirm this view. This means that the UK will not be able to enjoy above-trend growth any longer. A fair long run comparison of the UK's growth can therefore be made from 1979 to 1995 and, as Table 6.1 shows, while manufacturing productivity has undoubtedly improved, output and productivity in the whole economy are well below the long run trend (and are only very slightly better than the period between the two oil shocks of 1973 and 1978).

Moreover, Barrell and Sefton (1995: 72) conclude that the UK's long run per annum growth potential is now 'in the range 2–2.1%'. This is significantly below the estimates for the 1950s and 1960s (of about 3 per cent) and even below those made in the early 1980s (of 2.5 per cent). The implication of this downward revision to underlying growth is of fundamental importance. It means either that some factor (as yet unspecified) has been making the situation worse, or that all the supply-side reforms, introduced to make capitalism work better, have actually, in aggregate, had the opposite effect.

The reason to suppose that the supply-side reforms are at least partly at fault is that this result was predicted (Boltho and Graham, 1989) even while the economic miracle was being claimed. By the late 1980s it was clear that there had been a large and lasting rise in the share of output devoted to consumption and, corresponding to this, a balance of payment deficit and a decline in the share of fixed investment. Equally clear was a growing discrepancy between the UK and its major competitors in the proportion of output devoted to research and development, in the level of skills of the UK workforce and in the resources being devoted to training and education either publicly or privately. This lack of investment in both

Table 6.1   *Growth rates of output and productivity, 1960–95 (average annual percentage change)*

| | Output | Output per person | | |
	Whole economy	Manufacturing	Whole economy	Manufacturing
1960–73	3.2	3.1	2.9	3.6
1973–9	1.4	–0.7	1.2	0.6
1979–95	1.8	0.3	1.9	4.0

physical and human capital was bound to have adverse effects eventually (a factor confirmed by Rowthorn (1995), who finds low investment to be a major reason for the rise in unemployment in several European countries). Overall it is therefore hard to conclude anything other than (a) that the potential output has been diminished; (b) that this may be at least in part because of the supply-side policies.

Consider second, the evidence about inflation: one central thrust of Conservative policy was to make the labour market more 'flexible' and so to reduce the non-accelerating inflation rate of unemployment (the NAIRU). However, Davies (1994: 4) finds that the behaviour of wages in 1994 'is not a statistically significant difference'. In addition neither the OECD (1994) nor a recent extensive study by Barrell (1994) finds any evidence that the NAIRU has declined in the 1990s.

Third, the recent rapid fall in unemployment obscures the causes of that fall. Gregg and Wadsworth (1995) show that, whereas in 1981, 75 per cent of those leaving unemployment went into work, in 1993 only 60 per cent did so. Moreover, those in work faced greater insecurity as the result of higher turnover.

Consider fourth, inequality: the claim is that lower wages, particularly for the unskilled have been necessary to generate extra employment, the USA being held up as the example to follow. However, Nickell and Bell (1995) find no evidence to support the view that countries which maintained more equal wage distributions faced higher unemployment and Freeman (1995: 64) finds that in the USA 'the reduction in the pay of less-skilled Americans did *not* increase their employment' and that 'the weak job market for the less skilled and high degree of earning inequality contributed to the crime rate'.

Of course, none of these arguments deny that since 1992 the performance of the economy has improved. However, it would be truly surprising if, starting from the depths of a recession and following a large devaluation, a significant reduction in interest rates, a recovery in the world economy and a large budget deficit for several years in a row, anything else were to occur. Every instrument of macro-policy was set to stimulate the economy in 1992, and this is what occurred. But when we find that it is sharp changes in macro-economic policy that are producing extra output and employment and that micro-economic policies may have reduced long run growth potential, raised the equilibrium level of unemployment and increased poverty and crime, it is hard to know what (apart from the fall in inflation and the improvement in productivity in manufacturing) is left of the original version of Conservative capitalism.

Explanation

If Conservative capitalism has failed in this way, the fundamental question is why. One explanation might lie in a mixture of incompetence and of events beyond the government's control. This cannot be ruled out, but it is hardly plausible that a government should make so many mistakes and such obvious mistakes. The real explanation, I suggest, lies partly at the theoretical level and partly in that fluid domain of understanding and misunderstanding from which today's politicians distil yesterday's ideas.

The conventional account among economists of what went wrong is that serious errors were made in both macro- and micro-policy. There is much in this. For example, contrary to the rhetoric, UK macro-policy was positively destabilizing (Allsopp, 1985; Allsopp and Graham, 1987; Keegan, 1989; Boltho and Graham, 1989; Smith, 1992; Allsopp, 1993). Equally it has been well documented (Helm, 1986; Hahn, 1988; Boltho and Graham, 1989) that micro-economic policy proved to be extraordinarily ignorant of market failure and that, as a result, gross errors were made in policy towards industry, education, training, and research and development. Moreover, it is likely that the first error compounded the second: the supply-side reforms were not only sometimes poorly designed, but were further undermined by the lack of aggregate demand (Graham, 1994).

It is not sufficient, however, to describe these errors simply as mistakes. The theoretical underpinning of policy was grossly at odds with reality. The first gap between theory and reality lay in the appeal to Adam Smith's invisible hand. Ever since the work of Arrow and Debreu in the 1950s, most economists have been well aware of two points. One is that the invisible hand can be shown to be consistent with a perfectly competitive market economy and that such an economy is, in a certain sense, 'optimal'. However, the other is that these miraculous results require such demanding assumptions that the only sensible position to hold is that the fully competitive model not only does not exist, but could not exist.

The immediate contemporary relevance of these remarks is that mainstream micro-economic theory gives no reason at all either for favouring competitive markets everywhere or for assuming that the large cyclical movements which have taken place in the UK economy in the last fifteen years are in any way automatic. Yet throughout the 1980s the rhetoric of British macro-economic policy was that the UK economy would automatically find its way to its 'natural' rate of employment. It was claimed that there was no alternative, when economic theory proves no such thing.

Moreover, the reality of policy followed the rhetoric. Financial deregulation set off a rapid expansion of consumption from the mid-1980s. Yet, as the economy overheated and the balance of payments went into deficit in autumn 1986, the then Chancellor of the Exchequer, Nigel Lawson, announced public expenditure increases and, the following March, further tax cuts, claiming that consumers were responding rationally and that the boom would correct itself. Little more than a year later interest rates had to be gradually doubled (from 7.5 per cent in May 1988 to 15 per cent by October 1989), and, even prior to that, shortly before the UK entered its longest recession since the war, the country was informed that there would be a 'smooth landing'.

Conservative capitalism did not, however, rest entirely on a general equilibrium model of perfect competition, nor on the theory of rational expectations. Mrs Thatcher was as much influenced by Hayek as by Smith or Friedman. Hayek admitted that the coordination of the market would not be perfect, but argued that it would be far better than the alternative of planning by government. Also, and most fundamentally, he emphasized that it was the pursuit of profits that both moved the system forward and, in a Darwinian manner, drove out of existence the inefficient.

Reality, however, again proved more complex. In the two financial squeezes of 1981 and 1991 some firms which survived best were not necessarily the most profitable nor the most efficient, but the most cash rich. Another group that survived was those that shed labour fastest. Thus it was caution or ruthlessness rather than risk taking or profitability that was rewarded. In addition, following their theory that risk-taking capitalism based on a share-owning democracy would best promote economic growth, and believing in particular in the efficiency of financial markets, the Conservatives encouraged the distribution rather than the retention of dividends, only infrequently acted to prevent hostile takeovers, and promoted competition between the financial institutions. Yet, as Hay and Morris (1984) have shown, an unquestioning belief in the efficiency of capital markets is misplaced, since unquoted companies show better records than quoted companies. Moreover, after examining the international evidence and taking account of the tendency of UK capital markets to encourage short termism, Morris concluded that 'economic welfare is likely to be highest where this pressure (to maximize profits) is weakest' (Morris, 1994: 250).

Many other examples of mistakes in macro-economic and micro-economic policy could be given. In particular, many policies were adversely affected by a touching faith in the efficiency of the private sector (and its methods) combined with an attempt to cut public expenditure at all costs. The results were often perverse, with large sums spent on private-sector consultants with no identifiable benefits, with projects transferred to the private sector (where the financing costs were much higher), and with public-sector staff left highly demoralized. However, the more fundamental point remains the inadequacy of the theoretical underpinning of Conservative capitalism.

The central problem of Conservative capitalism (and indeed of much traditional liberal theory) is that the underlying theory is based on two interrelated fallacies: first, its concept of the person; and second, its idea of the society of which that person is a part.

Consider first the concept of the person. By the mid-1990s attempts were being made (for example, Willetts, 1994) to claim that 'true' Conservatives always believed in people's capacity to cooperate as well as compete. This may be true of some, but this was not the agenda of the 1980s and is still not the agenda of most Conservatives. That agenda, like the economics on which it was built, assumes that every individual is, and only is, a rational, self-interested calculator of his or her own utility. Such an idea fails on four counts:

1 It is too narrow. People have commitments, loyalties and affinities to many ideas and ideals that go well beyond their own self-interest or that of their families.
2 Despite being too narrow it is too demanding. Rational decision-making in the precise sense required by economists is impossible given the uncertainty of the future and our lack of knowledge about how others will behave.
3 It is inconsistent. Rational decision-making is too time consuming for individuals ever to consider fully all possibilities, let alone always to consider all possibilities. As a result, much of the time the truly 'rational' person does not rationally evaluate many outcomes but instead relies on rules of thumb and on custom and habit.
4 It is implausible. It sees people as no more than 'globules of desire', to use Veblen's phrase, or as mere 'wantons' (Frankfurt, 1988) responding to immediate stimuli. Such a notion is not only inconsistent with any idea of Kantian autonomy, but also totally at odds with our own immediate knowledge of ourselves as reflective agents and with our great mass of psychological and sociological evidence about how people learn and how they think.

Second is the idea of society on which free market theory rests. This theory requires that society play no role in forming individuals. People already know what they want and already have the ability and the information to make their choices. They are thought of 'as if' they arrive in the social world already endowed with their preferences. Society only comes along afterwards, so to speak, being no more than a scheme of cooperation to achieve individually determined ends. As a result, the society formed has no intrinsic value. Moreover, the society that emerges has no consequences beyond the purpose of the cooperation, no enduring value and no value other than the sum of the individual satisfactions derived by each of its members at the time. There could, for example, be no value in the activity of participation itself, nor any value in committing oneself to the 'common good' (since this does not exist), nor any notion of the self being developed by such 'public' activities (because, if it were, this would require that the public preceded the private whereas the theory assumes the opposite).

Such an account is manifestly unsatisfactory. It is also particularly inadequate when taken together with the criticisms made above of the concept of the person. If individuals act partly out of custom and practice, and if, also, their preferences are formed and developed by the society within which they find themselves, then explanations that begin and end with the individual must, at best, be only part of the story.

The two central theoretical problems that must be faced are therefore as follows. First, it is not merely that the world is composed partly of some individuals driven by the pursuit of rational gain, while others act altruistically and a third group is held in the grip of routine, but rather that each person is some complex mixture of all three. Second, the form that this mixture takes is itself a complex combination of genetic inheritance, cultural context, personal volition and institutional / societal influence.

The implication of this line of thinking for the practical application of Conservative capitalism is profound. It can be seen at many levels. For example, one obvious feature of Conservative capitalism was an increase in potential rewards combined with an increase in risk. This is the logical consequence of the increased dispersion of pre-tax pay that has occurred. However, the risk element was considerably compounded by the large rise in unemployment, by the growth in bankruptcies and insolvencies and, more generally, by the instability of the economy. According to the Conservative view of incentives this combination of sticks and carrots should have caused an increase in output and economic welfare. However, even within the conventional framework of economics, the combination of an increases in risk plus an increase in reward has an ambiguous effect on welfare (depending on whether or not the rewards compensate for the insecurity). Thus, even viewed in its own terms, the Conservative approach had its weakness.

However, what is at issue here is far more substantial. First, within a more complex view of the person there is the possibility that the increase in worry created by the insecurity might reduce either the work or the effectiveness of the individual (even if the employee felt compelled by insecurity to work more than the job strictly required, this could be offset by greater inefficiency). Black's study (1994) does not support the first of these suggestions, but this does not rule out the second. In addition, the benefits, if any, might be more than offset by loss of cooperation with others – a point confirmed by Walsh (1993), who concluded that performance pay systems, by disturbing customary notions of fairness and horizontal equity can have 'demotivating consequences and may, in fact, impede employees from securing the productive gains from teamwork'.

Second, and in the long run even more important, are the unquantifiable but insidious effects through which insecurity can dislocate traditional institutions and communities. Gray (1994: 9), for example, in a sweeping attack on the whole Conservative project comments that 'the desolation of communities by unchannelled market forces and the resultant pervasive sense of economic insecurity . . . [being] . . . crucial factors in an epidemic of crime that has probably had no parallel in national life since the early nineteenth century'.

Hard evidence for such remarks is difficult to establish. This is particularly true when, as here, the argument is about effects operating at the level of society as a whole. The counter-factual is even more elusive than normal. Nevertheless support for the adverse effects of insecurity on the social fabric might be seen from Wilkinson's (1994) extensive cross-country comparison of the relationship between health and inequality. As expected he found that, within any given country, rich people have better health than poor people. However, above a certain minimum, the same is not true of rich countries. What matters, he found, was not the level of income, but its distribution. What is more the increase in ill health in countries with unequal income distributions is found to occur virtually throughout the income scale. Such results would be consistent with a general increase in insecurity. In addition, Wilkinson found that, as inequality in the UK has risen in the 1980s so its health, compared with other countries with more equal income distributions, has declined. As Wilkinson remarks, it is hard in the face of this evidence to escape the conclusions: 'First, that inequality affects people more fundamentally than is usually recognized, and second, that such powerful psychosocial implications of inequality are unlikely to confine themselves to health.'

Still sharper evidence about the inadequacy of the underlying assumptions of Conservative capitalism can be seen in the labour market. Two central planks in the reforms were to decentralize pay determination (in the interests of making it more 'flexible' and more responsive to local conditions) and to individualize it through the introduction of performance-related pay. Serious research results are only now beginning to appear, but, so far, the results do not support the Conservative assumptions.

Walsh (1993) concludes that the decentralization of bargaining in the private sector may have led to 'competitive leapfrogging and increased bargaining costs' as well as 'more intense monitoring'. In the public sector the attempts to decentralize pay bargaining have been largely unsuccessful, but even where performance-related pay systems (PRP) have been introduced, the results on staff motivation are not encouraging. Marsden and Richardson (1994) found in a detailed study of Inland Revenue staff that the PRP scheme had manifestly 'undermined the integrity of the long-standing and well established appraisal system' and that the 'net effect on staff motivation could well have been negative'. Moreover these micro-economic studies should be seen in the context of the work of Soskice (1990b). If more decentralization reduces 'coordination' by wage setters, then it will have increased wage pressure, not reduced it as hoped.

Most important of all, the situation is not static. If people have the capacities to be both self-seeking and cooperative, then the balance between these will depend on the institutions within which individuals are embedded and on what they experience. The more direct the involvement with the market and the more that rewards are market rewards, then the greater will be the inclination to follow the individualist behaviour of *homo economicus*. Whereas if people are valued for their cooperation, their loyalty or their contribution to the community, it is these attributes that will be reinforced.

In other words it is suggested that the key strategists in the Conservative Party knew full well that by giving people property rights and experience of the competitive market they would embed a belief in the virtues of the market. However, by the same token it makes much larger the mistake of assuming that people could be made more rational calculators without any costs elsewhere. To put the same point another way: it is one thing to ignore (as most economists do) that people have loyalties, commitments, and a capacity to cooperate even without economic incentives, but to know that they do and then to choose to undermine these without considering the consequences is a far larger error, especially for a Conservative Party.

Seen from this standpoint it is no surprise that so many senior executives chose to reward themselves so highly in the 1980s and 1990s; or that salespeople rewarded on commission should have misled so many people over the value of their pensions; or, as the Committee on Public Accounts (1994) has shown, that standards of public business should have declined (since these were not valued); or that corruption in the City of London increased so much (as the payoffs rose and as the law became seen as a constraint on the market); or that morale in education or public broadcasting declined (since these public activities were constantly attacked); or that so much management time and money have been employed in the Health Service with so little results.

There was indeed a double mistake in the management of the public sector. This is the area where notions of commitment and cooperation were most likely to be found, yet the neo-Taylorian techniques of management that were imported destroyed much of this cooperation. Moreover this was being done at the very time when many successful private sector companies were dropping such techniques because they were not longer relevant to post-Fordist production techniques!

As Ayres and Braithwaite (1992) argue persuasively, the reality is that society does not face a choice between individualism and cooperation, nor between a contractual model and an associational model. A society based entirely on contract without implicit compliance collapses under the monitoring required; an associational model without enforcement collapses under the strains of self-interest. Neither extreme is either attainable or desirable. The great mistake of Conservative capitalism was to push towards the extreme of self-interest without regard to the cost.

Conclusions

The argument of this chapter has been that, except for the battle against inflation and the improvement in manufacturing productivity growth, Conservative capitalism failed, judged both against most of the normal social and economic indicators and its own core values. The causes of this are threefold. First, there were large macro-economic mistakes. Second, there were gross misunderstandings of how micro-economic markets work. Common to each was that ideology rather than analysis dominated policy-making.

In addition there was a third failure on which this chapter has concentrated. The underlying aims of Conservative capitalism were to make people more competitive in each and every part of the economy, more self-seeking, indeed more like *homo economicus* is supposed to be. The incentives, the institutional reforms and the language of everyday discourse were all geared to this end, and, to some extent, they succeeded. Yet – and this is the fundamental point – the project was self-destructive. Competition is emphasized only at the cost of cooperation, and self-interest at the cost of concern for others. When this occurs more regulation, not less is required; performance-related pay improves performance in one area, but less occurs elsewhere and the gaps have to be filled; and more insecurity combined with more self-interest leads to more fraud and more corruption – and this is what occurred. Like everything else in economics, competition is not a free good.

Two questions remain. First, what lessons will the UK draw from this experience? One might be that the experiment went too far and that there is much to be learnt from other countries who have built more cooperative arrangements. Regrettably this is unlikely. Conservative capitalism appealed to the UK in part because the UK was (and is) a highly individualistic society, especially in its business relations and especially among the managerial and financial classes. Britain, like any other country, has many networks and affiliations, but in the UK these have more to do with social class than with long-term cooperative business relationships. In particular, employers' organizations have been weak and remain so. In addition, many employers remain deeply distrustful of employee involvement in business decisions (as the attitude of the CBI to the Social Chapter illustrates). Moreover, the very embedding of individualism that was the goal of Conservative capitalism, together with the destruction of institutions such as the National Economic Development Council where cooperation and links between industry and finance might have been encouraged, make the lessons more difficult to learn. In addition, it is far easier to destroy morale, trust and cooperation than it is to create them. Institutions once destroyed or damaged take time to rebuild. The relationships are not symmetrical. As a result lessons, even if learnt, will be difficult to apply. Thus, even if there were agreement that a more cooperative set of relationships between employers and employees, or between industry and finance, would be useful, these will be difficult to establish.

Finally, contrary to its self-image as a pragmatic nation, the UK has in recent decades become highly and increasingly ideological. As a result, the alternative lesson that some have drawn (and will draw) is that the mistake was not to push the experiment far or fast enough. Thus, parts of the Conservative Party are, even now, calling for more privatization and for the extension to other members of the European Union of the 'successful' capitalism of the UK. Or, if this is not possible, this part of the Conservative Party wishes the UK to disengage from the European Union. But this is a dangerous game. At the moment the UK is to some extent free-riding on the EU. It will not be able to do so indefinitely, yet if it were to withdraw from the Union, the option to free-ride would no longer exist.

However, this brings us to the second question. Why is it that despite its overall failings, in arguments about the merits of free market capitalism versus collaborative capitalism (or 'Rhenish' capitalism as Albert (1991) has termed it), the UK experience is still frequently quoted with approval? There are two reasons. First, in the global marketplace one option for a country is indeed to compete on low wages (and not quite so low skills). This may also not be a route that most of the country's citizens would prefer, but they may have little choice in the matter (at least until after the results of the choice are obvious). Second, under Conservative capitalism a minority did well and a tiny minority did extraordinarily well. These were, of course, those at the top end of the income distribution and these are, equally inevitably, those who occupy most of the main positions of power and influence in society. That such people would both believe and promulgate the view that Conservative capitalism succeeded and that it is therefore a good model for other countries to follow needs no explanation. Power and objectivity are not natural bedfellows.

7

THE INSTITUTIONAL EMBEDDEDNESS OF AMERICAN CAPITALISM

J. Rogers Hollingsworth

This chapter makes several arguments: that contemporary American capitalism must be comprehended in terms of global economic changes; that the distinctive configuration of American capitalism has evolved over a long period and has a logic to its institutional evolution; that the dominant forms of governance of the American economy have been private hierarchies, markets, and the state, with associations being very weak; that variation in governance forms has made for varying performance of industrial sectors over time; that American economic institutions are part of a larger institutional context, and therefore are unlikely to converge with the configuration of capitalism elsewhere; and that the dynamism of American capitalism, with its heavy emphasis on a market mentality and widespread inequality in income distribution, threatens to erode the institutions which have, historically, shaped it.

Capitalism is contradictory, undermining the institutions essential for its continuation. Historically, a variety of social and political institutions have contained the destructive forces of capitalism, keeping firms in harmony with society, but the weakening of existing modes of regulation has recently created serious problems in American capitalism. In order to understand American capitalism, it is important to understand it as part of a social system of production which is characterized by the following:

1 an emphasis on short-term horizons in decisions;
2 a low capacity in most industrial sectors for making high-quality products, but high adaptiveness in some sectors to new product development;
3 a weak commitment to collective governance in the private sector but high reliance on the state as a regulatory agent;
4 a strong commitment to continuous economic change;
5 a weak commitment to economic equality.

The logic of development of American capitalism

Long-term historical factors explain why the market mentality became so pervasive in the USA, why Americans have a weakly developed civil society and have championed individualism over collective responsibility, and why they have historically preferred mass standardized products over customized and specialized ones. In the USA, there were no 'ancient' religious, aristocratic, or political authorities to overthrow, as the Americans attained democratic and modern institutions without a democratic revolution. Modernization developed without a modern state, and unlike most other advanced capitalist societies, Americans have had a decentralized state with diffused power and little policy coherence. This has resulted in the development of a conservative American political culture. In some European countries, socialist and social democratic parties gained strength by fighting for basic political rights. But not in the USA. Because working men in the USA early on enjoyed political and civil rights, there were fewer incentives for organizing along class lines.

Unlike nations with aristocratic traditions, Americans have historically highly valued entrepreneurship. American Puritanism provided spiritual legitimation for the virtues of enterprise, which, combined with the weakness of traditional communities, partly explains why Americans have historically had a weakly developed civil society. By the end of the eighteenth century, the ease of accumulating land and wealth stimulated a materialistic culture. In the absence of an aristocracy, this produced a class of merchants and manufacturers with a craving for material wealth. An egalitarian political culture, combined with Puritan traditions emphasizing hard work and achievement, reinforced the belief in the USA that one could 'get ahead' by hard work and individual initiative.

These social norms eventually became associated with the American system of standardized mass production, known as early as the 1850s as the 'American system of manufacturing'. That system came into existence before the development of a transcontinental railway system, before the accumulation of the great American fortunes, before availability of low-cost Mesabi range ores and cheap oil, and before the development of a large national market. Part of the reason for the early development of the 'American system' was the high costs of labour and the shortage of skills. But also of great importance were the norms and habits, the lack of sharp class distinctions, and the homogenized tastes of Americans. They tended to place a monetary value on almost everything and supported a market mentality more pervasive than in any other capitalist society.

As communication and transportation revolutions led to declining transportation rates, firms in numerous industries after the Civil War were able to extend product markets, increase output, utilize economies of scale and scope, and undersell smaller and less efficient firms. But after a few decades of expanding markets and impressive profits, they were faced with the classic problems of intense price competition, 'saturated' markets, idle plants, accumulating inventories, severe price declines, and the threat of bankruptcy. Efforts to cope with these problems resulted in a fundamental transformation of the American economy during the late nineteenth and early twentieth centuries.

Firms in many industries attempted to limit output and stabilize prices by resorting to ineffective informal agreements. Formal arrangements such as trade associations emerged, so that by 1900, associative behaviour had become quite common in a variety of industrial sectors. Trade associations, however, generally failed to stabilize output and prices, because the strong tradition of individualism sanctioned the freedom of American firms to behave as they wished. Also important was the large size of the country, with attendant large numbers of firms and diversity of interests among firms in the same industry. Business associations in the USA have been less developed and therefore have tended to have less autonomy, fewer resources, and less capacity to govern their members than in smaller countries. Moreover, American courts and legislatures declared cartel arrangements and many other forms of collective behaviour illegal, and in 1890 Congress passed the Sherman Anti-Trust Act.

Anti-trust law had the unintended consequence of accelerating the development of large corporate hierarchies. The courts ruled that 'loose combinations' (for example, 'gentlemen's' agreements, pools and other types of cartels) were illegal under the Sherman Anti-Trust Act, but that firms could not be held to be in violation of the law simply because of their size and market share. Before the courts would rule that 'tight combinations' were illegal, there had to be convincing evidence that the firm had engaged in abusive, restrictive, or predatory behaviour, that a company had acted with the 'intent to restrain trade', and that as a result of this 'intent', it had already succeeded or would succeed in the future in obtaining monopoly power. By acting reasonably toward competitors, firms were permitted to do things within a 'tight combination' that were illegal under a 'loose combination'. The Sherman Act encouraged firms to forsake practices of restraining competitors through loose combination, and to pursue internal strategies (for example, hierarchical arrangements) to enhance their market position and stabilize their industries. A long-term consequence of the Act was to enhance concentration of the American economy.

Horizontal and vertical mergers

There was an extensive merger movement in the late nineteenth and early twentieth centuries, with the USA having more mergers than any other country – both in absolute numbers and in proportion to the number of firms in the country. Horizontal mergers occurred with greater frequency in industries which were capital intensive, had undergone rapid expansion prior to the depression of the 1890s, and experienced severe price competition. Consolidations succeeded only when tight integration resulted in economies of scale and lower labour costs, or raised barriers to entry; in industries with high volume, large batch or continuous-process production; in industries with high energy consumption; and in those that had large markets. These included food processing, oil, chemicals, primary metals, paper, and consumer durables (for example, sewing machines, agricultural machinery, electrical equipment, elevators).

Firms in a number of other industries believed they obtained cost advantages over competitors by becoming vertically integrated. There were several motives for American firms to integrate vertically. The first was to reduce uncertainty about availability of raw materials and transport facilities by backward integration, and to attain outlets for products by forward integration. The second was to enhance market share by erecting barriers to new competition. In general, firms resorted to vertical integration because of distrust of actors on whom they were heavily dependent. Indeed, low trust among transacting partners has historically been a distinctive trait of the American economy.

Backward integration occurred when processors had few sources of supply; when it was difficult to write contracts for supply far into the future; the production technology was relatively stable; and the product was in a mature stage of the life cycle. Thus, the food processing and tobacco industries did not engage in backward integration, for they had large numbers of suppliers. But backward vertical integration was quite common in oil refining, steel, aluminium and copper, where processing firms believed sources of supply might be cut off, or supplies might become very expensive. Similarly, when firms were engaged in recurring transactions of highly specific assets, vertical integration was used to avoid monopolistic pricing (Williamson, 1975, 1985; Chandler, 1977; Lamoreaux, 1985).

There was also often an offensive strategy to backward vertical integration. Firms in some industries bought up raw materials in order to limit competitors' access. In the steel, copper, aluminium, and newsprint industries, a small number of firms gradually gained control of vital ore deposits and timber. Research and development also were increasingly vertically integrated, for it was exceedingly difficult for firms to write satisfactory contracts specifying research on new products. Firms feared that by contracting out research and development, they might lose their proprietary interests to opportunistic contractors. Firms such as American Telephone and Telegraph, General Electric, and Westinghouse used in-house research and patents to restrict competition and enhance market share.

The logic of networks in the American economy

Even after corporate hierarchies were established by horizontal and vertical integration, it was possible for firms to engage in ruinous price competition. Many first therefore looked for some form of industry-wide or collective stabilization of prices. Although it was illegal to fix prices through cartels, firms frequently employed price leadership (the dominant firm strategy) as an alternative way of collective price setting, with the price of a good being announced by one firm and the rest of the industry then adopting the same price.

The sectors in which price leadership occurred most frequently were steel, autos, copper, petroleum, agricultural implements, anthracite coal, newsprint, industrial alcohol, and the refining of sugar and corn products. While dominant firm pricing tended to stabilize prices in the short term, in the long run the leader's market share invariably declined, differences in firm size diminished, and leadership tended to decay as a result of competition. Because price leadership stabilized the industry in the short term, firms had few incentives to innovate or adopt new technologies. Hence, firms adopting price leadership as a strategy tended to decline in efficiency. While some American industries used dominant firm pricing to their advantage prior to and after World War II, Japanese firms in the same industries found themselves in fierce competition with one another for domestic market share, which helped them to be efficient and successful once they entered American markets. The Japanese pattern suggests that intensive price competitiveness without price leadership may lead to high efficiency over the long run.

To understand the importance of sources of capital for the coordination of American industrial sectors, one needs to think comparatively. In Japan and Germany, where industrialization occurred somewhat late and where mass markets were much smaller than in the USA, large firms before World War II were dependent for capital on outside financiers – the large banks in Germany and the major financial groups (*Zaibatsu*) in Japan. Historically it was common for Japanese and German firms to rely on one or two major banks for capital. Not only did those banks closely monitor the firms' operations, but they often held equity in them. In Japan there was also extensive cross-company stock ownership. These are important reasons why Japanese and German firms were able to forsake short-term profit maximization in favour of long-term goals.

In the USA, where equity markets are more developed, large firms have been much less dependent on commercial banks for financing. Indeed, during the last 35 years, the proportion of American industrial funds from commercial bank loans has been among the lowest among highly industrialized countries. Equity markets developed earlier and became more important in capital intensive industries in the USA because the country industrialized early. Substantial profits generated from textiles and sailing ships were available for investment purposes in the late nineteenth century. Specifically, investment banking houses in the USA served by the end of the nineteenth century as intermediaries between those needing and those having capital, and without this intermediary to monitor investments and corporate practices, many large firms could not have emerged.

The role of a few investment banks was so important in transforming and regulating the American railroad industry that they could determine which areas of the country would have railroad expansion, and how many railroads would be established between major cities.

After 1914, state policy was the most important reason for the declining role of investment banking in the coordination of the American economy. The Clayton Anti-Trust Act of 1914 made interlocking directorships among large banks and trusts illegal, and forbade a corporation from acquiring the stock of another if the acquisition reduced competition in the industry. In addition, in 1933 the American government forced a sharp separation between commercial and investment banking. From that point on, investment banks lost much of their access to capital and had diminished capacity to regulate or govern non-financial corporations. The net result was that both types of banks came to have little control over the modern American corporation.

American non-financial corporations thus became dependent on liquid financial markets for raising capital, on the whims of stockholders, who in turn have pressured the federal government to become involved in regulating the behaviour of the equity markets. When owners of American securities think their investments are not properly managed, they sell their assets. Since American management during the past half century has been evaluated more and more by the current selling price of the stocks and bonds of the company it manages, the American corporate structure has increasingly become embedded in an institutional arrangement placing strong incentives on short-term considerations and heavy regulation by the American state.

As a result of this short termism, shareholders in America have relatively little loyalty to the firms in which they are part owners. Individuals invest in companies for appreciation in the value of shares, and the boards of directors of American firms know that their primary responsibility is to assist shareholders in maximizing their returns or risk being removed, or worse, sued. Thus, American management is preoccupied with boosting stock prices (Garten, 1992: 122–4).

Industrial relations in hierarchically coordinated firms

During the late nineteenth century, mass production became the undisputed means of enhancing industrial efficiency in numerous sectors of the American economy, and the basic strategy for expanding markets and minimizing costs. Those firms that engaged in mass production followed a distinctive logic. Mass producers took seriously Adam Smith's prescription that the most efficient way of organizing a factory was to routinize and differentiate workers' tasks down to the smallest detail. The key to breaking manufacturing into ever more detailed operations was to employ specific purpose machinery for each task along an assembly line.

Employment was viewed as an impersonal economic exchange relationship, with machines easily substituted for workers when profitable. Whatever labour was needed to work on assembly lines could be hired or dismissed at short notice. As machinery became more and more specialized, the skill and autonomy of workers declined, and management had little incentive to engage in long-term contracts with workers or to invest in their skills.

Prior to 1960, American mass production strategies were dominant among:

1 producers of low priced, semi-perishable packaged products, with large batch, continuous process technology (for example, cigarettes, breakfast cereals);
2 processors of perishable products for regional and national markets (for example, meat packing and processing firms);
3 manufacturers of consumer durables produced with continuous process technology (for example, sewing machines, automobiles, office equipment);
4 makers of high margin production goods that were technologically complex but standardized (for example, elevators and pumps);
5 other industries which were capital intensive, energy consuming and reliant on continuous production technology (for example, chemicals, oil refining, rubber products).

In the USA, there has been considerable variation in the way that labour–management relations have been coordinated, over time and in different sectors of the economy. Despite the dominance of the standardized mass production paradigm for a number of decades, some industries were always organized differently. Indeed standardized mass production itself demanded the existence of industries organized along opposite principles as special purpose machines necessary for mass production cannot be mass-produced but have to be custom-made. In other words, industrial dualism was a logical necessity even when standardized production was the dominant technology (Piore, 1980).

Mass production was also inappropriate in industries where production was labour intensive and low in energy consumption, and where product markets were heterogeneous. Examples included lumber products, printing and publishing, and residential construction firms. These were industries where each product was relatively unique and required considerable worker autonomy. Such activities took place in settings involving long-term stable relationships among craftsmen.

Still, by 1950 numerous manufacturing sectors of the American economy were tightly integrated into a system of mass production, which was dependent on very large stable markets for products low in technological complexity and slow in their rate of technological change. American management tended to believe that hierarchically organized firms were particularly well suited for mass production and distribution. The system was complemented and supported by public sector mass education which provided a labour force with basic training in reading, writing, and discipline to work on assembly lines. American students decided voluntarily how much to invest in their own education. Over time, this voluntarism meant that the level of human capital investment was lower in the USA than in countries with apprenticeship training mandated for specific occupations. Comparing American and German workers, Hansen (1991) points out that American manufacturing workers received virtually no formal training on the job. Of the monies which American firms invested in human capital, most went to managers, technicians and supervisors. American systematic training of rank-and-file employees historically was brief, narrow, and job specific. And through the 1950s, this system struck most American managers as being quite effective.

Challenges from abroad: the postwar period

Many of the USA's industrial firms succeeded with a hierarchical form of coordination because the barriers to entry were too high for effective competition from other firms, both domestic and foreign. But the day of reckoning was to come. By 1960, various European and Japanese manufacturers were adopting some of the latest technology, at a time when transportation costs were declining and markets for high quality consumer goods were expanding. Moreover, manufacturers in Japan, Germany and several other countries had never been as committed to the hierarchical form of standardized mass production as the Americans. Indeed, those countries had very different ways of coordinating manufacturing sectors – geared more to flexible production, to strategic alliances instead of hierarchies based on vertical integration, and to collective forms of governance.

In Japan, Germany and other countries where industrialization occurred later and markets were smaller, modes of coordination which were less hierarchical and more network-like had long been common. They proved more effective once markets became unstable and consumers demanded products based on complex and changing technologies. Hierarchical coordination, by comparison, is effective when markets are stable, consumer tastes are homogeneous, and technology is not highly complex and slow to change.

Following the first world oil crisis in the 1970s, many American manufacturers producing standardized goods found themselves with products for which there was little demand, and with rigid systems of production that had little capacity to adjust. Many American firms responded to market saturation and decline in profits simply by trying to reduce costs. Some froze or rolled back their employees' wages. Others took advantage of the declining costs of transportation and communication to shift production to low-wage areas. Because of the pervasiveness of the market mentality and the widespread view of labour as a commodity, thousands of firms reduced labour forces and introduced automated equipment. Many firms and their trade associations – especially in the shoe, textile, steel and automobile industries – pressured the government for protection against foreign competitors. Despite these expedients, it became evident that standardized systems of production were incompatible with volatile and unstable markets. Even when the market demand for certain goods remained relatively stable, less developed countries with lower wage rates were able to copy standardized products and sell them in the USA at lower prices. Hence, American mass producers increasingly faced severe price competition and losses.

Eventually, it became obvious that a different coordinating strategy was needed in many manufacturing sectors. The question was whether industries in the USA, historically coordinated predominantly by corporate hierarchies, could shift to the more flexible coordinating strategies employed by their foreign competitors, to overcome their slow response time, their inability to develop in-house components with complex technologies, and their high production costs.

Some American firms adopted certain aspects of Japanese management (for example, just-in-time production, self-managing teams, quality circles and 'statistical process control'). But this was not sufficient to transform the American economy. A nation's financial markets, educational and industrial relations systems and other socio-political factors influence sectoral and national economic performance. And the American economy cannot mimic the Japanese economy simply by adopting some of the Japanese management and work practices.

Importance of multilateral and collective behaviour in advanced capitalist societies

The dominant social system of production in American society was historically coordinated by markets and corporate hierarchies, with firms embedded in a weakly developed civil society. At the same time, there has been, for some years, an emerging subordinate system, one in which economic coordination takes place, not within firms, but within networks of cooperating actors who have developed flexible long-term relations with one another. These networks exist in the absence of highly developed associative institutions like trade unions, business associations or training institutes organized by capital or labour.

Some of the most effective American networks involve cooperative relations among university-based firms with a strong knowledge base and state and federal governments. Where such networks have been successful, much of the leadership has come from the state. Significantly, the American state has rarely sought to develop coordinating networks among manufacturing firms in more traditional industries. Rather, it has been active during the past half century in developing networks for manufacturing firms in relatively new industries addressing military and health-related needs of society. The following are products and technologies coordinated by networks firmly embedded in environments involving cooperative relations with university-based scientists and engineers, the state (especially the military), and other firms, both suppliers and competitors: aircraft, semiconductors, integrated circuits, computers, nuclear power, microwave telecommunications, new materials such as high strength steel alloys, fibre-reinforced plastics, titanium, and metal fabrication such as numerical-controlled machine tools. Without such networks, these technologies and products could not have developed in the USA.[1]

One important feature of networks is their linking together organizations with different knowledge bases. This kind of coordination is not possible within a hierarchy, as no single firm has the knowledge and resources to develop any of the technologies and products listed above. Nor could a single firm linked with suppliers develop such products. They could be developed only because firms were engaged in established, cooperative, long-term relationships with other organizations. Networks have been vital in linking experts in industry, government laboratories and land grant universities with knowledge in many different areas.

Industries in which American manufacturing is strong are those in which knowledge is constantly changing at a rapid rate and in unpredictable directions, and in which the strategies of firms are ambiguous and rapidly evolving. Because the relationship of such firms with their suppliers of capital and knowledge is also changing, they can flourish only in an institutional environment that is extraordinarily flexible, one in which scientists, engineers and venture capital are highly mobile. Such firms are born and disappear with great rapidity, just as engineers and scientists are ever shifting from one product and industry to another.

Many Americans are socialized in their educational system to be highly individualistic and to excel in entrepreneurship. Because of the pervasiveness of the market mentality, the strong tradition of entrepreneurship, the flexibility of external labour markets and the presence of venture capital markets, it has been relatively easy for American researchers and engineers to set up their own firms to commercialize new products, especially when the federal government has blessed such ventures with research and development funds and immunity from anti-trust concerns. This has been especially common in information-based industries in and around Silicon Valley, as well as in the biomedical, biochemical, artificial intelligence, and defence-related industries. With a cross-national perspective, it is apparent that network arrangements have performed extremely well in American society in advancing knowledge at the frontiers of science and in developing new products from basic science.

The American R&D system has been less successful in improving upon older products for commercial markets. The Japanese system of research and development offers a contrast in styles. Although the Japanese are much weaker in basic science, have been somewhat less successful in developing radically new products, and may be somewhat deficient in entrepreneurial leadership, they have established close communication among researchers, engineers, and production and marketing personnel involved in existing product technologies. Japanese firms tend to be rather successful in linking scientists and engineers within established production facilities. In the USA, research and development tends to involve production personnel only in a very limited manner (Aoki, 1988; Powell, 1990; Powell and Brantley, 1992).

Because of the flexible external labour market in the USA, it is very difficult for American firms to keep knowledge proprietary. Movement of personnel from one organization to another undoubtedly facilitates communication, creativity, and development of new products. But because knowledge is so easily siphoned from American firms, they are limited in their ability to focus their talents on long-term development, whereas the less flexible internal labour market in Japan permits firms there to focus more energy on the improvement and refinement of products.

Differences in the underlying institutional structure in capitalist societies have led to substantial variation in their network structures. In the USA, networks are either state led or private–contractual in nature. In Japan, networks are socially or communally based, while in Germany they are quasi-public or associationally constructed.[2]

American-style capitalism and distributional issues

The relevance of this for the USA in the 1990s is that a number of major innovations during the past forty years has had a Schumpeterian clustering effect – innovations and discoveries in biotechnology, electronics, computers, communication, instrumentation, and new materials (synthetic and otherwise). Most of these innovations are occurring in industries in which product lives are short. The American social system of production with its institutional arrangements facilitating creativity, individualism, 'short termism' and flexible labour and capital markets fosters the development of totally new industries. Moreover, the same institutional environment has facilitated the rise of the USA to world leadership in the entertainment and publishing industries, sectors which place a great deal of emphasis on the development of new products with short lives.

There is considerable evidence that the American economy is becoming more concentrated without becoming more centralized. Large firms are becoming leaner and cutting back their in-house operations to essential 'core competencies', delegating other work to outside suppliers. While some scholars have speculated that dual labour markets would disappear in advanced industrial societies, there is increased evidence that they are becoming even more institutionalized in America. Ultimately, economic power and control is becoming not less but more concentrated within multinational manufacturing corporations and financial institutions (Harrison, 1994). While many who discuss the increasing flexibility of the American economy focus on small firms with good jobs and trained workers, there has been a tendency to ignore the low-wage, superexploitative character of many firms on the periphery that support the entire system by suppressing labour costs. For example, in Silicon Valley, an area associated with creativity, high skills, and high pay, nearly one-half of the workers perform production and maintenance tasks and are officially classified as semi-skilled and unskilled. For them, pay is extremely low and benefits are non-existent (Harrison, 1994: 115). In the meantime, the decline of the old industries, such as, steel, textiles, and construction has led to a workforce increasingly polarized between management and other highly skilled workers on the one hand, and low-skilled workers with little capacity to change their skill levels on the other. Viewing the American economy as a whole, the number of people that is highly trained is increasing, but skilled jobs are supported by a very large segment of the population with very low skills.

As American firms in both manufacturing and services engage in vertical disintegration, downsizing, outsourcing and network building across sectors and national borders, there has been a steady decline in union membership which in turn has contributed to increased wage inequality. The dramatic increase in immigration has also contributed to declining union density and rising inequality of wages (Borjas et al., 1992; Freeman, 1993). Indeed, since 1979 there has been a sharp acceleration in the growth of earnings inequality, especially among males (Levy and Murnane, 1992).

During the past decade, Americans had a larger number of new jobs than any other highly industrialized society, but a substantial proportion of these have been involuntary part-time positions with low wages and few fringe benefits, resulting in frequent job turnover. Since 1982, temporary employment in the USA has been gaining three times more rapidly than employment as a whole. Throughout the American economy, workers on average take home 7 to 12 per cent less income than in 1970 (Callaghan and Hartmann, 1991; Levy and Murnane, 1992; Karoly, 1993; Mishel and Bernstein, 1993).

Increasingly, more and more Americans have slowly been moving to the political right in response to promises of tax cuts and reductions in welfare spending. As Keynesian policies are discredited, politicians increasingly articulate political–economic views resembling those of the 1920s: there should be less state and social regulation of the economy, tight monetary and fiscal policies, and more economic coordination by the market. Although much of the American economic recovery is being driven by the expansion of new industries, these industries are embedded in an institutional framework and a political culture that are unlikely to be able to sustain the recovery.

Concluding observations

In assessing the relative roles of corporate hierarchies and networks in the USA, several points should be noted. First, since stable, homogeneous markets continue to exist for many products of low technological complexity, hierarchical coordination remains dominant in many industries. 'Dis-integration' may be occurring in other sectors, but hierarchical coordination is still widespread in American manufacturing, especially in market segments where there are relatively homogeneous tastes for inexpensive products, such as paper products, breakfast cereals, soft drinks, bug sprays, floor wax, deodorants, soaps, and shaving cream. Mass markets for these products are stable and far from saturated, and remain ready for products manufactured by semi-skilled workers and distributed by general purpose firms.

Second, the ability of the USA to produce high quality products in more traditional industries is drastically limited by the rules, norms, and arrangements which influence practices of industrial relations. An industrial relations system that facilitates diversified high quality production is one in which workers have broad skills and some form of assurance that they will not be dismissed. Indeed, job security tends to be necessary for employers as well to have incentives to make investments in worker skills. This type of incentive and skill system has become much more widespread in Japan and West Germany than in the USA, where downsizing of firms and 'sweating' of labour are more pervasive.

Third, the associational system of a country influences both its industrial relations system and its ability to engage in diversified quality production (Streeck, 1991). Where there is a well-developed civil society and associational system, firms have a greater capacity to enter into collective agreements with their competitors not to poach one another's workers. This encourages firms to develop more flexible internal labour markets, and to invest in the skills of their workforces. One consequence of the highly fragmented American associational system is a very flexible external job market combined with rigid internal labour markets, conditions which limit the development of a highly trained labour force in more traditional industries.

Fourth, capital markets in the USA have also placed constraints on the development of broad worker skills. American capital markets have encouraged firms to engage in short-term profit maximization. By comparison, firms in Japan and Germany have relied more on bank loans and cross-firm ownership as a source of capital. The short-term profit horizon of many American corporations has been due to their dependency on liquid equity markets, combined with the fact that American banks have been disinclined to provide long-term interest loans.

Fifth, as technology becomes more complex, changes more rapidly and becomes more expensive, firms are finding that various types of networks are an effective form of coordinating transactions, even in rather traditional industries. But to maximize their effectiveness as governance arrangements in more traditional industries, networks need to be embedded in a rich institutional environment involving various forms of collective behaviour. American firms with networks as a major form of coordination are very weakly embedded in institutional arrangements of a collective nature.

The social environment plays an important role in shaping the behaviour of firms, their types of products and their production strategies. If firms are embedded in an institutional environment rich in collective goods, flexible systems of production in more traditional industries are likely to be dominant. But in a society where there is a lack of such an environment, the market mentality becomes more important, and the collective goods necessary for the flexible production of high quality products and for international competitiveness in more traditional industries are lacking. On the other hand, precisely because American firms are not embedded in a rich institutional environment, they are extraordinarily adaptable, which has given them a distinct advantage in newer sectors that emphasize individualism and creativity and that have a need for well-developed venture capital markets. At the same time, underneath all the glamour of the new industries in the American economy, the institutional underpinnings requisite for sustaining a vibrant economy and a high degree of civility remain extremely weak. The long-term prognosis for American capitalism is therefore problematic, with two competing visions.

Those sharing a neo-Polanyian view (Hollingsworth, 1994) believe that effective civility and governance at the local level are in crisis, with law and order breaking down, social pathologies widespread, and boundaries among ethnic and racial groups becoming more rigid. In this view, the power to govern the states and metropolitan districts has now shifted to suburban areas. As a consequence, schools in large cities remain underfunded and become increasingly unsafe, and urban violence and despair are becoming more widespread. The gap between the life chances of minorities and those of white Americans is widening, and labour market opportunities for minorities are declining. Every American census since 1940 has demonstrated that the metropolitan areas of the country have become increasingly more segregated along lines of race and ethnicity, with middle-class whites moving to suburbia, and central cities populated by African-Americans, Hispanics, and other low-income Americans. In 1990, 60 per cent of Chicago's population consisted of ethnic minorities, while surrounding suburbs were 80 per cent white. As a result, monetary resources for coping with problems of inner American cities are in decline. The tax base of American cities has continued to diminish, while federal government spending on urban problems has declined from 18 per cent of the federal budget in 1980 to 6.4 per cent in 1990.

The implications of these trends for the next generation are threatening. If the USA is to adjust to the economic requirements of an advanced industrial democratic society during the twenty-first century, it must either rebuild or construct new institutions at the local level. If it fails in this endeavour, order and civility may well break down, and the USA would then lack the capacity to develop at local–regional levels the social institutions necessary for the governance of the economy in an advanced industrial society.

The alternative view is articulated by some centrist and conservative political leaders in the USA and is somewhat more optimistic about the nation's future. With low taxes, an inegalitarian income distribution, high immigration of both cheap manual labour and well-trained Asian engineers, the USA may be able to continue to be innovative in industrial sectors with short product lives. Also, as a result of American military power, the country can continue to offer incentives to the economic and political elites of other countries to be supportive of the American political economy, despite huge trade deficits and a falling dollar. In short, the social infrastructure of American society may be disintegrating, and crime and other social pathologies may be spreading among the surplus population, but the upper third of American society may be able to live extremely well, feasting on the social infrastructures of other countries and on the world market.[3] How long the band can continue to play on in such a world cannot be predicted with accuracy, and depends on the course of events both within and outside the USA.

Notes

1   American agriculture owes much of its success to the fact that agricultural producers have been embedded in a rich institutional environment, with cooperative activity among agricultural producers under an anti-trust exemption; dissemination by the state of university-based knowledge to agricultural scientists; and financial assistance from a number of public and quasi-public institutions.

2   I am indebted to Wolfgang Streeck for these insights.

3   These views were developed after extensive conversations with Colin Crouch and Wolfgang Streeck.

8

FOLLOWING THE COLLAPSE OF COMMUNISM, IS THERE STILL A MIDDLE WAY?

Jean-Paul Fitoussi

The end of the 1980s saw the triumph of the market economy, interpreted initially as an objective recognition that this was the form of organization which was most effective in assuring both the well-being of societies and their freedom. The collapse of socialism was proof of this and its downfall left no solution other than complete espousal of the system that remained. The recognition came, it is true, after more than ten years of conservative revolution, with the redistribution of incomes in reverse and a marked increase in inequality. Nonetheless, it was puzzling, the victor being in a somewhat sorry state, with mass unemployment on this side of the Atlantic and growing poverty on the other, a high national debt and deficits all round.

The truth is that Western economies were still not totally converted to the system which they recommended should be applied in the East. They still had some way to travel. Certainly contingency policies had already been sacrificed on the altar of financial propriety and monetary sovereignty renounced so as to profit effectively from unregulated financial markets. However, particularly in continental Europe a system of social security had been built up whose principled arrangements constituted many obstacles to the free operation of markets. Therefore the only solution – in France, Italy and Britain – was to organize an equally important body of reform so as to effect its transition to the market economy.

That is the substance of debate all over Europe. Europe will be neo-liberal or be nothing and even if the conviction holds that social cohesion is important, for some there is a still stronger belief that, far from affording effective protection to the weakest and most deprived, our system of social security serves to exclude them.

The motivation behind 'our error of judgement' is however clear. We were witness to the collapse of a system in the East and, faced with the issue of what was to become of the economies that ran that system, our reply was that they should adopt ours. But all we had as the dominant representation of our system was its theoretical descriptive categories. Our recommendation to these Eastern regions was therefore that they should devise the purest form of neo-liberal capitalism, conduct in effect a laboratory experiment. Hence we were in the trickiest of positions, given that our own system was far from representative of neo-liberal capitalism in its pure state and contained several flaws. Heartened by what we had recommended to others, we then realized that this should also apply to ourselves and that there were still transitions to make. Yet, if our thinking was eminently reasonable, in J.R. Oppenheimer's words such 'reasonableness is merely mistaken when it leads us to consider that what is familiar to us should necessarily materialise in unfamiliar surroundings and leads us to hope that one country will be much like the next'.

'The two outstanding vices of the economic world we live in are that full employment is not assured and that the distribution of fortune and income is arbitrary and unjust' (Keynes, 1936: ch. 24). At the time economists and governments would draw conclusions that were radically different from those we draw today.

This chapter will attempt to show that all forms of capitalism can be no more than a means to an end, applying this demonstration to a question that is much discussed at present, that of the relationship between competitiveness and social welfare.

Two systems and an intermediate position: an application to the concepts governing economic systems

The current state of thinking on the economic system is a good illustration of the trap into which we can fall merely by finding ourselves confronted with the apparent absence of an alternative.

The terms of the debate

Different forms of capitalism coexisted with different forms of socialism, which in the main have now disappeared. For some this signifies that all forms of capitalism, other than the purest, must also disappear, so that reality may at last accord with its reference model. Any potential third way between capitalism and socialism is itself condemned to disappear.

But I imagine that each of us has a different definition of the terms of the debate. What is capitalism? What is socialism? Are we referring to conceptual or to concrete systems? Too often discussion is obscured by an ideological connotation that leads us to compare the concrete functioning of one system with the pure theory of the other, and so conclude inevitably in favour of the second. The implications for well-being of the theory of the competitive general equilibrium – which is the reference model for capitalism – are clearly superior to the concrete result of the functioning of a socialist economy.

But one could equally well hold the view that capitalism and socialism demarcate a spectrum containing all possible systems, of which they represent extreme forms. In this sense, all existing systems would constitute alternative 'middle ways', combining in differing degrees the organizational principles that define each system, some approximating to capitalism, some to socialism. What has gone in the East is a particular subset of such middle ways, one close to the socialist extreme within the spectrum. And it is too early to know whether the failure of these systems was due to their socialist nature or to the particular institutional characteristics incorporated in the solution that predominated.

Likewise, what has gone in the East is a particular form of communism, more a totalitarian regime than an ideology. The confusion of one with the other was painstakingly nurtured since it provided a dictatorship with the pretext of a generous ideology. Yet it would be illusory to think that communism as an ideology has disappeared. If this were the case, other utopias would need to be invented, since it would be dangerous were capitalism as a theoretical system to be confronted only with itself.

It is true that the disappearance of communism in this form was unpredicted. The suddenness with which it occurred caught us unawares and allowed us no perspective on the event either politically or economically. We had not considered that an alternative might exist to the system in which we live, other than that identified with the Soviet model.

We were made orphans of that system, whose function it was to reflect a gratifying image of ourselves: after all, its existence testified that we in the West were enjoying the least discreditable of systems. But where can we find a reference now? There lies the danger. We catch ourselves saying, thinking even, that there is no possible alternative. But the collapse of a bad system is not in itself proof that the remaining one is the best that can be conceived.

This conceptual difference as to the nature of the economic system – should we seek a middle way that combines contradictory principles of organization, or a fully coherent extreme course – has always characterized economic thinking.

Two texts dating from 1931 provide a measure of the divergence in interpretation at the time. Here is what Keynes said in his Harris Lectures at the University of Chicago:

> Today we are witnessing the greatest economic catastrophe in modern times. I am told that in Moscow it is considered to be the last supreme crisis of capitalism and that the existing social order will not survive it. It is easy to believe what one wants to believe. But if this crisis turns out later to be analysed by economic historians, there is, it is true, a possibility – I shall not go further – of its being interpreted as a major turning. Nevertheless, no more than a possibility. For I profoundly believe our destiny is in our hands and that we can emerge from this crisis if we make the appropriate choices, or rather if those who hold power throughout the world make them.

Here again, in 1931, is what Jacques Rueff wrote in a celebrated article in the *Revue d'économie politique*:

The error in argument is here manifest: the crisis has not resulted from the capitalist system, since it has only now appeared and in areas where the mechanism that characterises the system, whose effectiveness it is claimed to demonstrate, has been prevented from coming into play.

What the unemployment in Britain proves is not the impotence of the price mechanism but on the contrary, the fact that when it fails to function economic equilibrium cannot survive.

So if, more than half a century after this exchange, we are condemned to re-enact the same debate, it is probably because the concepts we use to compare the economic systems are ill-adapted. In our thinking we generally stress difference, whereas because actual economic systems represent intermediate courses they are betwixt and between. To stress difference is to stress a static concept which fixes categories in an immutable typology: young and old; rich and poor; immigrants and nationals; socialist and capitalist systems, and so on. The middle ground on the contrary represents movement. It describes a dialectical space in which differences appear and interbreed, crossing their opposites in situations that are vibrant and remarkable (neither young nor old, spanning cultures, spanning systems).

Could it not be said that today economics spans two discourses? There is the discourse of necessity that gives itself to be 'natural', primary, conjugating the multiple constraints of economic activity. The laws of the market, however remorseless they are for some, are inescapable, and it is useless to try to evade them. And there is the other discourse – of ultimate purpose, in which the economic factor is only as good as the programme it presents and is shaped by political purpose: the project, that of raising the general well-being and creating a movement where each may find a place and fulfilment. The two discourses appear quite distinct. In fact, they display a highly intricate middle ground where the discourse of the programme is never far away from that of necessity, or that of necessity from ethical considerations. The duality between 'what is' and 'what ought to be' is covered. But now the collapse of socialist systems leaves a gaping hole in the purposive discourse. Does that imply regression towards the primary discourse of necessity? One might say that in the East the discourse of planning failed because it proclaimed itself to be ultimate – original and natural and covering every eventuality. Preventing as it did the middle ground to function, it blocked any possibility for displacement, and therefore of adaptation.

For the discourse of constraint, that of final purpose appears both as what it lacks and what it risks. Once, in the event of failure or serious dysfunction, one incurred the risk of socialism; but what is there to risk now? If the notion of purpose disappears, the primary discourse of necessity may appear faultless, flawless, occupying the entire space. In short, the agony of socialist systems contains the risk of making us totalitarian, turning us in on ourselves, identifying us with ourselves, as if there were no other alternative.

At bottom, the socialist – purposive – system was merely the symptom of the faults of our own. And now here we are deprived of the symptom rather than cured of what gave rise to it – the impossibility of meeting all human needs. At the present time our system incorporates elements of social purpose, and middle ways are widespread. But this is now being questioned in the name of competitiveness, that is, of the stern laws of necessity.

Pure capitalism does not exist, however. It would be as superficial to proclaim today the demise of communism as it would have been to announce the demise of capitalism in the 1930s. Yet capitalism in its extreme forms disappeared more than fifty years ago. It has been replaced everywhere by 'middle ways', in the USA too. These 'tertiary routes' have consisted in the progressive introduction of institutions destined to mitigate the excesses of the free market. Further, the capitalism that we know is 'contaminated' by the concern for justice and social welfare that springs from the spontaneous functioning of democracy. It is precisely because 'capitalism' has been able to recognize its dysfunctions and its failings and continually to adapt that it survives today.

On the other hand, the communist regimes in the East, because they were organized in every dimension by totalitarian states, were incapable of adaptation. The discourse they forged was totalitarian and as such was unable to accept its failings, intent on occupying the entire space of economic and social life, with no place at all for innovation and internal criticism. Thus debarred from adapting, the system could only seize up.

At the same time, two powerful motivations – democracy and the risk of communism – directed the evolution of capitalism towards forms that were socially acceptable, which explains why capitalism has a variety of forms, some achieving greater stability than others. Capitalism is a model that is constantly evolving, whose structure cannot be fixed in terms of what exists today. In the 1930s it was thought that mass unemployment was fatal to capitalism. It is ironic then that the system should triumph just when, in Europe, its most civilized ground, mass unemployment makes its reappearance. That is scarcely testimony to social equilibrium and it is highly likely that alternative forms will materialize out of the historical process.

Democracy and the search for justice, on one side, the risk of socialism on the other, hence constituted powerful motivations for resolving conflicts by way of compromise (the 'middle way'). It may well be true that conflicts should not be systematically avoided, representing as they do a dynamic element, but they need to be overcome. Toynbee himself thought that if conflicts were a mainspring for evolution, civilizations would die when they encountered an insurmountable obstacle, as certain conflicts can sometimes be. If, by way of reference model, capitalism acquires an absolute monopoly, there is a great danger that it may lose the motivation and the ability to reform itself. For there are elements that are of greater importance than the laws governing the market and production. As J.B. Clark wrote in the first edition of the Palgrave Dictionary (1894–9):

The primary fact of economic science is the production of wealth. The division of the product between those who create it is secondary in logical order and, in a sense, in importance. However, the most important subject for reflexion in social economics is distribution. If the term is given sufficiently wide meaning, it designates all the economic processes whose solution presents moral problems. Upon the solution of the ethical question of the division of income depends not only social harmony but the productivity of industry.

Gradualism and radicalism as part of tradition

One of the decisions of the G7, at the economic summit in Houston in July 1990, was to invite four international institutions – the IMF, World Bank, OECD and EBRD – to undertake a combined study of the Soviet Union, so as to determine the conditions for its receiving international aid. I was responsible for the EBRD team. Over the few months that the study lasted, we learnt a great deal about the disarray in which the Soviet economy found itself, but above all we became aware of the extraordinary complexity and institutional richness of what is known as a market economy.

It was by observing the Eastern economies across their failings that we grew aware of this complexity. For these institutions are so much part of our everyday surroundings that we tend to forget their existence. The degree of regulation required for a 'free' market economy to function – apart from the violence inflicted by government and private interests – is considerable. The difficulty lay precisely in that institutions which had been shaped in the West in the course of several centuries were in the East to be created out of nothing. Hence the prudence that has to be adopted in the face of those – and they are many – who advocate the 'Big Bang'.

I call to mind a remark made by Kenneth Arrow, a member of the EBRD team. He had realized, he said, that the institutional content of the theory of general equilibrium, if it had been made explicit, would have made up at least 90 per cent of the theory.

There exist two methods to reach the required objective, the democratic transition to a market economy: gradualism and radicalism. The consensus was for the choice of radicalism. It is worth noting that it is not customary for one hundred or so economists to reach consensus in resolving a problem. Ordinarily, it only requires two economists for three opinions to be expressed. Even so it may be that agreement was possible because each of us had interpreted the term radical in a different way. There is a number of radical approaches, some more progressive than others, and the radicalism we selected inclined, within the spectrum of possibility, towards progressive methods.

Why so? Reforms need to be sufficiently radical to impose a change of direction on the system, yet sufficiently gradual to be accepted by the population.

That it to say that it is important not to caricature the points of departure and arrival, and not to be mistaken about the desired outcome of the process. However, generally, when recommendations are made, they give the impression of being based on too simple a notion of transition – that from a pure system of ultimate aims, point A, to a pure system of necessity, point B. And as we know little about the dynamics of transition, our best recommendation is to say that it should be done in a single bound. As Jeffrey Sachs (the American economist who advised many eastern and central European post-communist governments) would have put it, you don't take a couple of steps to cross a precipice: a useful image, but haven't our civilizations long displayed their capacity for bridge-building? The task requires time certainly, but it avoids drawing too close to the abyss.

In truth, our consensus came about because we had a different conception of the arrival point of reform, system B. For all of us, it was an intermediate system, one which left an ample margin of manoeuvre for conceiving social institutions, redistributive systems and many other deviations from the market economy model attainable. In short, the distance between points A and B varied with each economist concerned, even if each was agreed on the fact that a critical mass of reforms was needed to impose a change of direction on the system.

All that, I fear, is evident, and points in the same direction. In our world where not all the conditions for general market equilibrium are brought together – because they cannot be – it is essential to devise policies and institutions so as to assure a minimum degree of social cohesion. Certainly one might act on the supposition that these conditions were assembled – under the frequently invoked constraint of competition between low-waged economies – but then the system 'rid of its social contaminations' would run the risk of break-up, since it would be activated by a single organizational principle. To take an example, one of the conditions that suffice for the existence of general equilibrium is that the initial emoluments of economic actors should be adequate for them to live without working. Otherwise, the wages paid to certain categories of workers, as they result from markets in equilibrium, might well settle at a level below that required for subsistence. One would then be within the frame of competitive general equilibrium, but with a population incapable of survival. To steer clear of such a consequence, a system of welfare protection needs to be put in place, that is to say a third, an alternative, course has to be found.

Constraints and objectives in the debate on the relationship between competitiveness and social cohesion

No sooner were our celebrations over at the collapse of the socialist system than we began to show concern at its effects on our competitive position. For those who press for Western economies also to commit themselves to the transition towards market economies and in the course of doing so to abandon intermediary forms of capitalism, the preoccupation with competitiveness is primary, the discourse of necessity inescapable. As a result the debate on the relationship between competitiveness and social cohesion merely constitutes another aspect of the debate on the possibility of a middle, an alternative, pathway.

European countries are divided between the desire for newfound inter-dependence and the necessity of pursuing their transition to a market economy, which got underway at the end of the 1970s. Imperceptibly, it is the latter that appears to be the more urgent. The emergence of newly industrialized countries seems to have markedly lowered their competi-tiveness and in this respect the future appears still more threatening. Simultaneously, the growth of public and welfare deficits seems to indi-cate that European countries no longer have the means to provide their public services, still less their systems of social welfare. In any event, the debate is engaged between those – and they are many – who, however reluctantly, consider it necessary to reduce the extent of the welfare cover at present accorded, and those – a minority – who consider other options possible.

The system is likely to collapse because the crisis is worse than expected. No economy possesses sufficient resources to support mass unemploy-ment over a long period. The financial costs of running a society where there is a high level of unemployment are considerable. In the main, these costs result from the normal mechanism of welfare protection, which is then seen as damaging to national competitiveness. I call this the concept of trade-off.

But there exists a second conception according to which, on the contrary, social cohesion is an essential factor in economic development, hence in competitiveness. The deficits in welfare protection are to a large extent a symptom of dysfunction in our economic system. It is possible to imagine solutions which would enable us to be rid of them, but if we fail to root out the ill which gives rise to them, the symptom will reappear in another, probably far uglier, form.

The concept of trade-off

According to the first concept, which today is dominant, there exists a process of political trade-off between competitiveness and social cohesion – more of one can only be obtained at the expense of the other. However veiled the discourse transmitting this idea, it implies that the cost of welfare protection reduces a country's competitiveness. Such a conception was expressed most clearly by John Major: 'We have jobs; you Europeans, welfare protection.' Public policies follow from this: labour market deregulation, increase in inequality, lower taxes, hence a drop in public expenditure and services provided by public authorities.

This conception is built upon a body of theoretical and empirical justifi-cation. Globalization of markets, whether for goods or capital, intensifies competition, in particular from countries where wages and the level of welfare protection are low. The problem is the more acute insofar as technological progress works to the detriment of unskilled labour, whose employment appears to be increasingly superfluous in the productive process. In view of the fact that the same methods can be implemented everywhere, the only resource left in order to compete on equal terms is to increase the flexibility of the labour market by at least significantly reducing – if not altogether removing – the obstacles to its smooth functioning: that is, guaranteed basic wage, unemployment benefit, over-restrictive clauses in the code of working practice, etc. This would be the price for a return to full employment. Our societies cannot remain rich unless certain categories of workers become poorer and their lot more precarious. For no forecast, not even the gloomiest one, assumes that there will no longer be increases in per capita income in the rich countries. Therefore the concept of trade-off holds that many will be excluded from sharing the fruits of future expansion.

The empirical justification seems to come from a simple observation. To take a superficial look at developments on both sides of the Atlantic over a period of twenty years, the impression forms that each region has chosen a different model for adaptation in the face of a common adversity. Europe is characterized by mass unemployment, whereas the USA is, no less alarmingly, registering growth in the number of poorly paid workers. The existence of a trade-off between unemployment and poverty is thus corroborated. A closer look, however, shows that things are not quite so simple: poverty is developing because of unemployment and non-employment because of poverty. The level of labour force participation of those who are most vulnerable has fallen in the USA, because of wage levels that offer too little incentive and the existence of means other than work for earning a living. The result is that unemployment statistics have fallen. Hence the trade-off appears for what it is: one between two forms of poverty, that which arises from unemployment and that resulting from wages which are too low. One avoids Charybdis only to encounter Scylla.

But what matters most in this argument is the idea of the social contract it carries. If for instance the debate over the SMIC (index-linked minimum wage) seems to me essential, it is not because of the bearing the SMIC has on labour costs, but because it deals fundamentally with the status of labour. Those who argue for the suppression of the minimum wage think of labour as merchandise: if it is abundant, in order to find a buyer its price must drop freely. Those opposed to this have a different conception: labour is the means whereby an individual is integrated in a community. When labour-as-project becomes labour-as-merchandise, the social bond disintegrates since labour is no longer a factor of integration. Individualism prevails over interdependence, and inequality fast becomes intolerable to a point where the very foundations of society are called into question.

The solution that consists in substituting for mass unemployment (the European case) a situation where a sizeable fraction of the population cannot really live from their labour (poor American workers) does not resolve the problem of social instability. This is because the labour market is much less a 'market' than the chosen area of the social contract. Merchandise has no need to consider its future. Conversely, it has taken countless years of social struggle to set up the institutions which today rule the labour market.

The evolution of the social contract

Why is the concept of trade-off dominant today? How has this situation come about? It is no pure coincidence that the rise in unemployment and the weakening of social cohesion have intensified at a time when the level of interest rates has been rising.

The abnormally high level of interest rates, from whatever cause, is an arresting symbol. It signifies that income from private wealth is – equally abnormally – favoured in relation to income from labour and industrial activity. Hence it amounts to the depreciation of effort and its reward. It further signifies that low growth has not had disagreeable consequences for all alike. It has been accompanied by a very considerable redistribution of wealth and income, with the consequence that the situation of some groups has improved more during the years of low growth than over the scores of years that preceded them. This in itself gives cause for concern, since it signifies that many people no longer necessarily have an interest in growth. Insofar as the incomes of a fraction of the population can grow through the redistribution of a given volume of wealth, rather than through growth in this volume, society becomes less interdependent and the common front for growth disappears. There takes place within a country what occurs in international relations, that is the substitution of a market share rationale for a rationale of growth or, if one prefers, the transition from a cooperative to a non-cooperative mechanism. Each country attempts to corner a larger share of the market, and one's gain is another's loss. Each actor attempts to increase his share of the national income. Those who hold a certain degree of power succeed in this.

This transformation of the game rules eventually leads, by a process of contagion, to a change in the attitude of those who constitute the workforce. One cannot for long expect them – those in particular who are under less of a threat – to show solidarity with the unemployed, if they feel themselves disadvantaged and unjustly treated in relation to other social categories. In these circumstances why would they accept that a decreasing proportion of the national income, represented by wages, should be divided between a larger number of people, without access to the proportion represented by growth? The currently fashionable notion of a further division between wages and jobs comes up against this problem: why should not profits and unearned income also be made to participate in this new social exchange? Why should profits or private income be the sole forms of income to benefit from the fruits of future growth? Hence, among the better protected wage earners one increasingly sees the development of insider attitudes, which because they are monopolistic cannot be to the advantage of employment. This group will try to benefit from the windfalls of their situation or from those given them by their human capital: their incomes may increase if the numbers in employment drop and they may then find an objective interest in this occurring.

All of this points to a change in the social contract. To simplify, the social contract in its old form may be represented as implicitly containing a complex of 'subsidies' between agents, subsidies that were favourable to employment. Low interest rates enabled a higher wage bill to be distributed, which in turn promoted a higher level of employment. A reduced wage spread implied that higher wage earners accepted a lower remuneration, and this allowed firms to give more attention to taking on workers with low or no skills. Young people accepted lower wages when they came on to the labour market, because they knew that their wage packet would show a constant increase throughout their careers. That enabled the older age group to be paid a higher wage.

It only needs this structure of support–subsidy to dissolve for unemployment to grow. It starts to dissolve if everyone is trying to obtain the maximum to be got from the market – and high interest rates make people more impatient, more eager to seek satisfaction in the here and now. The resulting unemployment will be concentrated among the less qualified, those who have no power, no private means of support.

What this rapid analysis of past trends shows is that one can interpret the rise in unemployment as resulting rather from a loosening of social cohesion than from a loss of competitiveness which would be the inevitable consequence of an over-generous welfare protection system.

The concept of complementarity

Where the first conception considers there to be contradiction, the second on the contrary finds that there is complementarity: competitiveness is a means the better to serve social cohesion, and social cohesion competitiveness. It inclines towards a preference for a rationale of growth to one where there are conflicts over share-out, whether such conflicts relate to market share or national income. Clearly it implies policies that are opposite in all respects. What matters is not so much the level of compulsory contributions as their use for investment and for the maintenance of social cohesion. Its theoretical and empirical foundations are at least as convincing as those of the previous argument.

Public investment expenditure has a knock-on effect in terms of the efficient functioning of the private sector. This is particularly the case with expenditure on education, research and development, health and infrastructure. In the absence of a public agency responsible for this expenditure, the level of investment in the economy will be sub-optimal. Expenditure on public investment thus has a long-term effect in raising the economy's path of growth. It follows that the level of compulsory contributions is not of great significance, since higher public expenditure could equally well accelerate income growth in the private sector.

Moreover, in a liberal democracy, public expenditure is a decisive element in the social contract, largely biased as it is towards projects which promote justice and equal opportunity: education, health, transport.

Finally, the redistribution of income through the medium of the fiscal and welfare system, provided it does not reach extreme levels, increases the degree of social cohesion, while modern labour market theories show that it favours productivity and hence competitiveness: wage levels that are too low give little incentive to those with lower skills and discourage firms from investing in in-house training. Turnover of manpower is very high when wage levels are too low, wage earners having little interest in establishing a long-lasting relationship with the firm or in showing themselves prepared to put their hearts into their work. Similarly, firms have little incentive to train a workforce, which by definition will not spend long with the firm, since they will not see the results of what they have invested in training. The theory of an efficiency wage shows that there is a margin of increase in wages which at the same time boosts competitiveness, because the increase in productivity outstrips that of wages, and that in itself cuts wage costs. In short, social cohesion is also an investment with which bonuses for employment and living standards are linked.

The empirical bases of this conception derive from the analysis of economic 'miracles'. It happens that those among developed countries which have suffered least from problems of unemployment and poverty are Germany and Japan, the ones in fact where the wage spread is most compact and where real interest rates have increased least.

Among newly industrialized countries, those where growth has been highest are at the same time those where the degree of inequality in income distribution has dropped fastest. Hong Kong, Singapore and Taiwan, among several other countries with remarkable performances, have all deliberately set out to reinforce social cohesion and spread the effects of growth. As is noted in a recent World Bank report, these countries have pointedly set up institutions and a body of regulation, the better to combine 'the advantages of competition and those of cooperation both between firms and between administration and private sector'. Hence each of these countries has devised explicit mechanisms to give credibility to its purpose of making the fruits of future growth benefit the entire population equally. Among developing countries there appears to be an inverse correlation between inequalities of income and growth, that is, a direct correlation between social cohesion and economic performance.

Conclusion

We live in a capitalist system today certainly; but it has little in common with that of the 1930s. It is a system that in fact derives from two organizational principles. There is the market governed by property values, where the acquisition of assets is proportionate to individual resources; and there is democracy governed by universal suffrage. The tension between the two is dynamic because it enables the system to adapt instead of breaking up, as systems governed by a single organizational principle (such as the Soviet one) generally do. The rise in unemployment and poverty at present, which appears to me to proceed from over-dogmatic application of neo-liberal principles (where once socialism constituted the risk, what is the risk now) creates an imbalance in this tension and could make us relive history in reverse.

A solution to the most serious problem that democracy has had to face in peacetime – mass unemployment – does not seem to me to be found in an attitude of resignation in the face of the formidable growth of inequality and the dismantling of our social security systems. On the contrary, it lies in greater cohesion, not merely on moral grounds but on grounds of efficiency. Anyhow I have tried to show that social justice ought not to be a secondary preoccupation, a manner of healing injuries that are accepted as the price of efficiency, but that it is the very condition of that efficiency.

9

A CHECK TO ENLIGHTENED CAPITALISM

Philippe d'Iribarne

Even in those countries most attached to a narrow conception of free enterprise and the market economy, institutions and attitudes temper their ascendancy. Experience of the damage done in the name of laissez-faire, which marked the nineteenth century, everywhere prompted various forms of socialization of the economy with the aim of removing innumerable aspects of its functioning in a strictly market perspective (Polanyi, 1983). So it is that whatever major capitalist economy one cares to take, with neither labour, nor housing, nor health, nor agricultural produce does a truly free market operate. And each country, in keeping with its particular social and political traditions, has devised specific ways of overseeing the market through the agency of government, corporate bodies or independent institutions, as the case may be. Yet today, possibly under the heady effect of the clear superiority shown by free economies over their socialist counterparts, together with the momentum of deregulation and the increasing globalization of competition, capitalist countries are again subscribing to a hard-line concept of the market; while the member countries of the European Union, under the vigilant eye of a Commission anxious to remove all restraints of trade, may well be at the forefront of this trend as active rather than passive participants. It is time to examine what this experience can teach us.

Economies embedded in systems which are national in their institutionalization and outlook

In real economies relations between economic actors (both within and between firms) are a long way from consistently observing the canonical form of exchange between strangers that constitutes the basic transaction of a free market. There is a host of relations based on trust and loyalty between firms and their personnel, between principals and subcontractors, between groups of firms pursuing common objectives, such as that of producing a quality labour force, between firms and banks. In some respects, of course, these relations impede economic efficiency, by interfering with the process of Darwinian selection which is the endpoint of out-and-out competition. But at the same time they occupy a very positive role in the way in which economies function. In addition to imposing bounds to the harshness meted out to the weak, they are sources of efficiency. They are essential if forecasts are to be dependable in enabling economic actors to make long-term plans. They enable 'transaction costs' to be limited, costs that economic theory is coming to discover after neglecting them for too long (Williamson, 1985). But for them it would be difficult to advance beyond the adventurer capitalism which Max Weber clearly showed to be quite different in nature from our industrial capitalism.

The establishment of these relations in a given context is linked to the manner in which each society allows its members to live one with another. Political requirements play a part – an appreciation of the balance of powers, of ways and means of limiting the domination of the strong over the weak and of resolving conflict. The emphasis given to market regulation is itself political in expression; one only needs to look at the manner in which firms and the American economy function. Within European societies, though all are marked by a 'modern' view of the social and political bond, one finds in practice widely contrasting notions as to how this bond, and therefore the overall economy, should be organized. This appears very clearly when one considers the case of France – and might well appear in considering Germany, Spain, Belgium and so on.

Anglo-Saxon faith in free competition as a cultural product

The merits of free competition in its undiluted version (which rules out consensual agreements, restraints of international trade and any sort of industrial policy) are in general discussed from the perspective of economic theory. Thus it is, at the same time appealing to the interests of the consumer, that the *Economist*, for instance, week in week out inveighs against anything which departs from strict competitive orthodoxy and against those who advocate a modicum of management of the economy. But in fact attachment to free competition is not first and foremost a question of economic efficiency but of political culture, one might say political faith.

In Anglo-Saxon political culture, the contract freely concluded for a strictly defined purpose is the very mark of the relationship between free individuals. It contrasts with submission to the arbitrary will of a master to whom one is entirely subservient (John Locke, 1690). The same fear attaches to the arbitrary nature of government.

This political culture characterizes the way in which both the American economy and industry function, informing institutions and mentality alike.

US legislation in regard to the economy (anti-trust and labour laws or legislation on stock exchange dealing) has the task of 'levelling the playing field', that is, of ensuring that no one will be advantaged or disadvantaged in negotiations undertaken between free individuals. In this perspective, an industrial policy is an offence insofar as it is conducive to government determining the winners and losers when interests are in play. Similarly, anything that 'distorts' competition, putting some into positions of strength, is to be condemned on ethical grounds.

The influence of American political culture is apparent within the firm itself (d'Iribarne, 1989), with the reference to a contractual relationship between equal citizens and the passionate refusal of any form of dependency on the arbitrariness, however benevolent, of a master. There too the pervading culture requires each citizen to remain autonomous and fully responsible for his actions, without interference from outside, within the limits set by respect for the contracts to which he abides.

Such a conception requires each to be judged on what he or she is personally answerable for, in line with criteria that are perfectly clear and known in advance and relying on proven facts. Here lie the basic conditions of fairness in the lot that falls to each and everyone. Such clarity and precision is, in the opinion of Americans, necessary protection against unacceptable arbitrariness. Moreover, a contractual relationship, with a specific purpose in mind, between customer as superior and supplier as subordinate, sets as great a limit as possible on any continuance of loyalty and provides the appropriate means of reconciling the subordinate role at work and the equality that pertains between citizens.

In accordance with this political ideal, the 'classical' mode of organization in the USA insists on a strict demarcation of tasks and responsibilities (between 'designer' and 'executant' as between services). Furthermore, it is based upon relatively short-term contractual relations, both within firms and in subcontracting, where centrality is given to the accountability of each party. Last, it assumes a financial market that operates in favour of short-term results.

That these notions are politically entrenched is clear too from the fact that they produce resistance to the implementation of methods of organization that are economically efficient. So much has been clear from the difficulties met in transferring Japanese methods of organization, built upon loyalty between favoured partners, to the USA, in areas where their greater effectiveness is nonetheless recognized. By way of example, one could cite the conclusions of the MIT survey of the worldwide motor industry in regard to the relationship between manufacturers and their suppliers – conclusions which are the more significant in that the survey is concerned to show that Japanese methods can be adopted whatever the context (Womack et al., 1990).

The types of relationship that pertain between car manufacturers and their subcontractors are characteristically different in Japan and the USA. In the USA, traditionally and in keeping with a strict market rationale, they are based on short-term contracts between independent firms which in relation to each other are jealously secretive about production methods, costs, etc.; whereas in the Japanese production model, the client-firm and the supplier to a large extent share information on internal operation, problems, production costs, etc. (Womack et al., 1990: 39). That implies the setting up of long-term partnerships, with the effect that suppliers are spared the risk of finding themselves ditched whenever a competitor comes up with a more tempting offer. The MIT survey shows that the method based on cooperation is more efficient than the traditional market-based one applied in the USA.

Does this mean that American firms are turning to the more efficient method? Realizing their appetite for new management techniques, one could well expect this to be the case. Not so in fact, as the authors of the survey testify; and they show that relations between manufacturers and suppliers in the USA are as distant as they have always been (Womack et al., 1990: 161).

There is not merely inertia but active resistance towards the adoption of new practices. The form of relationship between manufacturers and sub-contractors which is the rule in Japan is distasteful to Americans. Most suppliers hold strongly that 'what goes on in my factory is my business' (Womack et al., 1990: 144).

In fact, for all that, one is bound to choose one's suppliers, keep with some and discard others. Once the criteria are abandoned of instant price as to a precise offer at a given moment, others have to be found. 'We will stick with any supplier as long as we think they are making serious efforts to improve', in the words of one manufacturer's buyer. 'Only when we think they've given up that do we bring the relationship to an end' (Womack et al., 1990: 155); thanks to which, the authors declare, the suppliers 'can get on with the job of improving their own operations in the knowledge that they will be rewarded for having done so' (ibid., p. 168). But this type of relationship sits ill with American political culture.

When a supplier puts his faith in the fact that a manufacturer 'thinks' that he has done his best to improve, with the supposition unsupported by a battery of objective criteria defined in advance and susceptible to unquestionable – or at least no more than slightly questionable – appraisal, he accepts that he is prey to the arbitrariness of the manufacturer. In some degree he forgoes his status as citizen. When he is confident of being suitably rewarded for his labour by forsaking his right to obtain such reward on the basis of closely conducted negotiation, he thereby acknowledges a state of dependency.

It may be added that this type of relationship between clients and suppliers has repercussions on the way firms function internally. Here too there is a degree of incompatibility with American political philosophy. Let us return once again to the case of the buyer for the car manufacturer, who decides whether or not to maintain his firm's connection with a supplier on the basis of his 'thinking' that the supplier has or has not done his 'best' to improve. By what criteria does he 'think' that this 'best' has or has not been forthcoming? Is he not likely to have to resort to a somewhat intuitive, subjective view, and to factors too subtle to be conveyed by indicators that are clearly defined in advance (Ouchi, 1982). How will the buyer be able to justify his decisions to his own firm, especially if things fail to turn out as planned? More generally, how can the manner in which he explains himself to his superiors and is judged by them conform to the American conception, when the indisputable elements of reference tend to be missing?

Moreover, the limits to correspondence between market rule and efficiency are clearly shown by the fact that in the USA relations based on loyalty, hence alien to a contractual rationale, are widely resorted to, promising an effectiveness that is beyond that rationale to achieve. This has been well displayed in analysing the way that so-called 'high culture' firms function, where a major role is given to relations based on trust and loyalty between the firm and its personnel (Peters and Waterman, 1982). At IBM, a model for this category of firm, the 1940 song book produced: 'We know you and we love you, and we know you have our welfare in your heart', 'you' designating the 'senior Watson'. If times have changed, much effort still goes into ensuring that firms take the family as their role model.

The case of France

Given that France considers itself to be a society of citizens and takes as its model the social contract, one might expect to find allusions to the social and political bond and to economic organization of a type not unlike those that characterize American society. In fact the differences are very marked.

The French are attached to the concept of the general will. They have chosen to be ruled by a government whose direction they accept on condition that it is the emanation of their sovereignty as citizens and not the prerogative of a master. They place their trust in this government to be the guardian of the common interest and the arbitrator between individual interests. In economic affairs they require of government not only that it 'levels the playing field' where these separate interests are in confrontation, but they count on its active intervention in the choices made by entrepreneurs.

At the same time, the French do not have the same faith as the Anglo-Saxons in the virtues of the invisible hand of free competition and are less inclined to see it as an indispensable condition of fairness. They remain attached to professional bodies whom they expect to show active concern for the general interest, while protecting the common interests of their members. If 'deals' are officially frowned upon in France, it is scarcely considered 'normal' that they should incur prosecution so long as they do not lead to 'abuse'. There is a greater readiness than in Anglo-Saxon countries to accept strictly economic arguments in favour of imposing certain limits on competition – concern for the long term, recognition of the fact that consumers are also producers, and so on. In many areas greater reliance is placed on public services, as upholders of the general interest, than on competition between independent firms, for the provision of a quality service in economically satisfactory conditions.

Similarly, the way French firms are run brings into play a different conception of the social bond than in the USA. The French have of course developed a theoretical view of the firm as contract based. Labour and commercial legislation are founded on a similar view. The practical results, however, remain limited. Members of each professional group, in fact, stubbornly defend their customary privileges. They go to some lengths to show that they are in no one's 'service', that they are master in their 'domain'. But once the dignity of their state is respected and nothing is asked of them that might be deemed dishonourable, they are prepared to accept forms of loyalty, towards firm and superiors, that would be unthinkable under the contractual ideal. From this standpoint, they will be judged on the manner in which they have performed the duties of their state, duties established largely by custom not by their bosses, rather than, as in the USA, on the extent to which they have attained their precise objectives as defined by the contract (d'Iribarne, 1989).

The question of the relations between chiefs and subordinates has an especially significant place in French society. The refusal – frequently expressed, though less than in the past – of 'class collaboration' or of 'integration into the firm' conveys a highly developed sensibility in this respect. But while they passionately desire to be treated with dignity and respect, the French on the whole would like this to be so without their being afforded the protection of contract.

French society is inclined to make a radical distinction between two types of personal loyalty that bind an individual to his firm and to those who exercise authority there. One corresponds to integration into a kind of 'domestic' community, gathering servants around a master; the other to integration into a kind of 'feudal' community, gathering vassals around a suzerain. The firm to which the French aspire corresponds in the main, now as in the past, to a form a community where each, whatever his rank, has escaped the indignity of servant and acceded to the prerogative of vassal. Both suzerain and vassal possessed the full dignity attaching to the freeman. Far from being the mere creature of the suzerain, the vassal was someone in this own right, with his own privileges and his own honour, which the suzerain was duty bound to respect. It is true that the French Revolution brought about the destruction of the political and social order which characterized the *ancien régime*. But the effect was largely to replace an aristocracy of blood by an aristocracy of talent – see Article VI of the Declaration of the Rights of Man. Around this new aristocracy, distinguished from the common herd by the eminence of its 'intellectual nobility', it recreated a type of social relationship that to a great extent reproduces that which formerly prevailed.

In the Middle Ages this relationship became the model par excellence of relations between freemen in France, but its impact in Europe was far from uniform (Bloch, 1968). In this respect the contrasts between European countries already foreshadow what is distinctive in the organization of their firms and their economies. The Anglo-Saxon world was already, even in its feudal relations, much closer to a contractual model, allowing a vassal to leave his lord at any moment, provided he had fulfilled his obligations. In the Germanic world, the image of the community of freemen maintaining relations as peers provided the main reference.

The limitations of the model in terms of efficiency have frequently been stressed. The French frequently deplore the fact and, depending on the time and the circumstances, would like to become American or Japanese or German. The limitations are unquestionable. Pride in the corps is the cause of countless quarrels over demarcation or precedence, engendering problems of cooperation in the line and, doubtless even more, between services with different missions. Even so, the efficiency it generates should not be underestimated. Pride in the corps goes along with a degree of commitment to work which transcends what may be explicitly laid down in the instructions of superiors. Such commitment is particularly efficacious in situations where the existence of uncertainty does not allow one to determine in advance what needs to be done (for example, the record of French firms in public works). Furthermore, the part played in the economy by a government which, unlike many others, can rely on an administration that is competent, enterprising and devoted to its mission is also in certain areas (for example, telecommunications or armaments) a source of economic success.

The destabilizing effect of the growing preponderance of the market

These types of organization of firms and economies, diverging as they do in a great many respects from exclusively market relations, are now destabilized. The opening up of frontiers, the resulting intensification of competition, the question mark over public services and the monopoly position they enjoy, the renewed drive against 'deals', the privatization of firms in the public sector, the extolling of the profit motive – the sum effect of all this is driving every system towards adopting the theoretical pattern of a market economy. It is expected that unproductive activities will be dispensed with and greater pressure put on firms to modernize and increase productivity. Indeed several factors incline one to think that the objective has to a large extent been attained. More or less everywhere firms are shedding employees in large numbers. In some sectors (for example, air transport in the USA) many firms considered to be inefficient have been ruthlessly eliminated. Even Japanese retail trade, a model of low productivity, is undergoing rationalization and, from the consumer's point of view, is leading to spectacular price reductions in some sectors. But there are also disturbing elements. At the very least one may question the long-term effects of what is taking place, and one may wonder whether there is not a threat to the social and ethical foundations of economic efficiency, when the existence of relations between economic actors is seen as inconsistent with the rationale of the market.

The social aspects

It has long seemed self-evident that economic progress provides the basis for all genuine social advancement. It is true that the development of Western economies in the period following World War II was clearly marked by the close interdependence of spectacular economic growth and the initiation of a range of social policies, affording both protection against the misfortunes and hazards of life, such as sickness, old age and unemployment, and, by way of investment in education and infrastructure, a foundation for sustaining growth. In this perspective, the loss of traditional forms of solidarity and loyalty towards a firm or supplier, which involved a degree of market distortion, is unarguably a benefit, representing a factor of both social and economic progress. Although some may see a temporary decline in their situation with the disappearance of certain activities, clearly appropriate social policies are always able to administer the corrective needed for the general situation to show improvement in the end.

But this kind of approach to the problem seems to accord less and less with what is now happening. The distinctive features of the postwar period were largely instrumental in making progress relatively painless. For all that the modernizers clamoured for unfettered competition and the rejection of outmoded practices, in the main these practices endured. Many firms which in fact remained shielded from too severe competition (a contrast in itself with the current situation) continued to operate with outdated installations, overmanned head offices and auxiliary services (canteens, grounds maintenance, etc.) of dubious efficiency. Added to which, in many instances personnel management was highly paternalistic, prepared always to keep on old retainers or those who for one reason or another were in difficulties, even if their contribution to productive efficiency was uncertain. And those concerned fitted in quite naturally where little was expected of them. Similarly, recruitment of young people did not always show concern for immediate returns. Doubtless the picture varied from one country to another, but even where the market ethos was most marked, paternalism was rife.

It should be added, as a further contextual element, that in a country like France where the major upheaval in the productive apparatus involved a contraction of the agricultural sector and the spread of mass production methods, the transition was made easier. Those who left the land were able virtually to move across into expanding industries where manpower was in demand; while those for whom such redeployment presented a problem could carry on doing odd jobs in obsolete concerns or in the obsolete remnants of concerns that had modernized.

But the context is no longer the same. Gradually as the intensification of competition has become a reality, firms have changed their attitudes to human resource management and the process of change continues. With accounts in the red, or threatening to become so, it has been increasingly a case of rooting out what management gurus have termed the 'phantom factory': all the types of activity which give people employment but contribute little to the sum of production. Clearly, by applying pressure to increase productivity, the escalation of competition has achieved what was intended by the modernizers, but it has cost, or at least threatened, the low-return occupations linked with these phantom activities.

In fact it has had an effect on jobs at all levels. It is frequently observed that global competition endangers jobs that compete directly with their counterparts in low-waged economies. As often as not this is followed up with the comment that the consequences are minimal since the bulk of our trade is carried on with other developed countries. But the questioning of traditional methods of human resource management under the impact of an increase in the pressure of competition affects more than low-paid jobs and unskilled workers. It affects anyone, whatever his or her qualification (highly qualified engineers even), who presents their employers at any specific moment with an unfavourable ratio between quality and price. All it requires to be under threat is that one's productive contribution appears not to match the remuneration that one is legally entitled to and which appears appropriate for the job (d'Iribarne, 1990).

Moreover, and here too the context has altered, social problems brought about by current amendments to the productive apparatus are of an altogether different order to those that the postwar changes produced. For someone who had worked on the land to take an unskilled job in an electronics firm was one thing, but it was quite another for a shopfloor worker in the car industry to become a software programmer.

As a result of this transformation, social policies have appeared – and continue to appear – increasingly impotent to correct the negative effects of economic modernization spurred on by escalating competition.

This impotence is immediately discernible in the figures. Unemployment has soared, so that there is some uncertainty over the financing of unemployment benefits, pensions and early retirement. The capability of systems for the redistribution of income to aid the casualties of economic progress is becoming increasingly doubtful. When a significant number of those who lose their jobs through the pressures of competition, far from being redeployed in more productive occupations, find themselves unemployed or reluctantly removed from the working population, the strictly economic benefit manifestly ceases to be positive.

Moreover, and this is perhaps the main point, it is more than just a question of levels of income. There is no correspondence between a living wage and compensatory income. However generous the compensation they receive, the unemployed feel excluded. Most of those on income support (RMI) consider their situation demeaning, so much so that there are many who decline to take up their entitlement (Paugam, 1993). Conversely, many obsolete forms of activity, in industry in particular, which stand condemned by increased competition and the resultant drive for efficiency, underlay whole communities. These occupations and their interrelationships brought a strong sense of identity to those who formed part of them and gave their lives a meaning. When all this is destroyed in the name of 'progress', without other activities of equal social potential taking their place, social policies can offer no substitute.

Economic efficiency in question

Setting up an effective productive apparatus involves two quite distinct processes. First – and this is stressed by the proponents of undiluted market rule – the elimination in conditions of ruthless competition of those who underachieve, insofar as it does away with the practice of making use of a sheltered position to vegetate and provides a constant incentive for improvement, is a factor of progress. But this is merely one aspect of the question. The methods that enable a productive apparatus taken as a whole to progress are not limited to a process of Darwinian selection. Wolfgang Streeck, for instance, elsewhere in this volume, draws attention to associations of producers in Germany whose members are held to respect standards that are at once technical and social. Associations of this type comprise agreements to withstand competitive pressure to lower prices and to uphold standards; hence they give rise to restraints of trade. But by the same token they 'prevent the pressures of a competitive market bringing about solutions based on low prices, low levels of quality, low skills and low wages'. The example of Japan makes it clear that this kind of resistance to market pressure is likely to encourage investment in human resources and product quality as well as in the productive process that will lead to long-term benefits.

However – and this may well be what the sum of studies comprising the present volume teaches us – the ongoing process of deregulation, wherever it has been observed, is remarked as being a threat to forms of regulation that are outside the market and at the source of such long-term benefits.

It is frequently thought that only French forms of economic regulation are at risk, with the place they give to major public services acting as monopolies, the call they make upon government that is traditionally interventionist and the limited role they assign to competition; and that the model students of the neo-liberal class, such as Britain or Germany, have always benefited. In fact, here too, the benefits are by no means obvious. The growth of opportunism, whereby each economic actor seeks to maximize his own interest rather than display loyalty to the overall interest of groups that are interdependent, can only be detrimental to overall efficiency.

Thus, the effects produced in Britain by Margaret Thatcher's market-driven policies led one of her advisers, with piquant historical irony, to recall Schumpeter's celebrated prophecy about the destruction of bourgeois values – in many respects the fount and source of economic efficiency – by capitalism (Graham, p. 128 of the present volume). Top executives take handsome pay rises even when firms are doing badly without apparent concern for the effect of their conduct on the quality of cooperation within the firm. Yet it is well known that poor cooperation weighs heavy on industrial performance in Britain and that Japanese firms there have had considerable success in improving performance, the self-restraint shown by their own top executives being not wholly unconnected with this. Neglect of educational and training provision for personnel is aggravated by having as its consequence that, in a world where the norm is to be out for oneself, the firm commands little loyalty. Training schemes are not considered to be cost effective and there is little cooperation between firms to develop them. In the final analysis, after a period of euphoria, the long-term consequences of the Thatcher administration on growth and employment are hardly felt to be positive.

Similarly, in Germany, some destabilization is discernible in practices which, though departing from a strict market rationale, boost economic efficiency in the long term (Streeck, p. 43 of this volume). Certainly, as compared with France, such practices are more often culture bound or connected with 'voluntary' associations (to which in effect it is socially obligatory or quasi-obligatory to belong) than promoted by government. This is particularly the case with the organization of the labour market (which is not truly a market) or the capital market (compare the role played by firms in provision for training and their relationship with banks). Such forms of regulation are thus better equipped than is the case in France to resist pressure from European institutions or international authorities to deregulate the economy. Nonetheless the threat to them is there; and anxieties surface as to how long the apprenticeship system can last if every firm, adopting strict market reasoning, starts to take a narrow view of its own interest.

The myth of progress

Such evidence as this to show that the rule of the market is not synonymous with economic efficiency and social progress is at hand all the time. Even so it is blithely ignored in pronouncements that form the basis of the policy that governs our economic organization. Why? Probably because to face certain facts in the official representation of the way our society functions would do grave damage to the myths which are its source.

The representations we ordinarily make use of place great emphasis on the contrast between modern and traditional, progress and decline, innovative and obsolete, expressed as it is in countless ways. Thus whatever confines human destiny to the inertia of the past, to habits that are routine bound and rigid, is to be condemned; whereas whatever provides a release from all that and builds expectations for the future is good and to be encouraged. Within this dichotomy, traditional situations of dependency are of their nature bad; individualism disencumbered from ties of any sort is of its nature good.

Grasping reality in all its complexity means abandoning the coherence of myth and confronting a state of affairs where progress takes different forms. It means allowing that a resourceful and determined construct for the future, by emancipated individuals, must in part embody the need to respect and protect the heritage transmitted by societies. Hence it involves relinquishing sacred dogmas.

Meanwhile, however, our problems remain and increase. It is time for us to 'get real'.

10

INTERNATIONAL FINANCE AND THE EROSION OF CAPITALIST DIVERSITY

Philip G. Cerny

In order for people to behave as 'efficient' capitalist economic actors, they must be able to exchange the surpluses they produce (or own) with a range of other specialist producers of commodities, owners of assets, or providers of services. Measuring the relative value of the things exchanged must be done through the price mechanism. An efficient financial system is, therefore, the essence of Adam Smith's 'invisible hand' – which in ideal conditions might theoretically permit the capitalist system to be both self-regulating and truly international. The actual history of capitalism, of course, has not been that of a genuinely self-regulating system, and the capitalist 'world system' has developed on a playing field composed of distinct nation-states characterized by diverse varieties of capitalism. The nineteenth-century attempt to move toward a global 'self-regulating' market failed in the face of social, political and economic instability and upheaval; in consequence, an expanding capitalist state took on the main burdens of regulating and stabilizing capitalist markets (Polanyi, 1944). As the twenty-first century approaches, however, that process is being reversed in a wave of finance-led marketization or commodification of the world economy. The very concept of the national economy – and the continued effectiveness of national capitalist diversity – has come into question (Reich, 1991).

The economic power of the modern national state derives essentially from its character as a multi-purpose institutional structure, integrating distinct tasks, roles, and activities in different functional issue areas under a single, territorially based umbrella. In theory, however, in a pure system of economic exchange, national states are by their very nature a distortion of the market mechanism. As markets expand, they subsume other social, political and economic relationships – what Marx called the process of 'commodification' – in a global market system. Rather than having a whole range of social, political and economic processes integrated in nationally unique ways, market processes find their own level. The world economy would not, therefore, be divided vertically into nation-states with separate national economies, but into different types of market-based activities spread horizontally across different 'virtual spaces'. National diversity would be replaced by diversity rooted in distinct types of economic activity (finance, different kinds of manufacturing, services, agriculture, etc.), rendering the territorial state less and less effective as a regulator and stabilizer of those activities.

Finance constitutes the central mechanism which links diverse market processes together in a single web through which the prices of all assets, goods and services are determined. Furthermore, financial markets are inherently the most spatially cross-cutting of all types of exchange. Finally, those diverse activities are once again being reintegrated at a global level – not, this time, through traditional political structures analogous to the state, but through the financial markets themselves. This not only erodes national capitalist diversity, but also raises questions about how global markets can be effectively regulated and stabilized in case of market failure.

The internationalization of finance

In the 1980s many states modified the system of regulating their financial markets, including banks and securities markets. There was an ideological backlash against government interventionism in general. There had already developed in the 1970s – on the left as well as the right – a widespread perception that the welfare state and Keynesian demand management had reached a plateau of effectiveness and were leading to a vicious circle of stagnation and inflation. Pressures from more complex and volatile international capital flows led to the increasing impossibility of insulating national economies at both macro-economic and micro-economic levels. Governments experimented with a variety of measures intended to improve their competitive advantage in a relatively open world – the 'competition state' (Cerny, 1997). The importance of finance to this process cannot be overemphasized (Cerny, 1993).

Global finance incarnates the fungibility of capital at its most abstract and far-reaching. States can no longer control their own domestic financial systems as they learned to do in the 1930s. Furthermore, financial globalization severely restricts wider economic policy, making it increasingly difficult for states to follow an autonomous path driven by domestic – democratic? – economic goals. Finally, tensions are growing between financial globalization and the requirements of production and trade. Even within the financial arena, the most abstract and 'dematerialized' financial markets, involving the pure trading of complex financial instruments, increasingly predominate. This may lead, as supply-side economists argue, to a renewed surge of stable growth in the world economy. Or it may lead to the emergence of a new embedded financial orthodoxy:

a system prone to unstable cycles of boom and slump, the use of blunt policy instruments such as interest rates to the exclusion of others, and the call for monetary stability above all else. The predominant climate is government austerity and private frenzy.

Since the first 'financial revolution' of the late eighteenth and early nineteenth centuries, government intervention in financial markets has been driven by the imperatives of the nation-state and the state-based international system. Governments have supported and guaranteed both domestic banking systems and, more sporadically, securities markets. These have been shaped by differences in endogenous state capacity, by the structural distinctiveness of particular national economies, and by their relative degree of vulnerability to transnational market forces. Two competing models of capitalism have emerged: open, market-driven systems; and closed, state or corporate-driven systems. The 'open' model was characterized by 'arm's-length' financial systems, combining active financial markets and a diversified banking system and providing relatively short-term credit. The 'closed' type was characterized by integration of industrial and financial decision-making through what Lenin called 'finance capital', that is, structured linkages between the state apparatus, banking and finance, and large-scale industry. In each major phase of capitalist development, however, the 'leading economy' has been of the open type (Maddison, 1982). Nevertheless, finance in both types of system was seen as a vital strategic industry, too important to be left to the market alone. After World War II, state support for an increasing flow of credit to the economy allowed governments to promote economic growth through diverse types of mixed economy at home and expanding trade abroad.

Against this background, the 'second financial revolution' of the 1980s and 1990s is challenging the very foundation of the relationship between the state and the financial system. A deep structural tension has emerged between the internationalization of finance and national financial regulation. The overwhelming response to this tension – financial 'deregulation' – has altered both the scope and the substance of economic intervention. Governments increasingly measure their performance according to criteria acceptable to the financial markets. They must be seen as 'strong' or 'sound' if they are to retain the confidence of the transnational financial community. Gross financial exchange transactions, estimated at $60–70 trillion a year in the mid-1980s, even then dwarfed exchanges of goods and services, which totalled around $4 trillion. Gross capital exchanges between the USA, Europe and Japan (excluding intra-European exchanges) grew at an average annual rate of 54 per cent per year between 1980 and 1986, while trade grew at an average of only 8 per cent per year over the same period. The amount has ballooned since then (Goldstein et al., 1993a, b); the world stock of 'derivatives' alone has recently been put at $25–30 trillion.

Although the major trends are still towards global integration, some markets are highly globalized, some still mainly national despite some transnational inroads, and others a more complex mixture. In currency and short-term capital markets, instruments are relatively simple, forward markets liquid, and information about the main price signal, interest rates, easy to obtain. New technological developments make complex arbitrage profitable with low transaction costs from minimal spreads, and price changes have an immediate impact across markets. Risk assessments are far more complex in bond markets, especially private sector primary markets, where interest rate levels and ratings provide more comparable international price signals than in secondary markets. It was the role of unregulated Euromarkets in this sector in the 1970s and 1980s which provided the main linkage between transnational capital flows, securitization, and the process of regulatory arbitrage (see below). Finally, although share markets are still relatively national, there is increasing globalization, especially in secondary markets, for portfolio diversification purposes.

State action has not merely reinforced but also initiated market restructuring. Although there are significant differences in the restructuring process from state to state, governments in all of the major financial powers have decompartmentalized their financial markets, promoted increased disintermediation and securitization, and supported or even forced the pace of financial innovation. Driving this transformation has been technological change in the financial services sector. This has led to a quantum jump in the sensitivity of prices of financial instruments across the world, drawing market actors big and small – and their capital – into the search for paper profits. These global changes have in turn driven the evolution of a range of structural developments both in the wider economy, national and international, and in the forms of the state apparatus engaged in financial market regulation and wider economic policy.

Cross-border price sensitivity is much easier to foster and expand in financial markets than in other markets because of the abstract character of finance itself. No physical goods need be produced or exchanged. At one level, genuinely price-sensitive financial markets attract holders of capital because of the ease and scope of participation compared to the slog and the longer term risks of actually making things. At another level, even those who wish to make things need capital and are forced to go to the financial markets to find it and are subject to the rules and the utilities of those who operate on them full time or who have a high level of financial market power or market share. The price sensitivity of the 'paperless world' of the global financial marketplace is increasingly controlling market – and political – decisions elsewhere.

In product terms, finance has become the exemplar of a flexible industry. Financial innovation has been rapid and far-reaching, affecting all parts of the financial services industry and shaping every other industrial sector. Furthermore, product innovation has been matched by process innovation. Management structures have evolved a long way from the traditional staid world of domestic banking. Traders and firms are expected to act like entrepreneurs (or intrapreneurs) as a matter of course. The ownership and transfer of shares and other financial instruments are increasingly recorded only on computer files, without the exchange of paper certificates. With the greater globalization of production and trade, market demand for financial services products is continually segmenting. Exchange rates and interest rates, essential to business decision-making as well as to public policy-making, are increasingly set in world markets. As the post-Fordist production structures of the third industrial revolution develop, they will be increasingly coordinated through the application of complex financial controls, rapidly evolving accounting techniques, and financial performance indicators (because non-financial performance measures are more and more complex and difficult to apply in a globalizing world).

An international 'ratchet effect' has been at work. Each deregulation has led to increased structural complexity and price sensitivity, making a return to tighter national-level regulation less possible. The same process can be seen in the 'securitization' and 'disintermediation' of finance, that is, the trend away from traditional bank loans and 'relationship banking' towards the selling of negotiable securities, from certificates of deposit to complex mixes of debt and equity. These instruments can later be traded in a secondary market, and the most attractive and efficient of such markets – the most liquid – are international. Price margins are finer and price sensitivity is growing across an elaborate range of securitized financial products. New, complex and often specially tailored instruments have been designed to find new marginal price niches. A notable example is the development of 'derivatives' markets – mainly futures and options – in which imaginary financial instruments are traded, ostensibly to hedge against loss in volatile markets. These are the most 'abstract' markets of all – they do not require the actual buying and selling of the 'underlying' securities – and are rapidly becoming the most globalized.

The essential mechanism of change in the area of financial regulation is regulatory arbitrage. Once the dykes have been breached of domestic regulatory compartmentalization and international capital controls in key sectors and the centrality of money and financial markets reasserted – as in the expansion of the Euromarkets and the breakdown of the Bretton Woods system – other market sectors seek to reduce existing regulatory barriers in their own areas in order to compete for business. Governments and regulatory agencies promote the health and profitability of their 'own' national financial systems and their 'own' domestic sectors. They seek to 'level the playing field' – to remove their clients' competitive disadvantages – and even to provide them with new competitive advantages vis-à-vis rival nations or sectors. Competition between states, and between different branches and agencies within states, interacts with structural changes at the international level to promote further deregulation.

The distinction between domestic and international levels now makes little difference to the markets themselves. The biggest institutions, often dealing with only the biggest non-financial firms, have the economies of

scale to be both flexible and profitable in a highly competitive international environment where profit margins are cut to the bone. Smaller
firms need to find niches in this global marketplace. Some believe that
globalization is not yet sufficiently comprehensive and inexorable to
prevent governments from taking back control, at least to the extent of
mitigating the worst dangers. The cooperation between finance ministers
of the developed world in keeping the financial markets liquid after the
October 1987 crash is often cited, as is the Basle Accord of 1988 (Kapstein,
1994). Governments are still sovereign, and may be able to use legal
restrictions to increase the 'friction' between different markets. But the
limits to such re-regulation – and thereby to any meaningful recuperation
of state autonomy – are growing daily.

Dilemmas of deregulation and re-regulation

Financial deregulation can be seen as a transfer of responsibility for the
allocation of financial resources to more efficient – financial – markets; or
it can be seen as an abdication of responsibility for managing the international financial system. The main political advantage of deregulation as
a policy option is that it can play both of these roles at the same time. It
can appear to be a non-policy; it involves, ostensibly at least, the simple
removal of regulations.[1] Unlike the multilateral decision-making processes embodied in the IMF or the GATT, the decision to deregulate can
be a unilateral one. Deregulation, then, is a policy option which is possible to pursue in an anarchical international system when there exists what
public choice theorists call an 'empty core' – the systematic lack of sufficient shared preferences for the emergence of a collectively agreed
outcome. It represents a non-cooperative equilibrium in policy terms. In
the financial arena, multilateral action is necessary to control financial
flows in an open world; otherwise abstract money would simply flow
around and through most national-level controls. Unilateral action, in contrast, has the effect of 'opening' the world financial system. A widening
circle of deregulation reflects an interactive series of unilateral actions by
states to deregulate first limited, but later more sweeping, classes of financial markets, institutions and transactions.

Deregulatory moves have included not only the end of Bretton Woods
and the move to floating exchange rates, but also the deregulation of
securities trading, the lifting of a range of exchange controls and interest
rate controls, deregulation of money markets, deregulation of savings and
loans in the US and building societies in the UK, and a variety of other
measures – especially those designed to attract foreign funds (e.g., increasingly footloose American funds) from the unregulated Euromarkets.
Together, these measures have had the effect of removing barriers between
distinct kinds of financial markets. This decompartmentalization has permitted banks, brokers and market-makers to engage in 'arbitrage' between

different financial markets at home and abroad in a wave of financial innovation in order to get the highest rate of return on their capital. Financial deregulation has promoted, reinforced and accelerated the integration of American and other financial markets into the transnational financial structure. US banks and financial markets (and those of other countries) are not merely 'interdependent' but structurally interlocking. Arbitrage between these markets can theoretically take place in a variety of different centres in a range of different countries, in effect on a 24-hour basis, if the players are determined and knowledgeable enough, and if they have the necessary resources to participate in the game.

In this context, the most effective form of re-regulation might be to evolve new multilateral mechanisms or to breathe new life into old ones (see Ruggie et al., 1992). This 'new multilateralism' in theory could be achieved in two distinct ways: either by developing more effective forms of intergovernmental cooperation or by establishing and/or reinforcing more autonomous transnational regimes. The problem is that international cooperation and transnational regimes are easy to prescribe, but hard to establish and to work effectively. Unless there is a cumulative and simultaneous mobilization of different states' perceptions of their shared national interests – in a fundamentally additive rather than hierarchical process – even well-established regimes are likely not only to lack clout but in practice to be rudderless and fragile.

Although international-level regulatory solutions may be potentially the most effective response to the problems of volatility, market failure, etc., in internationalized financial markets such solutions are not likely to be forthcoming to anything like the extent necessary to deal with the legacy of deregulation. The most important resulting agreement – the 1988 Basle Accord on bank capital adequacy ratios – represents only limited success. The success lies in the fact that an apparently workable intergovernmental agreement was reached on a significant aspect of prudential regulation, and that it is actually being implemented, despite setbacks. The limitations, however, are twofold. First, as we have already noted, capital adequacy is only one ingredient in effective prudential regulation, and indeed, some argue that agreement on ratios might become a substitute for wider regulation so preventing more effective action. Secondly, the adoption of strict capital adequacy standards may have perverse consequences, causing banks to retrench and reduce lending in order to bolster capital ratios. They were thought to have contributed in this way to the 'credit crunch' of the early 1990s. Finally, the process of adjustment to the new standards has been problematic and further multilateral steps are proving more difficult to achieve.

Future projects are likely to require special conditions to be successful. Four such conditions can be identified from a look at the Basle case. First, an effective international coalition must be formed in such a way that no major state can impose a blocking veto.[2] Second, the substance of any agreement must be limited enough in scope that it can be treated as a technical issue and dealt with by experts away from the political limelight; politicization might well prove to be an insuperable barrier, especially to effective implementation. Third, state actors charged with undertaking both the negotiation and the implementation of such an agreement need to have the legal and political autonomy and discretion to carry out these tasks without having to engage in turf battles or competitive politicking at a party or interest group level. The fourth and final condition is quite simply that the form of international regulation agreed upon must be effectively enforceable. The success of the Basle negotiations depended upon (a) the capacity of the Federal Reserve to take an effective lead role, (b) the deference with which the Fed was treated by American bureaucrats and politicians on this issue, and (c) the ability of national regulators to ensure compliance by the private sector (Kapstein, 1994). However, it may turn out to be the exception that proves the rule.

A second critical ramification of the level shift entailed by financial deregulation and internationalization is its impact on domestic political processes. This effectively involves 'whipsawing' the state between growing transnational financial constraints and a growing demand for political action to counteract the effect of those constraints. In liberal democratic political systems, politicians are expected to pursue policies which prevent financial crises and market failures. When crisis and market failure occur in political systems with widespread access for individuals and groups to a range of different governmental levels, demands for re-regulation at the domestic level will grow. Politicians must at least address the issue, and may attempt to seize the opportunity to propose domestic-level solutions. On the other hand, the state may be required by international constraints to pursue unpopular and damaging monetary policies in order to prop up exchange rates, or even to bail out speculators with taxpayers' money.[3] The contradiction between politicians' promises of national solutions and what governments actually can do will grow.

Conclusions

A country without efficient and profitable financial markets and institutions will suffer multiple disadvantages in a more open world. It will lose yet more investment and it will suffer worse real interest rates in the attempt to attract or keep foreign capital, thereby making it prone to recession. Its government will be limited in its general economic policy by the threat of capital flight, the long-term erosion of its tax base, and its inability to attract internationally dynamic firms and sectors to locate there. The kind of state financial control which enabled national capitalist diversity to flourish in the Long Boom is fast disappearing. In today's world, the global markets and big transnational institutions are 'where the money is', as nineteenth-century bank robber Willie Sutton said of banks. Furthermore, there is no government with the 'extraterritorial' power to control its allocation. These processes in turn lead to the whipsawing of states between market pressures and organizational levels which they cannot control.

National varieties of capitalism will be tolerated only so long as they do not undermine profits in international financial markets. If genuinely new forms of transnational regulation are not forthcoming from states acting in concert, then the transnational financial structure is increasingly likely to be run by a de facto private regime centred in the financial markets themselves (Filipovic, 1994), further eroding state authority. Polanyi's 'Great Transformation' is over, and a new Great Transformation will be required at a global, supranational level if values other than the establishment of a global self-regulating market are to be realized.

Notes

1   This is, of course, a contested view of what deregulation actually entails. For a critique of the notion that deregulation is a simple removal of regulations, see Cerny (1991).

2   Kapstein (1994) argues that the alliance between the Fed and the Bank of England was strong enough to impose its approach on a somewhat divided group of central bankers from other states.

3   As is well known, the cost to 'the American taxpayer' of bailing out failed savings and loan institutions alone has been estimated at $300–500 billion over several years. For a wider critique of the 'socialization' of finance, see Grant (1992).

11

THE FUTURE OF GLOBAL CAPITALISM; OR, WILL DIVERGENCE PERSIST FOREVER?

Susan Strange

As an international political economist, I am more interested in the pace and direction of change in the whole world market economy than in the pace and direction of change in particular parts of it contained within the rather arbitrary territorial borders of states. I therefore lack sympathy with the preoccupation of comparative political scientists and the 'new institutionalists' with questions such as those posed by the editors of this volume: which of the many diverse forms of capitalism are more likely to 'succeed' in competition with others and why; and what national institutional and other factors would affect the outcome of the competition between states for world market shares and, incidentally, for social cohesion and political stability as well as economic growth.

My approach is fundamentally different although I begin with the same question of the future of capitalist diversity. It is this. Given that the seeds of a capitalist mode of production grew to maturity in very different gardens, and evolved under the hand, as it were, of very different gardeners, within very different cultures and social structures and under the influence of very different state laws, constitutions and policies, would the forces of global structural change allow these differences to persist indefinitely? Or, alternatively, would the common logic of integrated world markets for more and more goods and services slowly but surely modify the old differences and bring national versions of capitalist production and exchange ever closer to a common pattern? My bet was, and is, on the latter. Crouch and Streeck seem to agree, but there still remains a gap between their approach and mine. As comparative sociologists, they are still looking within national societies for possible alternatives to government intervention to modify the social consequences of global economic integration.

As someone who started academic life teaching about international society, my focus is on the world system, on the world economy and world society. If national differences are disappearing, my concern is more with the social and economic consequences of their disappearance for the whole system, for its viability and for the changed mix of values within it. My bottom-line question is how much 'good governance' – in the partial absence of state power – can the system manage without; what transnational substitutes might be found for the nation-state? Some enquiry is necessary therefore to establish where authority over future outcomes might be found. If experience suggests it is unlikely to be found in inter-governmental organizations, then perhaps in trans-national enterprises or in transnational social movements, whether these are concerned with environmental protection, with human rights, with the relief of hunger or sickness or with the development of professional standards and autopœtic, or self-made, law for the settlement of inter-firm disputes.

As an international political economist, I am more interested in the webs of structural power operating throughout the world system than in com-parative analysis of discrete parts of it, bounded by territorial frontiers dividing states. It has always seemed to me that comparative social scien-tists are misnamed; they do not compare nearly as much as they contrast. This seems true whether they are economists, sociologists or political scientists. That is to say, their attention is mainly directed at the differences between states, or economies or societies than at their similarities. They are asking how states or societies differ, and why they differ. For example, the experts in the study of neo-corporatism, so far as I can see, have always spent their energies trying to explain why neo-corporatist practices in Austria, the Netherlands, Sweden or Japan differ from each other. They seldom bother to inquire into what seems to me the rather more impor-tant question – why is it that all these states adopted broadly similar system-sustaining policies and institutions at about the same point in their social, economic and political development?

Similarly, the question about why the capitalist mode of production and a market-based system of exchange for goods and services evolved at different times and in different places, suggests to me more fundamental questions about the necessary and sufficient conditions for it to emerge at all (Baechler, 1975; Hall, 1985; Mann, 1986; Cox, 1987). That is a prior ques-tion to the reasons for some divergence between versions of capitalism. I look therefore more to Weber and Schumpeter or more recently to Baech-ler and Hicks, and to economic historians such as Cipolla or Braudel, or even Polanyi, than to Albert, Katzenstein or Thurow, Zysman, Hart and company in the USA. Although *Modern Capitalism* was mainly concerned with the divergence between Italian and British, French and German forms of capitalism as they had developed in the postwar decade, Shon-field, I believe, was also interested in the common problems faced by their respective governments in a world of growing economic integration and interdependence. (Like the editors of this volume, he cherished a belief in the ability of a European Community of pooled sovereignties to resist the forces of structural economic change and to preserve the values of the European welfare state and social democracy.)

My quarrel with most comparativists is that they seem to me not to see the wood for the trees, to overlook the common problems while concentrating on the individual differences. It is as if an ecologist specializing in forestry spent his or her time describing and explaining the differences between oak trees, beech trees and birch trees – their shape, the form of their leaves, the look of the bark – to the point where the common characteristics of deciduous trees were taken for granted: the fact that all transpire moisture through the leaves; that all convert carbon dioxide to oxygen; that all shed their leaves in the autumn, first turning from green to yellow and russet, and then, in winter becoming 'bare ruined choirs where once the sweet birds sang'. Concentrating on the differences instead of the similarities immediately obscures the wider character of the wood: its ecological functions, as a habitat for wild animals, birds and insects; its effect on micro-climates; its role as provider of resources available for human political economy from fungi and nuts to timber; on the politically determined uses of the forest as a hiding place for outlaws; as a hunting preserve for the ruling classes, or as a recreational playground for town dwellers.

The editors in their introductory chapter do mention some of the major challenges to the concept of diversity in patterns of capitalism. The speed of technological change and the growth of global financial markets, they say, have produced a world economy in which a premium is placed for all capitalist economies on their speed of reaction, their adaptability to technical change and their capacity to relocate manufacturing or processing where costs are lower. But at this point they confuse the state with the firms located within its jurisdiction. The success of the economy does indeed depend heavily on quick responses, on adaptability and competitive costs. But these are attributes of corporate management, not of government officials or politicians. All these are merely the handmaidens of firms. The state becomes a kind of landlord for the enterprises inhabiting the national territory. It can be helpful or unhelpful to them. If the roof of law and civil order the landlord provides does not leak, and if the infrastructure provides cheap and dependable heat, light and water, and the drainage system does not clog up, the tenants can get on with adapting to change in the external environment. If the landlord fails in these matters, the tenants will fare badly or will leave for more congenial places.

The importance of agility in adapting to changing circumstances is a feature of the late twentieth century world economy that John Stopford and I had remarked on in *Rival States, Rival Firms* (1991). We tried to explain how and why it was that some national institutions were better able than others to help firms respond promptly and effectively to these new challenges. But we also tried to explain that the need to respond at all was due to structural changes in the whole world market economy. And that these changes were brought about by policy decisions and corporate strategies taken by those with structural power – as opposed to relational power. To understand change in the world economy, we needed to be able to identify those with the capability, in other words, to change the way in which the system operated, and the priority they gave to certain values over others – for example, the preference for free (or freer) markets over state planning, the substitution of capital for labour through automation in agriculture, in manufacturing, transport and services.

To overlook these common systemic trends, beginning with the accelerating rate of technological change but not ending there, is to bias analysis towards the factors leading to divergence and away from those leading towards convergence. It creates a limited concept of what constitutes politics and too narrow an understanding of power, and how it is used and by whom. It overlooks the seminal insight of young Stephen Hymer when he observed that enterprises engaging in international production were more often motivated by considerations of power, the importance of gaining and keeping control over products or processes or both, than by considerations of cost and profit, as neo-classical economic theory would have suggested.

Moreover, the new institutionalists, by concentrating on the formal and informal networks, through which firms operate within different national societies, were inevitably inclined to overlook the common systemic or transnational factors affecting political economic and social outcomes. To correct this comparative bias, it may be helpful briefly to suggest what these factors may be, and how they affect the conclusions to be drawn about the future of capitalism in a progressively integrated world market economy.

Common factors of global change

The first of these – and the least recognized by social scientists – is the acceleration in the rate of technological change. In combination with a coincidental change in the organic composition of capital – in plain language, the steady substitution of capital-intensive production for labour-intensive production – this accelerating secular change has meant that the profitability of many enterprises cannot be sustained on the basis of local or national markets alone. As machinery replaces workers, the combine harvester and the robots on car assembly lines are two obvious examples, the costs of capital invested in the business in relation to total operating costs rise, and the costs of labour and of raw materials fall. The enterprise must make sufficient profits to amortize these capital costs if it is to survive. But the accelerating rate and the rising costs of technological change do not allow it time to make sufficient profit if it depends only on the local market. Willy-nilly, it is obliged to seek new markets. And the most obvious way to find them is to look in other national economies than the home base of the enterprise. Hence, in brief, the internationalization of production occurs (Stopford and Strange, 1991).

First in the field in seeking world market shares were the big so-called multinationals. But they have been followed into these markets by many formerly 'national' firms, and by many smaller and middle-sized enterprises. They are no longer just American and European enterprises; multinationals today are as likely to be Japanese, Korean, Taiwanese, Indian or Hungarian. Concurrently, there has been a radical change in the attitude of host governments towards foreign firms. The basic explanation lies in what has been called the revolution in expectations in economically underdeveloped societies. To survive in power, governments in these societies have been obliged to find the means to raise living standards and rates of economic growth. This inevitably requires imports of capital goods which have somehow, sometime, to be paid for. Borrowing alone is not enough, nor secure. Foreign exchange also has to be earned by exporting. Hence the same dependence on world markets experienced by enterprises. The new symbiosis makes the developing countries recognize their need for the help of the foreign firms, while the firms have to recognize their dependence on new host states as gatekeepers to new national markets. Both have to revise old attitudes. The great attraction of the foreign firms, besides their control of technology, is the access they have already established to the rich markets of North America and Europe – and of Japanese firms to the Japanese market.

This is the broad picture in which, to an unprecedented degree, firms today have to 'think global; act local', while host governments have to exchange the access they can give to local markets for the access the firms can give to local production in foreign markets. Typically, they are allowed to sell locally if they produce locally, and in producing, train workers and managers, pay at least some taxes to the state, and even relocate research activities in the new host state.

But the relevant point for the capitalism versus capitalism debate is that this new symbiosis does not occur uniformly across sectors of product and services. There are some products and some services where local taste or habits make the local market less accessible to the transnational enterprise. There are others where consumers' preferences are much the same the world over. Think of Coca-Cola, TV sets, cameras, watches, microwave ovens, fax machines. There are capital or infrastructural goods – airport construction or hydroelectric dams – where local preferences are less important than transnational standards and needs. Technology, too, has not advanced at an even pace across products and services. There are some where world markets have been closed to exports until refrigeration and rapid air transport opened new opportunities. Flowers are a good example. Countries such as Kenya and Colombia now have access not only to the technology for mass commercial production of flowers and pot plants, but also to the means of supplying them direct to American and European markets. The development of iceberg lettuce in the USA similarly opened up foreign markets hitherto closed both by the perishable quality of most lettuces and by the low cost of local salad crops. Most consumer products, durable and non-durable, can now be sold on multiple national markets. Some brand names have had this access for decades; for others, the structural changes have quite recently incorporated local markets into the world market. Beer is such a product. Until about the 1970s, the beer for sale in most countries was locally produced by local breweries. Now, the big American, German, Danish and Irish brewing enterprises market their products worldwide. Even Chinese or Mexican beer has an export market.

The big preserve of local enterprise is still in some, but not all, service sectors. Local producers command the market in life insurance, while reinsurance is dominated by a small number of large, established transnational enterprises such as Swiss Re or Munich Re. Hairdressers (with the exception of a few 'designer' enterprises) operate free of international competition, although many of the products they use are sold on a world market. Drycleaning, too, is localized, while hotel management, thanks to franchising, is rapidly becoming a competitive world market. Lawyers and accountants compete locally, although both are having to concede growing market shares to big transnational firms or partnerships that have established a worldwide reputation. Retail banking, similarly, is still predominantly national, although increasingly ownership of local retail banks may be shared with foreign banks. The more specialized financial services such as bond marketing, securitization of corporate assets and transnational share dealing are apt to be taken over by transnationals.

What this adds up to is that the divergence in the operation of capitalist forms of production in services as well as manufactures, and in processed primary products as well as 'raw' materials, is apt to be greater across sectors of the economy than across national frontiers. The widespread failure to recognize this truth is just an indication of the extent to which social science has been 'colonized' by the concept of the state not only as the major actor, but also as the principal differentiating factor in the material life of men and women.

Since the technological changes and the new mobility both of capital and of knowledge have been substituting world markets for local markets at such a rapid pace in recent decades, while national institutions affecting competing enterprises have changed relatively little, it is arguable that the largely static forces of divergence between modern capitalism have been overwhelmed by the largely dynamic forces of convergence derived from structural changes in the world economy. Compared with differences between national laws and institutions, the differences may be much greater between largely oligopolistic sectors – oil, steel, aluminium, aircraft, for example – and highly competitive ones like textiles or cars. Even in the competitive sectors, there are differences between sectors where barriers to entry set by the minimum costs of capital investment are low (textiles), and where they are high (cars, aircraft or newspapers). To overlook these sectoral differences is a natural consequence when political scientists or sociologists pay more attention to the nature of states as the major independent variable than they do to the nature of markets.

There are three further reasons for thinking that the approach of most comparativists greatly overstates the role of national institutions and national policies. One is the general decline in the ability of governments to manage their national economies as they might like. As Crouch and Streeck concede, this 'dirty secret' of the impotence of government results in much empty rhetoric and a good deal of symbolic politics. While the decline in autonomy has not been even, it has been universally experienced to greater or lesser degrees even by the USA. Second is the growth in transnational regulation of capitalist behaviour, by means of which national regulation is steadily supplanted and national differences eroded. Third is what could be described as the de-nationalization of firms, the loss of identity between the location of the firm's headquarters and its behaviour in the world economy. Each of these deserves a word or two of explanation.

First, it is worth recalling that from the earliest days of the industrial revolution the responsibility of government for the wealth of the nation was unquestioned. Debate only centred on the necessary and sufficient conditions for that responsibility to be discharged, and also on the best means for carrying it out. Liberals took the minimalist view – but one that acknowledged responsibility for the defence of the realm, the value of the national currency, the collection of revenue and the administration of clear legal rules regarding property rights and the execution of contracts, whether to buy and sell or to lend and borrow. Socialists took a more maximalist view, holding that the injustices of a capitalist economy, and its inherent tendency to excessive booms and slumps, required the state to own the means of production and much more closely to oversee, if not directly manage, economic transactions of all kinds. The Keynesian compromise suggested that within each national economy it was possible to reap the advantages of both the capitalist system's productivity and the socialist system's regard for social stability and equity. Progressive taxation, the welfare state, neo-corporatist resolution of partisan conflicts of interest – these were the means by which society could have its cake and eat it.

The clearest demonstration that this happy solution was no longer possible came when President Mitterrand of France was forced by international financial markets into a political U-turn in the early 1980s. Once exchange controls had gone, once financial markets were globally integrated so that markets not governments determined the exchange rates of national currencies, the game was up. National Keynesian demand management would lead only to a vicious circle of capital flight, foreign debt and de-valuation. (James Callaghan had experienced the same rude awakening in the mid-1970s, but the lesson for Britain was obscured by the special international role, and vulnerability, of the pound sterling and by intervention of the International Monetary Fund.)

The substitution of inflation for deflation and unemployment as the public enemy number one for national policy-makers is an almost universal phenomenon of the last decade. It is in itself an acknowledgement of the vulnerability of state policies to world market forces. For inflation, more than deflation, exposes national government to the debilitating effects of a declining currency, capital flight, and a loss of competitiveness.

The extent of this vulnerability is still imperfectly understood. When the Bundesbank in the 1990s put its interest rates up or down, it always insisted that its decisions were made for the good of the German economy – usually to check domestic inflation, but occasionally, as in 1995, to encourage investment and growth. Market operators, watching with bated breath, knew that the decision to cut rates, for instance, was forced on Germany by the foreign exchange markets. When the markets decided that President Clinton was weak, indecisive and ineffectual, the dollar fell – and the mark and yen consequently rose – to the dismay of German and Japanese export industries.

For more than a decade, American academics have been looking for other explanations for the vulnerability of state policies to market forces. Upset and anxious about the declining competence of the US government in economic management, they looked everywhere but the international financial structure for the answer: it was the result of military overstretch during the Cold War; it was the result of Japanese competition – by implication, unfair competition; it was the price paid by the systemic hegemon for discharging its extra-national responsibilities and for short-sightedly allowing its firms to relocate off-shore.

Moreover, the very sources of US hegemonic power – its unrivalled military capabilities, its capacity through the acceptability of the dollar to borrow abroad but in its own currency, its guardianship of the world's largest single, rich market – have insulated it from the degrees of vulnerability experienced by others. Its public fiscal deficits could be financed by recourse to the international financial markets, if not indefinitely, at least for longer than was possible to other developed countries, let alone poorer ones.

That same combination of American structural power – military, financial and commercial – underlies the second reason why an institutional approach seems to me inadequate for the understanding of modern capitalism. There is a growing asymmetry of regulatory power among the governments of capitalist countries. The government of the USA exercises a global reach over enterprises and markets in other countries. It is a global reach unmatched by any other government. Some have more power than others to block or frustrate this influence by insisting on administering national rules, even if this makes them appear eccentric. Japan is the extreme case of such eccentricity, but even Japan finally agreed to conform to the Anglo-American rule agreed by the G7 that all banks should maintain a capital : assets ratio of 1 : 8. American global reach over the world market economy can also be seen in such matters as food and drug regulation, car emission standards and other environmental issues, classification systems for libraries and, more important, accounting and transparency standards for private and public companies. (To be listed on the New York stock exchange, Daimler-Benz recently had to revise radically the amount of information it made public about its business.) This asymmetric regulatory power can also have negative effects; if the US government decides that there is no need to regulate a market or business practice, it is very hard for others to do so. An example here is the fast-expanding but so far unregulated e-mail network linking personal and institutional computer systems by telephone lines.

The third reason for questioning the validity of the institutional approach is that it appears too limited to recognize a growing feature of modern capitalism, which is the widening gulf between national government and transnational business. This is de-nationalizing the firm. Some authors deny this by pointing to the fact that boards of directors even of major transnational enterprises only rarely include non-nationals. Corporate strategy is decided at (national) headquarters no matter how many other countries the firm operates in. Research and development is kept at home – although the fact is that this is rapidly changing thanks to pressure from host governments and the new possibilities of easy communication between scattered research centres. But the real point is that while firms may continue to appear and are recognized as American, British, German or Japanese, their behaviour is becoming, of necessity, much more responsive to multiple governments and not just to the government of their country of origin. If the institutional framework in which the enterprise operates is no longer that of one country but of several, it is inevitable that a process of homogenization is at work. As the firm becomes multinational in behaviour, if not in outward appearance, capitalisms are set to converge more than to diverge. The process can only be hastened by the growing practice of joint ventures and strategic alliances between two or more enterprises of different formal nationality.

There is a fourth structural change that may in the long run be more important for the future of the whole capitalist system than any of the other three. It is the growing tendency of governments to finance their spending with borrowed money rather than with tax revenues. Recall that in the 1970s many governments, and their regional or local authorities, borrowed heavily on the Euromarkets and from foreign banks. Some of them lived to regret their imprudence when, in the 1980s and as a result of American structural power in international finance, interest rates rose sharply and the big international banks refused to roll over loans or make new ones. By the 1990s, the preference of many governments switched to financing spending by issuing bonds – as governments used to do in the nineteenth century. The Bank of England in 1994, for example, floated a new issue of 16-year bonds at 6.5 per cent – a price which, if the 17.5 per cent discount offered to bondholders is included works out at about 8.5 per cent a year. British inflation rates being low, this was cheaper than the price that some other governments were obliged by the markets to pay. In Canada the 10-year bond yield was 9.2 per cent and in Australia 9.6 per cent even though their 1994 rate of inflation was zero or below 1.5 per cent respectively. By 1992, Japan's government shortfall between tax revenues and spending reached 45 per cent of GNP. By 1991, the US federal deficit amounted to 54 per cent of national GNP, and has for many years now been financed by the issue of government debt. But although the US deficit was larger in dollar terms than all others, as a proportion of national GNP it was exceeded by that of Belgium, for instance, or Denmark. The trend is so pervasive that even Taiwan, second only to Japan as the holder of the world's largest reserves of gold and foreign exchange, recently resorted to borrowing for current government expenditure in a big way. In 1991–3, it issued bonds worth over $22 billion – five times the government bond issues in 1990. One-quarter of all government spending is financed by borrowing. The proportion in relation to GNP has doubled since 1990 and may rise to 36 per cent of GNP by the end of the century, or as much as 40 per cent if government spending rises at 3 per cent a year.

The significance of this tendency to bond financing is clear enough. It means that all developed states are under pressure from public opinion to maintain a generous welfare system and to ensure an adequate infrastructure of transport, communications, energy supply, education and research. All these are becoming more and more costly to finance. But as the military defensive function of states seems less vital to the citizens than it did in the past, the other benefits they get from state government become more indispensable to a government's survival. In developing countries, too, the popular appetite for modernization, industrialization and higher living standards pushes governments into borrowing money rather than raising it by taxes.

Governments – the US government more especially – have the advantage in the financial markets that they are believed to offer a secure investment for pension funds, mutual funds, and other institutional investors. They are therefore in a position to outbid the private commercial borrowers competing for the same pool of savings or accumulated capital. But for many of these private borrowers, the return on capital from trade or production may sometimes and in some sectors where competition is fierce be less than the price of borrowed capital.

When that happens, governments grabbing too much of the pool of savings for themselves may be in danger of killing the capitalist goose that lays the golden eggs of economic growth and rising living standards. By continuing to spend heavily on defence, while allowing the costs of welfare to escalate, they are essentially playing symbolic politics. The result could be that the stagflation of the 1970s could be repeated at a much higher level both of economic stagnation in the real economy and of inflation in the financial system. That seems to me to be an issue in world political economy which is rather more important for future generations than whether capitalisms are diverging or converging. When the whole town is in danger from flood or fire, it does not matter too much which landlords have kept their roofs in good repair. But that would be a topic for another debate altogether.

BIBLIOGRAPHY

Acs, Z.J. and Audretsch, D.B. (eds) (1993) *Small Firms and Enterpreneurship: An East–West Perspective*. Cambridge: Cambridge University Press.

Aglietta, M. (1997) *Régulation et crises du capitalisme*. Paris: Odile Jacob.

Ahrne, G. and Clement, W. (1994) 'A new regime?', in W. Clement and R. Mahon (eds), *Swedish Social Democracy*. Toronto: Canadian Scholars Press, 233–44.

Albert, M. (1991) *Capitalisme contre capitalisme*. Paris: Le Seuil. Trans. *Capitalism against Capitalism* (1993). London: Whurr Publishers.

Allen, C. (1989) 'The underdevelopment of Keynesianism in the Federal Republic of Germany', in P. Hall (ed.), *The Political Power of Economic Ideas*. Princeton: Princeton University Press. pp. 263–90.

Allsopp, C. (1985) 'The assessment: monetary and fiscal policy in the 1980s', *Oxford Review of Economic Policy*, 1(1).

Allsopp, C. (1993) 'The assessment: strategic policy dilemmas for the 1990s', *Oxford Review of Economic Policy*, 9(3).

Allsopp, C. and Graham, A. (1987) 'The assessment: policy options for the UK', *Oxford Review of Economic Policy*, 3(3).

Amable, B., Barre, R. and Boyer, R. (1997) *Les systèmes d'innovation à lére de la globalisation*. Paris: Economica.

Aoki, M. (1988) *Information, Incentives and Bargaining in the Japanese Economy*. Cambridge: Cambridge University Press.

Ayres, I. and Braithwaite, J. (1992) *Responsive Regulation: Transcending the Deregulation Debate*. Oxford: Oxford University Press.

Baechler, J. (1975) *The Origins of Capitalism*. Oxford: Blackwell.

Bagnasco, A. (1977) *Tre Italie: la problematica territoriale dello sviluppo italiano*. Bologna: Il Mulino.

Bagnasco, A. (1988) *La costruzione sociale del mercato*. Bologna: Il Mulino.

Bagnasco, A. and Sabel, C.H. (1994) *PME et développement économique en Europe*. Paris: La Découverte.

Barca, F. and Magnani, M. (1989) *L'industria fra capitale e lavoro*. Bologna: Il Mulino.

Barrell, R. (ed.) (1994) *The UK Labour Market*. Cambridge: Cambridge University Press.

Barrell, R. and Sefton, J. (1995) 'Output gaps. Some evidence from the UK, France and Germany', *National Institute Economic Review*, 151, February.

Becattini, G. (ed.) (1987) *Mercato e forze locali: il distretto industriale*. Bologna: Il Mulino.

Becker, G.S. (1980) *Altriusm in the Family and Selfishness in the Market Place*. Discussion paper no. 73. London: Centre for Labour Economics, LSE.

Benassy, J.-P., Boyer, R. and Gelpi, R.-M. (1979) 'Régulation des économies capitalistes et inflation', *Revue économique*, 30(3): 397–441.

Béranger, P. (1987) *Les nouvelles règles de la production*. Paris: Dunod.

Berggren, C. (1991) *Von Ford zu Volvo: Automobilherstellung in Schweden*. Berlin: Springerverlag.

Best, M. (1990) *The New Competition*. Oxford: Polity.

Black, B. (1994) 'Labour market incentive structures and employee performance', *British Journal of Industrial Relations*, 32(1).

Bloch, M. (1968) *La Société féodale*. Paris: Albin Michel.

Bloch-Lainé, F. and Bouvier, J. (1986) *La France restaurée 1944–1954*. Paris: Fayard.

Boltho, A. (1995) Data supplied to the author. Private communication.

Boltho, A. and Graham, A. (1989) 'Has Mrs Thatcher changed the British economy?', *Rivista di Politica Economica*, year LXXIX, third series (IV).

Borjas, G., Freeman, R.B. and Katz, L. (1992) 'On the labor market effects of immigration and trade', in R.B. Freeman and G. Borjas, *Immigration and the Work Force: Economic Consequences for the United States and Source Areas*. Chicago: University of Chicago Press. pp. 213–44

Bouvier, J. (1987) 'Libres propos autour d'une démarche révisionniste', in P. Fridenson and A. Straus, *Le capitalisme français*. Paris: Fayard.

Boyer, R. (ed.) (1988) *Labour Market Flexibility in Europe*. OXford: Oxford University Press.

Boyer, R. (1986) *La Théorie de la régulation: une analyse critique*. Paris: La Découverte.

Boyer, R. (1987) 'The eighties: the search for alternatives to Fordism'. Paper presented at the Sixth International Conference of Europeanists, Washington, DC, 30 October–1 November.

Boyer, R. (1990) *The Regulation School: A Critical Appraisal*. New York: Columbia University Press.

Boyer, R. (1991a) *New Directions in Management Practices and Work Organisation*. Paris: CEPREMAP.

Boyer, R. (ed.) (1991b) 'Les Paradoxes de la crise française de l'entre-deux-guerres', *Le Mouvement social*, special issue, 154.

Boyer, R. and Dore, R. (eds) (1994) *The Return to Incomes Policy*. London: Pinter.

Boyer, R. and Durand, J.-P. (1997) *After Fordism*. London: Macmillan.

Boyer, R. and Saillard, Y. (eds) (1995) *Théorie de la régulation: l'état des savoirs*. Paris: La Découverte.

Braudel, F. (1979) *Civilisation matérielle, économie et capitalisme*. Paris: Armand Colin.

Callaghan, P. and Hartmann, H. (1991) *Contingent Work: A Case Book on Part-Time and Temporary Employment*. Washington, DC: Economic Policy Institute, for the Institute for Women's Policy Research.

Cassese, S. (1987) 'Stato ed economia: il problema storico', in P. Lange and M. Regini (eds), *Stato e regolazione sociale*. Bologna: Il Mulino.

CBI (1995) *Industrial Trends Survey*, April.

CEDEFOP (1987) *The Role of the Social Partners in Vocational Training in Italiy*. Berlin: CEDEFOP.

Cella, G.P. (1989) 'Criteria of regulation in Italian industrial relations: a case of weak institutions', in P. Lange and M. Regini (eds), *State, Market and Social Regulation. New Perspectives on Italy*. Cambridge: Cambridge University Press. pp. 167–85.

Cerny, P.G. (1991) 'The limits of deregulation: transnational interpenetration and policy change', in P.G. Cerny, (ed.), *The Politics of Transnational Regulation: Deregulation or Reregulation*. Special issue of the *European Journal of Political Research*, 19(2&3), March/April: 173–96.

Cerny, P.G. (ed.) (1993) *Finance and World Politics: Markets, Regimes, and States in the Post-Hegemonic Era*. Cheltenham: Edward Elgar. pp. 51–85.

Cerny, P. G. (1997) 'Paradoxes of the Competition State: The Dynamics of Political Globalization', *Government and Opposition*, 32(2), Spring: 251–74.

Chandler, A.D. (1977) *The Visible Hand: The Managerial Revolution in American Business*. Cambridge: Harvard University Press.

Chartres, J.-A. (1995) 'Le changement de mode de régulation. Apports et limites de la formalisation', in R. Boyer and Y. Saillard (eds), *Théorie de la régulation: l'état des savoirs*. Paris: La Découverte. pp. 273–81.

Cipolla, C. (1962) *Economic History of World Population*. London: Penguin.

Cipolla, C. (1970) *The Economic Decline of Empires*. London: Methuen.

Clark, R. (1978) *The Japanese Company*. New Haven: Yale University Press.
Committee on Public Accounts (1994) *The Proper Conduct of Business*. House of Commons Paper 154, Session 1993–4.
Cox, R. (1987) *Production, Power and World Order: Social Forces in the Making of World History*. New York: Columbia University Press.
Crafts, N. (1992) 'Institutions and economic growth', *West European Politics*, 15(1).
Current Population Survey (annual). Washington, DC: Office of the Government Printer.
Davies, G. (1994) 'A UK supply side improvement?'. Report prepared for HM Treasury's Panel of Independent Forecasters. London: HMSO.
Davis, H. and Stewart, J. (1993) *The Growth of Government by Appointment: Implications for Local Democracy*. Birmingham: INLOGOV.
Delorme, R. and André, Ch. (1983) *L'État et l'économie*. Paris: Le Seuil.
d'Iribarne, Ph. (1989) *La Logique de l'honneur. Gestion des entreprises et traditions nationales*. Paris: Points-Seuil.
d'Iribarne, Ph. (1990) *Le Chômage paradoxal*. Paris: PUF.
d'Iribarne, Ph. (1994) 'L'économique et le social. La fin d'un dogme', *Commentaire*, 66.
Dore, R. (1986) *Flexible Rigidities: Industrial Policy and Structural Adjustment in the Japanese Economy 1970–80*. London: Athlone Press.
Dore, R. (1987) *Taking Japan Seriously*. London: Athlone Press.
Dore, R. (1993) 'What makes the Japanese different?', in C. Crouch and D. Marquand (eds), *Ethics and Markets*. Oxford: Blackwell.
Dumez, H. and Jeunemaître, A. (1991) *La Concurrence en Europe*. Paris: Le Seuil.
Economist Book of Vital Statistics (1990). London: The Economist.
Esping-Andersen, G. (1990) *The Three Worlds of Welfare Capitalism*. Princeton: Princeton University Press.
Federal Republic of Germany (1991) *Statistisches Jahrbuch für die Bundesrepublik Deutschland*. Bonn: Government Publications Office.
Filipovic, M. (1994) 'A global private regime for capital flows'. Paper presented to the annual conference of the British International Studies Association, University of York, December.
Financial Times (1994) 'A survey of France'. 12 July. pp. I–VI.
Fourquet, F. (1980) *Les Comptes de la puissance: histoire de la compatibilité nationale et du Plan*. Clamecy: Éditions Recherches.
Frankfurt, H. (1988) *The Importance of What We Care About: Philosophical Essays*. Cambridge: Cambridge University Press.
Freeman, R. (1988) 'Labour market institutions and economic performance', *Economic Policy*: pp. 64–80.
Freeman, R. (1995) 'The limits of wage flexibility to curing unemployment', *Oxford Review of Economic Policy*, 11(1).
Freeman, R.B. (1993) 'How much has de-unionization contributed to the rise in male earnings inequality', in S. Danziger and P. Gottschalk (eds), *Uneven Tides: Rising Inequality in America*. New York: Russell Sage.
Freeman, R.B. (1994) 'How labor fares in advanced economies', in R.B. Freeman (ed.), *Working Under Different Rules*. New York: Russell Sage Foundation.
Gamble, A. (1988) *The Free Economy and the Strong State: The Politics of Thatcherism*. London: Macmillan.
Garten, J.E. (1992) *A Cold Peace: America, Japan, and Germany, and the Struggle for Supremacy*. New York: Twentieth Century Fund.
Golden, M. (1994) 'Collective Bargaining and Industrial Change: A Case of Disorganization?' Ms.
Goldman Sachs (1995) *The UK Economics Analyst*, May.
Goldstein, M., Folkerts-Landau, D. et al. (1993a) *International Capital Markets. Part I, Exchange Rate Management and International Capital Flows*. Washington, DC: International Monetary Fund.

Goldstein, M., Folkerts-Landau, D. et al. (1993b) *International Capital Markets. Part II, Systemic Issues in International Finance*. Washington, DC: International Monetary Fund.

Goodman, A. and Webb, S. (1994) *For Richer, For Poorer. The Changing Distribution of Income in the United Kingdom, 1961–1991*. Institute for Fiscal Studies Commentary, 42.

Grabher, G. (1993) *The Embedded Firm*. London: Routledge.

Graham, A. (1994) 'Did Keynesianism Work?', in S. Pollard (ed.), *Jobs and Growth: The International Perspective*. London: Fabian/Unison Special.

Grant, J. (1992) *Money of the Mind: Borrowing and Lending in America from the Civil War to Michael Milken*. New York: Farrar Straus Giroux.

Gray, J. (1994) *The Undoing of Conservatism*. London: Social Market Foundation.

Gregg, P. and Wadsworth, J. (1995) 'A short history of labour turnover, job tenure, and job security, 1975–93', *Oxford Review of Economic Policy*, 11(1).

Gruson, Cl. (1968) *Origine et espoirs de la planification française*. Paris: Dunod.

Hadenius, K. (1990) *Jämlikhet och frihet*. Stockholm: Almqvist & Wicksell.

Hahn, F. (1988) 'On market economics', in R. Skidelsky (ed.), *Thatcherism*. London: Chatto and Windus.

Hall, J. (1985) *Powers and Liberties: The Causes and Consequences of the Rise of the West*. Oxford: Blackwell.

Hall, P. (1986) *Governing the Economy: The Politics of State Intervention in Britain and France*. Oxford: Polity.

Hansen, H. (1991) *Manufacturing Skills: Institutionalizing Vocational Education and Training in the United States and Germany, 1870–1918*. Madison: Department of History, University of Wisconsin.

Harrison, B. (1994) *Lean and Mean. The Changing Landscape of Corporate Power in the Age of Flexibility*. New York: Basic Books.

Hatchuel, G. (1993) 'Les grands curants d'opinion et de perceptions en France de la fin des années 70 au début des années 90', in J.B. Dé Foucault (ed.), *La France et l'Europe d'ici 2010*. Paris: La Documentation française. pp. 127–35.

Hay, D. and Morris, D. (1984) *Unquoted Companies*. London: Macmillan.

Helm, D. (1986) 'The economic borders of the state', *Oxford Review of Economic Policy*, 2(2).

Herrigel, G. (1989) 'Industrial order and the politics of industrial change', in P. Katzenstein (ed.), *Industry and Politics in West Germany*. Ithaca: Cornell University Press. pp. 185–220.

Hollingsworth, J.R. (1994) 'Re-thinking democratic theory in advanced capitalist societies'. Annual Meeting of American Sociological Association, Los Angeles, 5–9 August.

Hollingsworth, J.R. and Boyer, R. (1997) *Comparing Capitalist Economies: The Embeddedness of Institutions*. New York: Cambridge University Press.

Hollingsworth, J.R., Schmitter, Ph.C. and Streeck, W. (eds) (1994) *Governing Capitalist Economies: Performance and Control of Economic Sectors*. Oxford: Oxford University Press.

Hollingsworth, J.R. and Streeck, W. (1994) 'Countries and sectors', in J.R. Hollingsworth, P. Schmitter and W. Streeck (eds), *Governing Capitalist Economics*. New York: Oxford University Press.

ISFOL, (1989) *Rapporto ISFOL 1989*. Oxford: F. Angeli.

Jürgens, U., Malsch, T. and Dohse, K. (1989) *Moderne Zeiten in der Automobilfabrik. Strategien der Produktionsmodernisierung und Arbeitsregulation im Länder- und Konzernvergleich*. Berlin: Springerverlag.

Kapstein, E.B. (1994) *Governing the Global Economy: International Finance and the State*. Cambridge: Harvard University Press.

Karoly, L.A. (1993) 'The trend in inequality among families, individuals and workers in the United States: a twenty-five year prospective', in S. Danziger and

P. Gottschalk (eds), *Uneven Tides: Rising Inequality in America*. New York: Russell Sage. pp. 19–97

Katz, L., Loveman, G. and Blanchflower, D. (1993) 'A comparison of changes in the structure of wages in four OECD countries', Discussion Paper no. 144. Centre for Economic Performance, London School of Economics.

Katzenstein, P. (1987) *Policy and Politics in West Germany*. Philadelphia: Temple University Press.

Kay, J.A. (1993) *Foundations of Corporate Success*. Oxford: Oxford University Press.

Keegan, W. (1989) *Mr Lawson's Gamble*. London: Hodder & Stoughton.

Kenworthy, L. (1995) *In Search of National Economic Success: Balancing Competition and Cooperation*. Thousand Oaks: Sage.

Kern, H. and Schumann, M. (1989) 'New concepts of production in West German plants', in P. Katzenstein (ed.), *Industry and Politics in West Germany*. Ithaca: Cornell University Press. pp. 87–113.

Kerr, J.C., Dunlop, J.T., Harbison, F. and Myers, C.A. (1960) *Industrialism and Industrial Man*. Cambridge: Harvard University Press.

Keynes, J.M. (1936) *The General Theory of Employment, Interest and Money*. Vol. VII. London: Macmillan.

King, D. and Rothstein, B. (1993) 'Institutional choices and labor market policy: a British–Swedish comparison', *Comparative Political Studies*, 26(2): 147–77.

Kogut, B. (ed.) (1993) *Country Competitiveness: Technology and Organizing of Work*. New York: Oxford University Press.

Kommers, D. (1993) 'Germany', in M. Curtis (ed.), *Introduction to Comparative Government*. New York: Harper Collins.

Lamoreaux, N. (1985) *The Great Merger Movement in American Business 1885–1904*. New York: Cambridge University Press.

Lane, C. (1991) 'Industrial reorganization in Europe: patterns of convergence and divergence in Germany, France and Britain', *Work, Employment and Society*, 5(4): 515–39.

Lange, P. and Regini, M. (eds) (1989) *State, Market and Social Regulation, New Perspectives on Italy*. Cambridge: Cambridge University Press.

Levy, F. and Murnane, R. (1992) 'U.S. earnings levels and earnings inequality: a review of recent trends and proposed explanations', *Journal of Economic Literature*, 30: 1333–81.

Locke, J. (1690) *Two Treatises of Government*. P. Laslett (ed.), Cambridge: Cambridge University Press.

Locke, R. (1994) *Remaking the Italian Economy: Local Politics and Industrial Change in Contemporary Italy*. Ithaca: Cornell University Press.

Loveman, G. and Sengenberger, W. (1990) 'Introduction: economic and social reorganization in the small and medium-sized enterprise sector', in W. Sengenberger, G. Loveman and M. Piore (eds), *The Re-Emergence of Small Enterprises: Industrial Restructuring in Industrialized Countries*. Geneva: International Institute for Labor Studies. pp. 1–61.

Maddison, A. (1983) *Phases of Capitalist Development*. Oxford: Oxford University Press.

Maddison, A. (1987) *Les phases du développement capitaliste*. Paris: Economica.

Maddison, A. (1991) *Dynamic Forces in Capitalist Development: A Long-Run Comparative View*. Oxford: Oxford University Press.

Mann, M. (1986) *The Sources of Social Power, Vol. 1*. Cambridge: Cambridge University Press.

Marsden, D. and Richardson, R. (1994) 'Performing for pay? The effects of "merit pay" on motivation in a public service', *British Journal of Industrial Relations*, 32(2).

Marseille, J. (1984) *Empire colonial et capitalisme français*. Paris: Albin Michel.

Maurice, M. and Sorge, A. (1989) *Dynamique industrielle et capacité d'innovation de l'industrie de la machine-outil en France et en RFA*. Aix en Provence: Laboratoire d'économie et de sociologie du travail.

Minc, A. (1991) *Français, si vous osiez.* . . . Paris: Grasset.

Mishel, L. and Bernstein, J. (1993) *The State of Working America, 1992*. Armonk: Sharpe.

Morin, F. and Dupuy, Cl. (1993) *Le Cœur financier européen*. Paris: Economica.

Morris, D. (1994) 'The stock market and problems of corporate control in the UK', in T. Buxton, P. Chapman and P. Temple (eds), *Britain's Economic Performance*. London: Routledge.

New Earnings Survey (annual). London: HMSO.

Nickell, S. and Bell, B. (1995) 'The collapse in demand for the unskilled and unemployment across the OECD', *Oxford Review of Economic Policy*, 11(1).

OECD (1992) *Economic Outlook: Historical Statistics*. Paris: OECD.

OECD (1993) *Employment Outlook*. Paris: OECD.

OECD (1994) *The OECD Jobs Study, Organization for Economic Co-operation and Development*. Paris: OECD.

Okazaki, T. (1994) 'The Japanese firm under the wartime planned economy', in M. Aoki and R. Dore (eds), *The Japanese Firm*. Oxford: Oxford University Press. pp. 350–78.

Ouchi, W.G. (1982) *Theory and How American Business Can Meet the Japanese Challenge*. New York: Avon Books.

Oulton, N. (1987) 'Plant closures and the productivity "miracle" in manufacturing', *National Institute Economic Review*, August.

Paci, M. (1989) *Pubblico e privato nei moderni sistemi di welfare*. Naples: Liguori.

Pastré, O. (1992) *Les Nouveaux piliers de la finance*. Paris: La Découverte.

Paugam, S. (1993) *La Société française et ses pauvres; l'expérience du revenu minimum d'insertion*. Paris: PUF.

Pavitt, K. (1984) 'Sectoral patterns of technical change: towards a taxionomy and a theory', *Research Policy*, 13: 343–73.

Peters, T. and Waterman, E. (1982) *In Search of Excellence*. New York: Harper and Row.

Piore, M.J. (1980) 'Dualism as a response to flux and uncertainty. The technological foundations of dualism and discontinuity', in S Berger and M.J. Piore (eds), *Dualism and Discontinuity in Industrial Societies*. Cambridge: Cambridge University Press. pp. 13–81.

Piore, M. and Sabel, C. (1984) *The Second Industrial Divide*. New York: Basic Books.

Pizzorno, A. (1978) 'Political exchange and collective identity in industrial conflict', in C. Crouch and A. Pizzorno (eds), *The Resurgence of Class Conflict in Western Europe since 1968*, vol. 2. London: Macmillan. pp. 277–98.

Polanyi, K. (1944) *The Great Transformation: The Political and Economic Origins of Our Time*. New York: Rinehart & Co.

Polanyi, K. (1983) *La Grande transformation*. Paris: Gallimard.

Pontusson, J. (1992a) *The Limits of Social Democracy*. Ithaca: Cornell University Press.

Pontusson, J. (1992b) 'At the end of the third road', *Politics and Society*, 20: 305–32.

Pontusson, J. (1995) 'Explaining the decline of European social democracy', *World Politics*, 47(4) 495–533.

Pontusson, J. and Swenson, P. (1996) 'Labor markets, production strategies, and wage-bargaining institutions', *Comparative Political Studies* 29(2): 223: 50.

Powell, W.W. (1990) 'Neither market nor hierarchy: network forms of organization', in L.L. Cummings and B. Staw (eds), *Research in Organizational Behavior*. Greenwich: JAI Press. pp. 295–336.

Powell, W.W. and Brantley, P. (1992) 'Competitive cooperation in biotechnology: learning through networks', in N. Nohria and R. Eccles (eds), *Networks and Organizations*. Boston: Harvard Business School Press. pp. 366–94.

Regalia, I. and Regini, M. (1995) 'Between voluntarism and institutionalism: industrial relations and human resources practices in Italy', in R. Locke, T. Kochan and M. Piore (eds), *Employment Relations in a Changing World Economy*. Cambridge: MIT Press.

Regini, M. (1981) *I dilemmi del sindacato*. Bologna: Il Mulino.

Regini, M. (1995) *Uncertain Boundaries. The Social and Political Construction of European Economies*. Cambridge: Cambridge University Press.

Regini, M. and Sabel, C. (eds) (1989) *Strategie di riaggiustamento industriale*. Bologna: Il Mulino.

Reich, R. (1991) *The Work of Nations: Preparing Ourselves for 21st-Century Capitalism*. New York: Alfred A. Knopf.

Reyneri, E. (1989) 'The Italian labor market: between state control and social regulation', in P. Lange and M. Regini (eds), *State, Market and Social Regulation. New Perspectives on Italy*. Cambridge: Cambridge University Press. pp. 129–45.

Ross, G., Hoffmann, S. and Malzacher, S. (1987) *The Mitterrand Experiment Continuity and Change in Modern France*. New York: Oxford University Press.

Rowthorn, B. (1992) 'Corporatism and market performance', in J. Pekkarinen, M. Pohjola and B. Rowthorn (eds), *Social Corporatism*. Oxford: Clarendon Press. pp. 44–81.

Rowthorn, B. (1995) 'Capital formation and unemployment', *Oxford Review of Economic Policy*, 11(1).

Rueff, J. (1931) 'L'assurance chômage, cause du chômage permanent', *Revue d'économie politique*: 211–51.

Ruggie, J.G. (1983) *The Antimonies of Interdependence: National Welfare and the International Division of Labour*. New York: Columbia University Press.

Ruggie, J.G. et al. (1992) 'Symposium: multilateralism', special issue, *International Organization*, 46(3): 561–708.

Sabel, C. (1994) 'Bootstrapping reform: rebuilding firms, the welfare state and unions?' Paper delivered at the Confédération des syndicats nationaux, Montreal, 15–16 November.

Sabel, C., Herrigel, G., Deeg, R. and Kazis, R. (1989) 'Regional prosperities compared: Baden-Württemberg and Massachusetts in the 1980s', *Economy and Society*, 18(4).

Sako, M. (1992) *Prices, Quality and Trust: Inter-Firm Relations in Britain and Japan*. Cambridge: Cambridge University Press.

Scharpf, F. (1991) *Crisis and Choice in European Social Democracy*. Ithaca: Cornell University Press.

Schumpeter, J. (1955) *Imperialism and Social Classes*. New York: Meridian.

Shonfield, A. (1964) *Modern Capitalism*. Oxford: Oxford University Press.

Shonfield, A. (1967) *Le Capitalisme d'aujourd'hui: l'État et l'entreprise*. Paris: Gallimard.

Smith, D. (1992) *From Boom to Bust: Trial and Error in British Economic Policy*. London: Penguin.

Soskice, D. (1990a) 'Reinterpreting corporatism and explaining unemployment', in R. Brunetta and C. Dell'aringa (eds), *Labour Relations and Economic Performance*. London: Macmillan. pp. 170–211.

Soskice, D. (1990b) 'Wage determination: the changing role of institutions in advanced industrialized countries', *Oxford Review of Economic Policy*, 6(4): 36–61.

Stewart, J. (1992) *Accountability to the Public*. European Policy Forum.

Stopford, J. and Strange, S. (1991) *Rival States, Rival Firms, Competition for World Market Shares*. Cambridge: Cambridge University Press.

Strange, S. (1993) *States and Markets: An Introduction to International Political Economy*. Revised edn, London: Pinter.

Strange, S. (1996) *The Retreat of the State: The Diffusion of Power in the World Economy*. Cambridge: Cambridge University Press.

Straw, J. (1993) *The Growth of the Unelected State*. London: Labour Party.

Straw, J. (1994) *The Unelected State Exposed*. London: Labour Party.

Streeck, W. (1989) 'Skills and the limits of neo-liberalism: the enterprise of the future as a place of learning', *Work, Employment and Society*, 3(1): 83–104.

Streeck, W. (1991) 'On the institutional conditions of diversified quality production', in E. Matzner and W. Streeck (eds), *Beyond Keynesianism: The Socio-Economics of Production and Unemployment*. Aldershot: Elgar. pp. 21–61.

Streeck, W. (1992) 'Productive constraints: on the institutional conditions of diversified quality production, in W. Streeck, *Social Institutions and Economic Performance: Studies of Industrial Relations in Advanced Capitalist Economies*. London: Sage. pp. 1–40.

Streeck, W. (1993) 'The social dimension of the European economy', in D. Mayes, W. Hager, A. Knight and W. Streeck, *Public Interests and Market Pressures*. London: Macmillan.

Streeck, W. (1994a) 'Modérations salariales sans politique des revenus: institutionalisation du monétarisme et du syndicalisme en Allemagne', in R. Boyer and R. Dore (eds), *Les Politiques des revenus en Europe*. Paris: La Découverte. pp. 147–64.

Streeck, W. (1994b) 'Pay restraint without incomes policy: constitutionalized monetarism and industrial unionism in Germany', in R. Boyer, R. Dore and Z. Mars (eds), *The Return to Incomes Policy*. London: Pinter. pp. 118–40.

Sweden (1991) *Statistical Abstract of Sweden*. Stockholm: Government Publications Office.

Swedish Metalworkers Union (1989) *Solidarisk arbetspolitk*. Stockholm: Swedish Metalworkers Union.

Swedish Ministry of Industry (1990) *Svensk industri i utveckling*. Stockholm: Swedish Ministry of Industry.

Swenson, P. (1989) *Fair Shares*. Ithaca: Cornell University Press.

Swenson, P. (1993) 'The end of the Swedish model in the light of its beginings'. Discussion Paper. Berlin: Wissenschaftszentrum.

Trigilia, C. (1986) *Grandi partiti e piccole imprese*. Bologna: Il Mulino.

Thelen, K. (1991) *Union of Parts*. Ithaca: Cornell University Press.

Thelen, K. (1993) 'West European labor in transition', *World Politics*, 46: 23–49.

UN (1993a) *World Investment Directory 1992*. New York: UN.

UN (1993b) *National Accounts Statistics*. New York: UN.

Visser, J. (1991) 'Trends in trade union membership', *OECD Employment Outlook*, July: 97–134.

Vitols, S. (1994) *German Banks and the Modernization of the Small Firm Sector*. Berlin: Wissenschaftszentrum.

Walsh, J. (1993) 'Internalization v. decentralization: an analysis of recent developments in pay bargaining', *British Journal of Industrial Relations*, 31(3).

Walton, D. (1995) 'How tight is the labour market?', *The UK Economics Analyst*, February.

Weber, M. (1970) *The Protestant Ethic and the Spirit of Capitalism*. London: Allen and Unwin.

Weiss, L. (1988) *Creating Capitalism*. Oxford: Blackwell.

Wiener, M.J. (1981) *English Culture and the Decline of the Industrial Spirit*. Cambridge: Cambridge University Press.

Wilkinson, R. (1994) 'Health, redistribution and growth', in A. Glyn and D. Miliband (eds), *Paying for Inequality: The Economic Cost of Social Injustice*. London: IPPR/Rivers Oram Press.

Willetts, D. (1994) *Civic Conservatism*. London: Social Market Foundation.

Williamson, O.E. (1975) *Markets and Hierarchies: Analysis and Anti-Trust Implications*. New York: Free Press.

Williamson, O.E. (1985) *The Economic Institutions of Capitalism*. New York: Free Press.

Winock, M. (ed.) (1990) *Les Années trente: de la crise à la guerre*. Paris: Le Seuil.

Womack, J.P., Jones, D.T. and Roos, D. (1990) *The Machine that Changed the World*. New York/Toronto: Rawson Associates, Collier Macmillan Canada and Maxwell Macmillan International.

INDEX